EDWARD GREY
WITCHFINDER

~~~

BY MIKE MIGNOLA

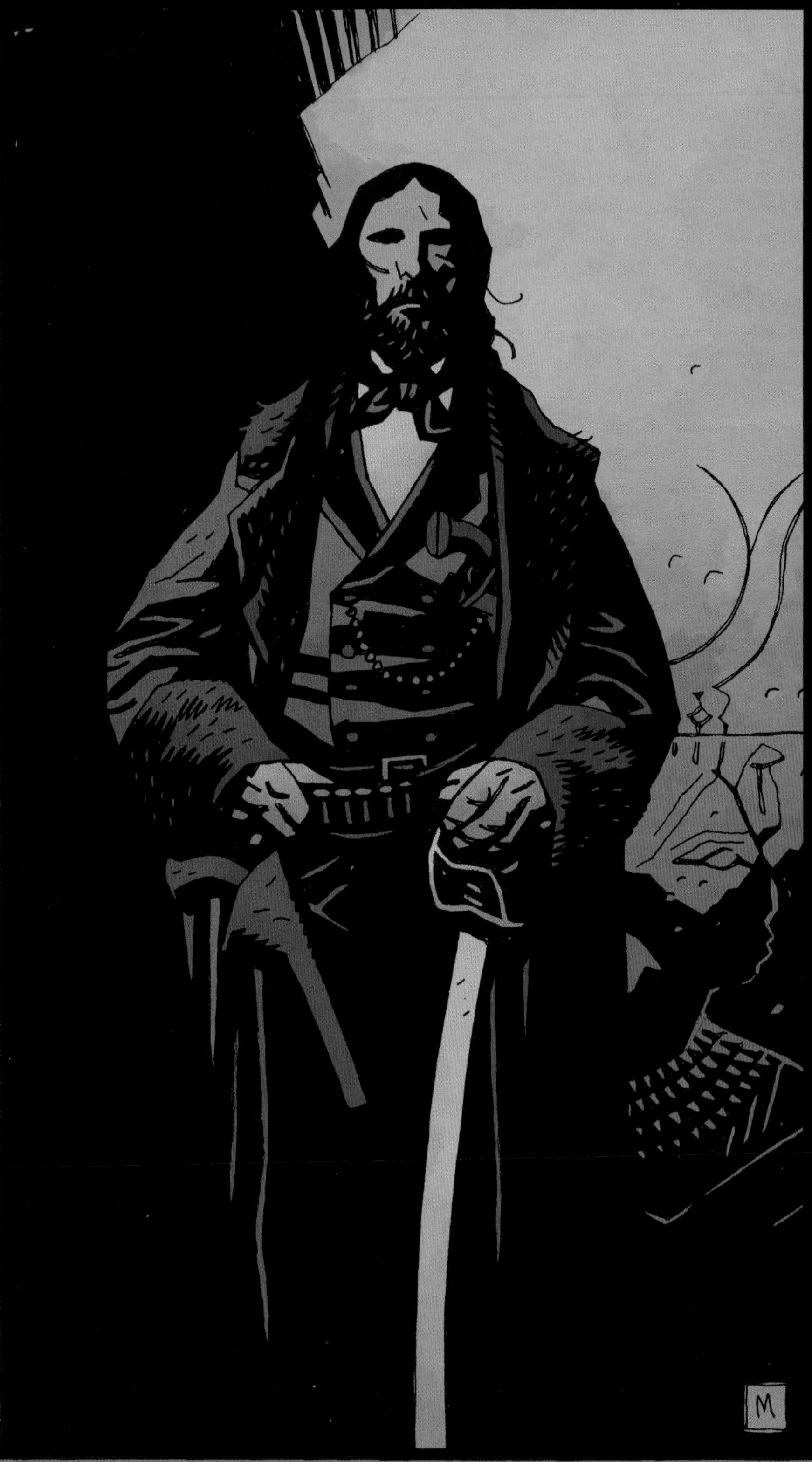

SIR EDWARD GREY

WITCHFINDER™

In the Service *of* Angels

story
MIKE MIGNOLA

art
BEN STENBECK

colors
DAVE STEWART

letters
CLEM ROBINS

editor SCOTT ALLIE

associate editor SAMANTHA ROBERTSON

book designer AMY ARENDTS

publisher MIKE RICHARDSON

DARK HORSE BOOKS®

Published by
Dark Horse Books
A division of Dark Horse Comics, Inc.
10956 SE Main St.
Milwaukie, OR 97222

First Edition:. April 2010
ISBN 978-1-59582-483-7

This volume collects *Sir Edward Grey, Witchfinder: In the Service of Angels* #1–#5, as well
as stories from *Hellboy: The Wild Hunt* #7 and *MySpace Dark Horse Presents* #16,
published by Dark Horse Comics.

1 3 5 7 9 10 8 6 4 2

Printed at Midas Printing International, Ltd., Huizhou, China

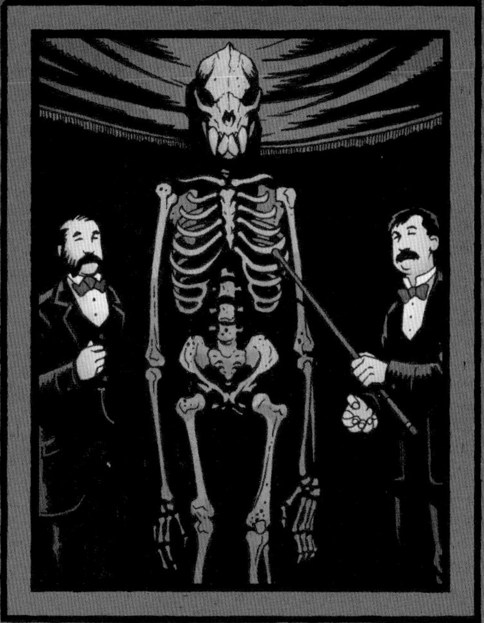

CHAPTER ONE

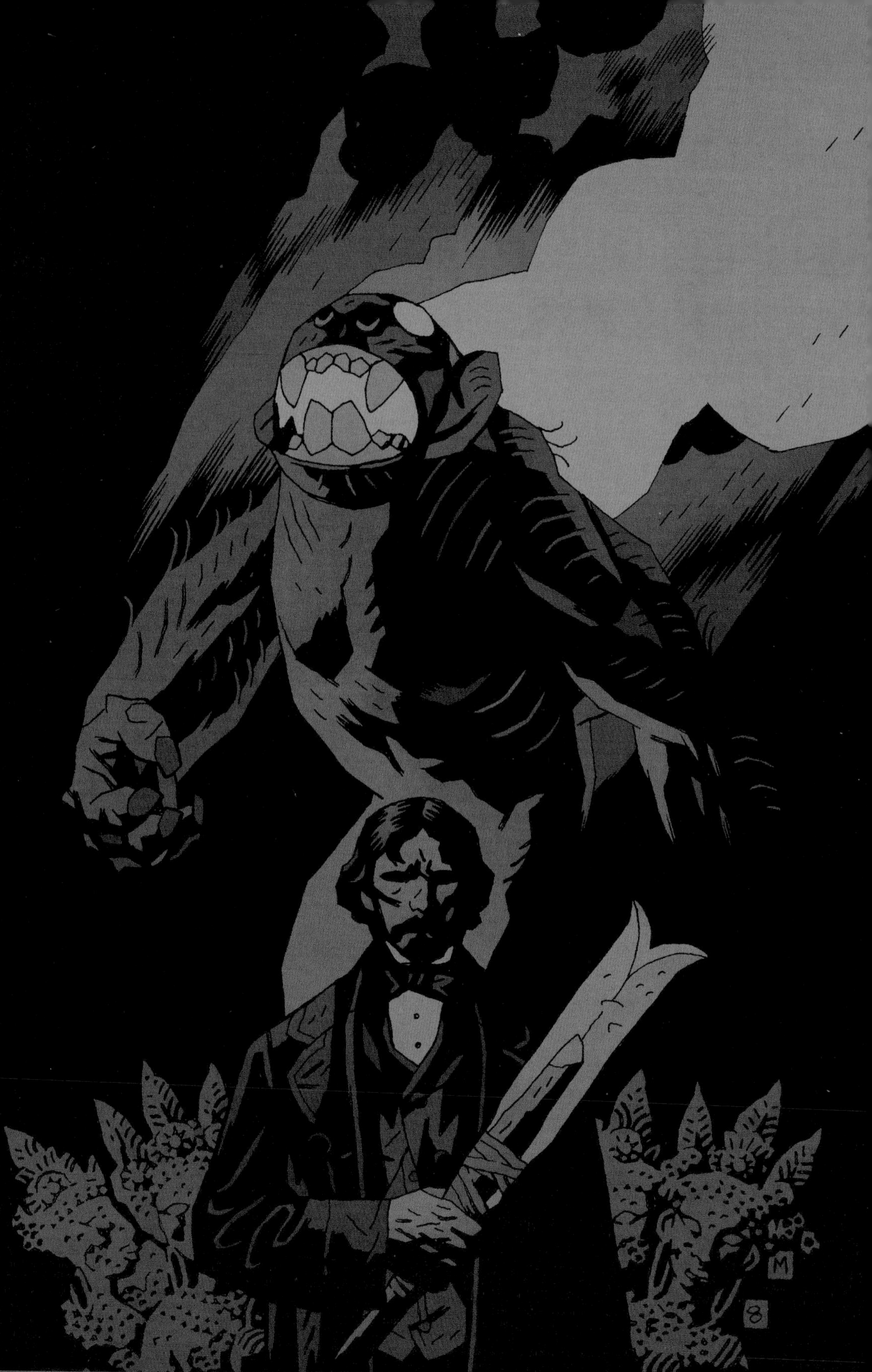

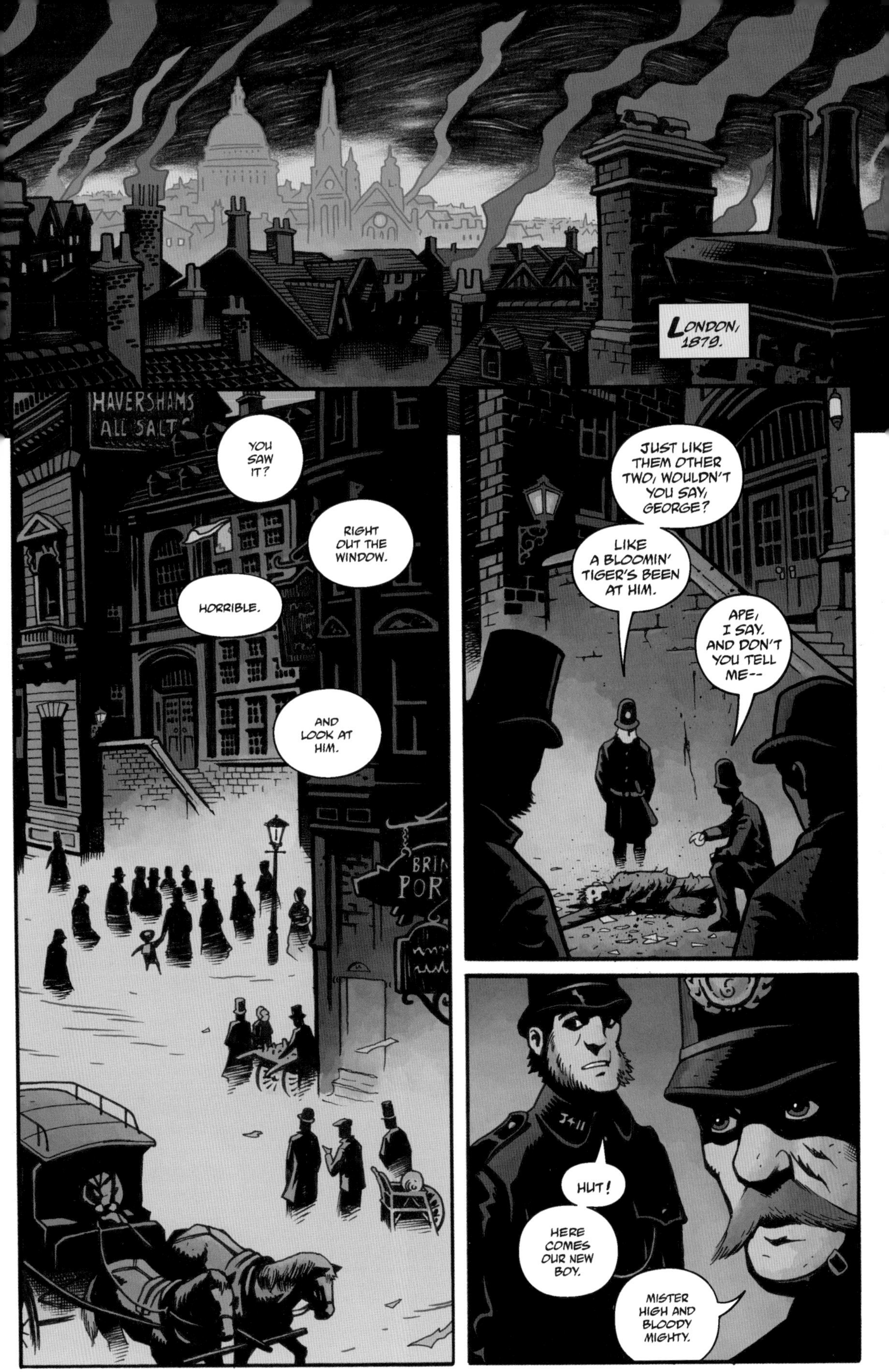
LONDON, 1879.
HAVERSHAMS ALL SALTS
YOU SAW IT?
RIGHT OUT THE WINDOW.
HORRIBLE.
AND LOOK AT HIM.
JUST LIKE THEM OTHER TWO, WOULDN'T YOU SAY, GEORGE?
LIKE A BLOOMIN' TIGER'S BEEN AT HIM.
APE, I SAY. AND DON'T YOU TELL ME--
HUT!
HERE COMES OUR NEW BOY.
MISTER HIGH AND BLOODY MIGHTY.

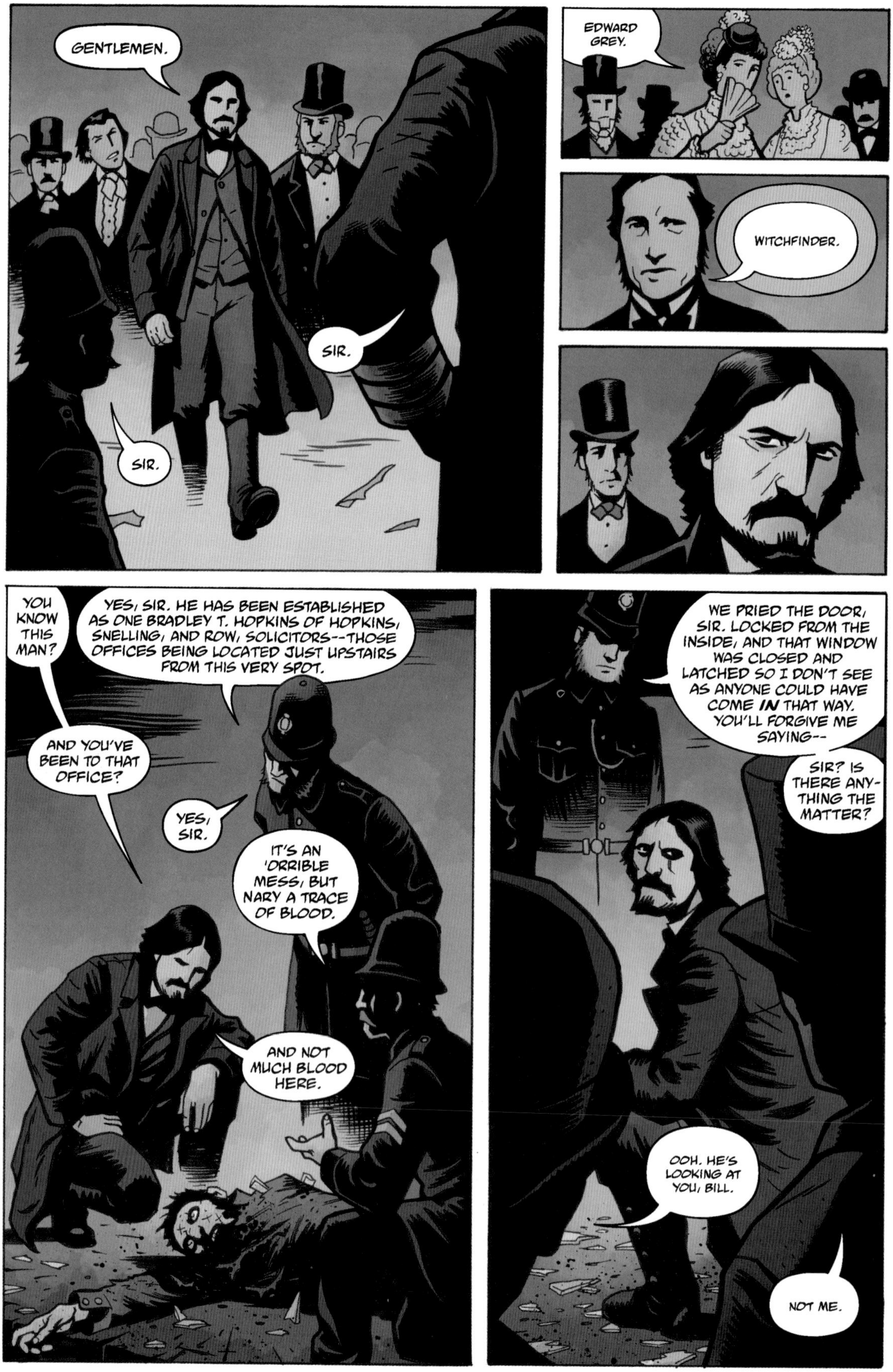
GENTLEMEN.
SIR.
SIR.
EDWARD GREY.
WITCHFINDER.
YOU KNOW THIS MAN?
YES, SIR. HE HAS BEEN ESTABLISHED AS ONE BRADLEY T. HOPKINS OF HOPKINS, SNELLING, AND ROW, SOLICITORS--THOSE OFFICES BEING LOCATED JUST UPSTAIRS FROM THIS VERY SPOT.
AND YOU'VE BEEN TO THAT OFFICE?
YES, SIR.
IT'S AN 'ORRIBLE MESS, BUT NARY A TRACE OF BLOOD.
AND NOT MUCH BLOOD HERE.
WE PRIED THE DOOR, SIR. LOCKED FROM THE INSIDE, AND THAT WINDOW WAS CLOSED AND LATCHED SO I DON'T SEE AS ANYONE COULD HAVE COME IN THAT WAY. YOU'LL FORGIVE ME SAYING--
SIR? IS THERE ANYTHING THE MATTER?
OOH. HE'S LOOKING AT YOU, BILL.
NOT ME.

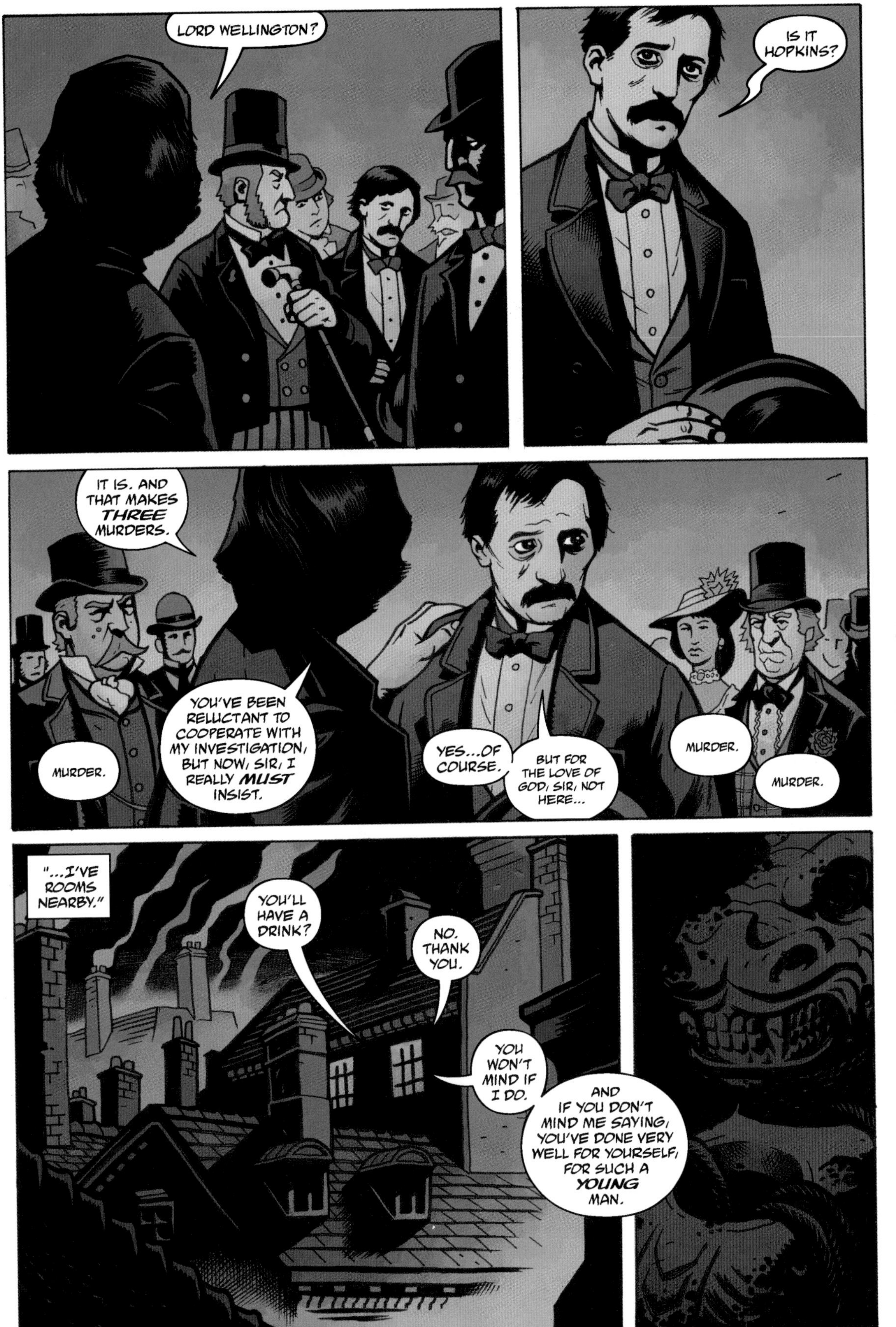
LORD WELLINGTON?
IS IT HOPKINS?
IT IS. AND THAT MAKES THREE MURDERS.
MURDER.
YOU'VE BEEN RELUCTANT TO COOPERATE WITH MY INVESTIGATION, BUT NOW, SIR, I REALLY MUST INSIST.
YES...OF COURSE.
BUT FOR THE LOVE OF GOD, SIR, NOT HERE...
MURDER.
MURDER.
"...I'VE ROOMS NEARBY."
YOU'LL HAVE A DRINK?
NO. THANK YOU.
YOU WON'T MIND IF I DO.
AND IF YOU DON'T MIND ME SAYING, YOU'VE DONE VERY WELL FOR YOURSELF, FOR SUCH A YOUNG MAN.

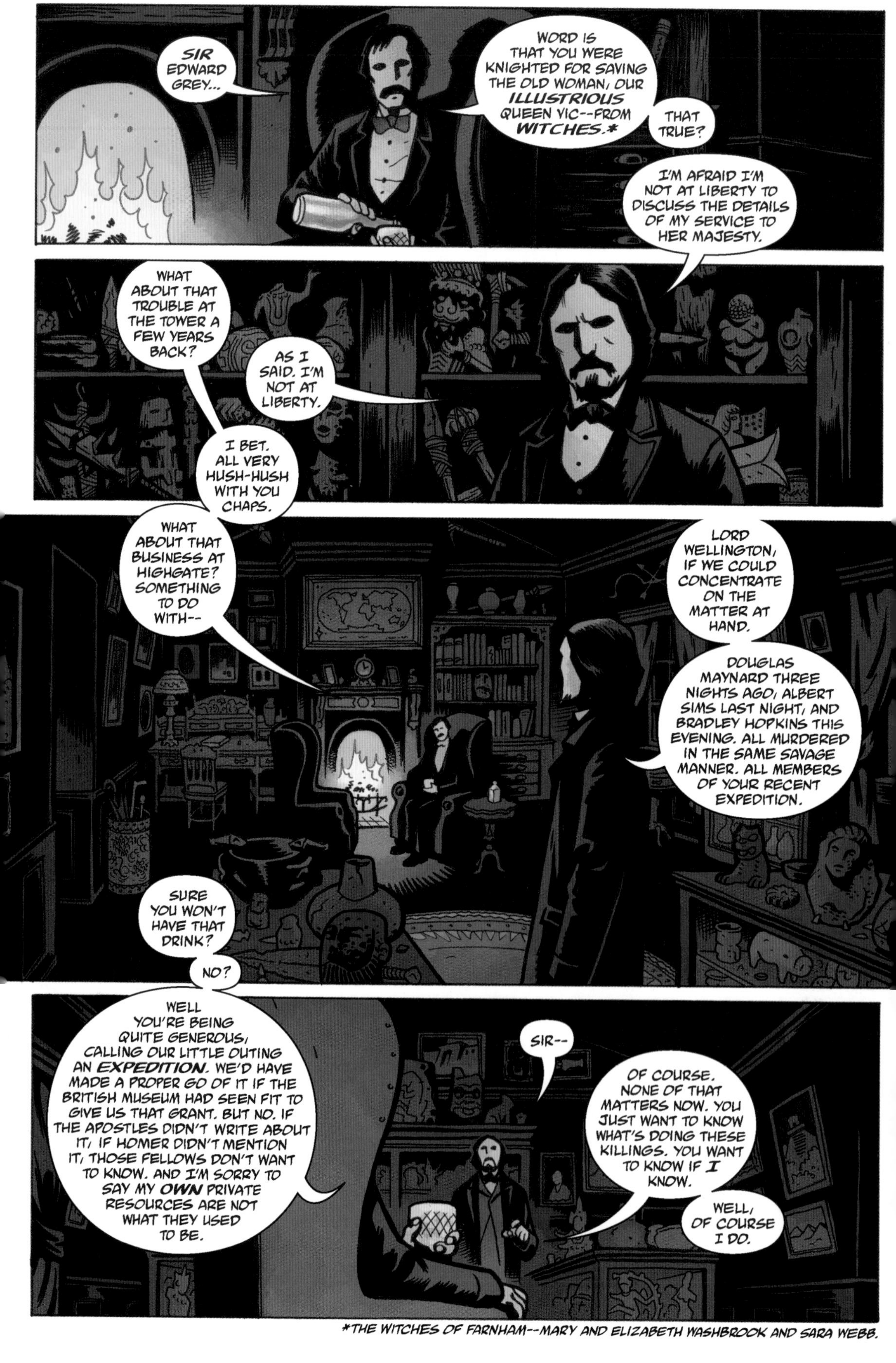
SIR EDWARD GREY...
WORD IS THAT YOU WERE KNIGHTED FOR SAVING THE OLD WOMAN, OUR ILLUSTRIOUS QUEEN VIC--FROM WITCHES.*
THAT TRUE?
I'M AFRAID I'M NOT AT LIBERTY TO DISCUSS THE DETAILS OF MY SERVICE TO HER MAJESTY.
WHAT ABOUT THAT TROUBLE AT THE TOWER A FEW YEARS BACK?
AS I SAID. I'M NOT AT LIBERTY.
I BET. ALL VERY HUSH-HUSH WITH YOU CHAPS.
WHAT ABOUT THAT BUSINESS AT HIGHGATE? SOMETHING TO DO WITH--
LORD WELLINGTON, IF WE COULD CONCENTRATE ON THE MATTER AT HAND.
DOUGLAS MAYNARD THREE NIGHTS AGO, ALBERT SIMS LAST NIGHT, AND BRADLEY HOPKINS THIS EVENING. ALL MURDERED IN THE SAME SAVAGE MANNER. ALL MEMBERS OF YOUR RECENT EXPEDITION.
SURE YOU WON'T HAVE THAT DRINK?
NO?
WELL YOU'RE BEING QUITE GENEROUS, CALLING OUR LITTLE OUTING AN EXPEDITION. WE'D HAVE MADE A PROPER GO OF IT IF THE BRITISH MUSEUM HAD SEEN FIT TO GIVE US THAT GRANT. BUT NO. IF THE APOSTLES DIDN'T WRITE ABOUT IT, IF HOMER DIDN'T MENTION IT, THOSE FELLOWS DON'T WANT TO KNOW. AND I'M SORRY TO SAY MY OWN PRIVATE RESOURCES ARE NOT WHAT THEY USED TO BE.
SIR--
OF COURSE. NONE OF THAT MATTERS NOW. YOU JUST WANT TO KNOW WHAT'S DOING THESE KILLINGS. YOU WANT TO KNOW IF I KNOW.
WELL, OF COURSE I DO.

*THE WITCHES OF FARNHAM--MARY AND ELIZABETH WASHBROOK AND SARA WEBB.

IT'S A STRANGE WORLD, GREY.

I SUPPOSE YOU KNOW THAT BETTER THAN MOST.

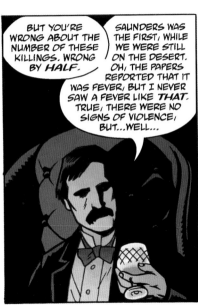

BUT YOU'RE WRONG ABOUT THE NUMBER OF THESE KILLINGS. WRONG BY *HALF*.

SAUNDERS WAS THE FIRST, WHILE WE WERE STILL ON THE DESERT. OH, THE PAPERS REPORTED THAT IT WAS FEVER, BUT I NEVER SAW A FEVER LIKE *THAT*. TRUE, THERE WERE NO SIGNS OF VIOLENCE, BUT...WELL...

"POOR SAUNDERS.

"AND YET ISN'T IT FITTING THAT HE SHOULD BE FIRST TO GO? IT WAS HIS MAD DREAM STARTED THE WHOLE THING, AND HIS MADNESS CLAIMED US ALL IN THE END."

THERE ARE THEORIES, GREY... IMAGINE WHOLE CIVILIZATIONS RISING AND FALLING BEFORE THE COMING OF MAN. HOW WOULD *THAT* SQUARE WITH YOUR BIBLE STORIES?

WHAT WOULD IT MEAN TO *PROVE* A THING LIKE THAT?

I WON'T TELL YOU WHAT SAUNDERS LEARNED, OR HOW HE LEARNED IT, OR HOW HE LED US TO THE PLACE, BUT THERE'S A CITY OUT THERE IN THE SAHARA A THOUSAND TIMES OLDER THAN TROY...

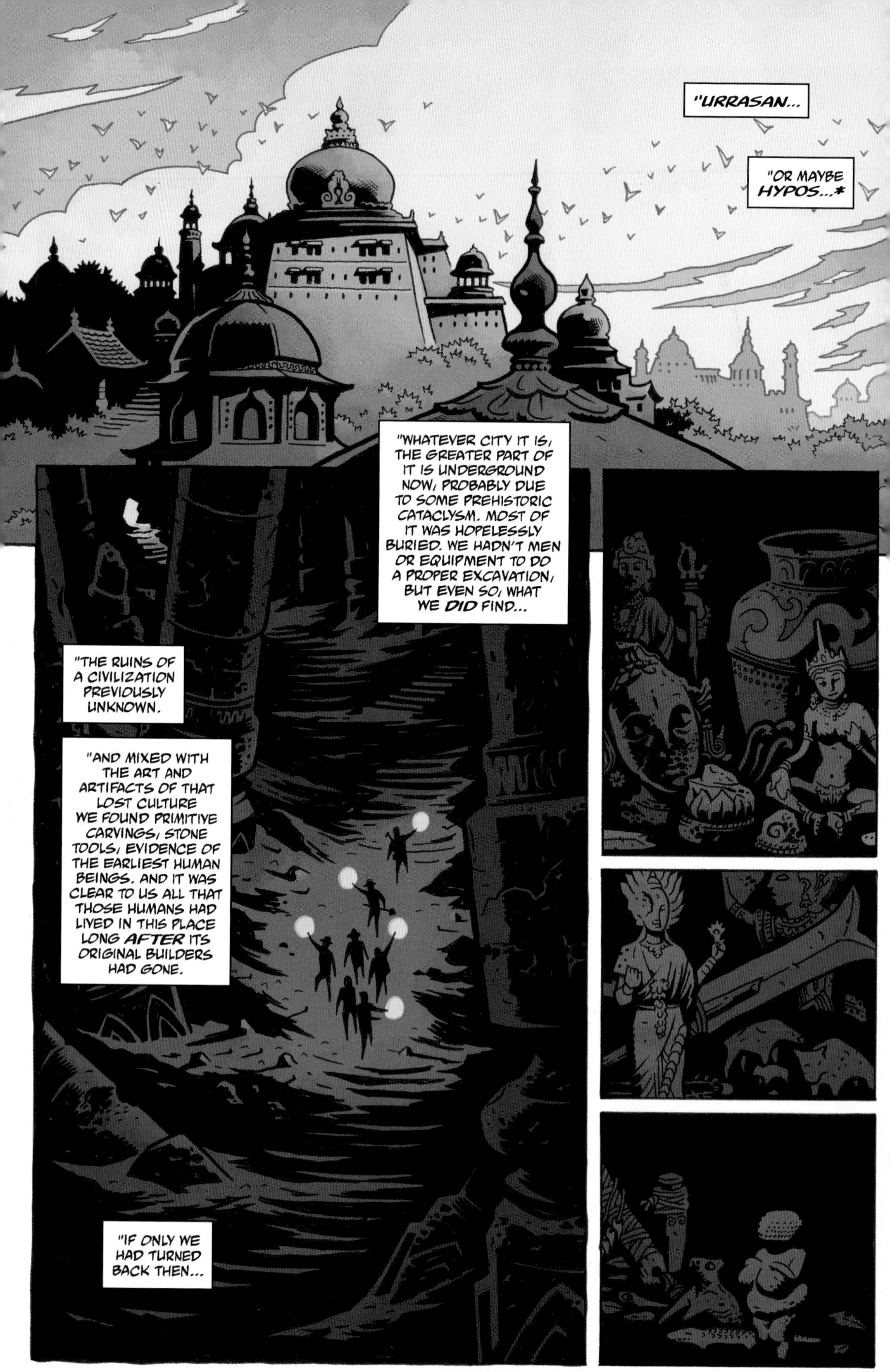
"URRASAN...
"OR MAYBE HYPOS...*
"WHATEVER CITY IT IS, THE GREATER PART OF IT IS UNDERGROUND NOW, PROBABLY DUE TO SOME PREHISTORIC CATACLYSM. MOST OF IT WAS HOPELESSLY BURIED. WE HADN'T MEN OR EQUIPMENT TO DO A PROPER EXCAVATION, BUT EVEN SO, WHAT WE *DID* FIND...
"THE RUINS OF A CIVILIZATION PREVIOUSLY UNKNOWN.
"AND MIXED WITH THE ART AND ARTIFACTS OF THAT LOST CULTURE WE FOUND PRIMITIVE CARVINGS, STONE TOOLS, EVIDENCE OF THE EARLIEST HUMAN BEINGS. AND IT WAS CLEAR TO US ALL THAT THOSE HUMANS HAD LIVED IN THIS PLACE LONG *AFTER* ITS ORIGINAL BUILDERS HAD GONE.
"IF ONLY WE HAD TURNED BACK THEN...

*ACCORDING TO AMELIA DUNN'S THE SECRET HISTORY OF THE WORLD (UNPUBLISHED), THESE WERE TWO OF SEVEN CITIES (ATLANTIS BEING ANOTHER) ESTABLISHED BY THE LATER HYPERBOREAN EMPIRE.

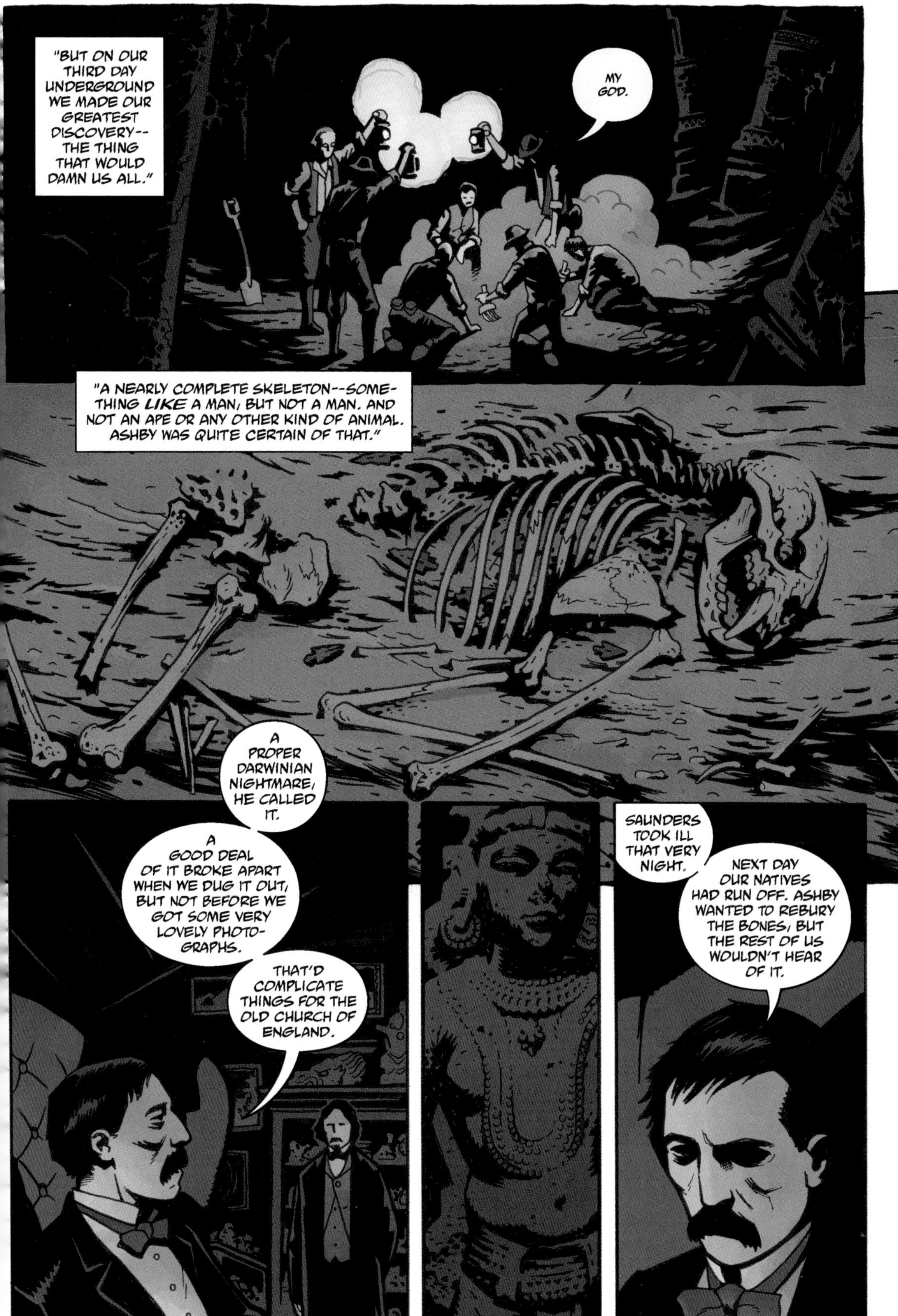
"BUT ON OUR THIRD DAY UNDERGROUND WE MADE OUR GREATEST DISCOVERY-- THE THING THAT WOULD DAMN US ALL."
MY GOD.
"A NEARLY COMPLETE SKELETON--SOMETHING LIKE A MAN, BUT NOT A MAN. AND NOT AN APE OR ANY OTHER KIND OF ANIMAL. ASHBY WAS QUITE CERTAIN OF THAT."
A PROPER DARWINIAN NIGHTMARE, HE CALLED IT.
A GOOD DEAL OF IT BROKE APART WHEN WE DUG IT OUT, BUT NOT BEFORE WE GOT SOME VERY LOVELY PHOTOGRAPHS.
THAT'D COMPLICATE THINGS FOR THE OLD CHURCH OF ENGLAND.
SAUNDERS TOOK ILL THAT VERY NIGHT.
NEXT DAY OUR NATIVES HAD RUN OFF. ASHBY WANTED TO REBURY THE BONES, BUT THE REST OF US WOULDN'T HEAR OF IT.

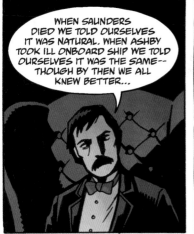

WHEN SAUNDERS DIED WE TOLD OURSELVES IT WAS NATURAL. WHEN ASHBY TOOK ILL ONBOARD SHIP WE TOLD OURSELVES IT WAS THE SAME-- THOUGH BY THEN WE ALL KNEW BETTER...

"HE KEPT CRYING OUT THAT SOMETHING WAS AT HIM, THAT HE COULD SEE ITS FACE--AND ALL THE WHILE BEGGING US TO THROW THOSE BONES OVERBOARD."

THEN HE DIED. AND A FEW DAYS LATER GRIFFIN STARTED COMPLAINING OF NIGHTMARES, AND A WEEK LATER WE FOUND HIM DEAD OUT ON THE DECK.

"UNLIKE SAUNDERS AND ASHBY, HE HAD MARKS ON HIM, LIKE SOMETHING SMALL HAD BEEN GNAWING AT HIM--RATS, WE THOUGHT. ALL SHIPS HAVE RATS..."

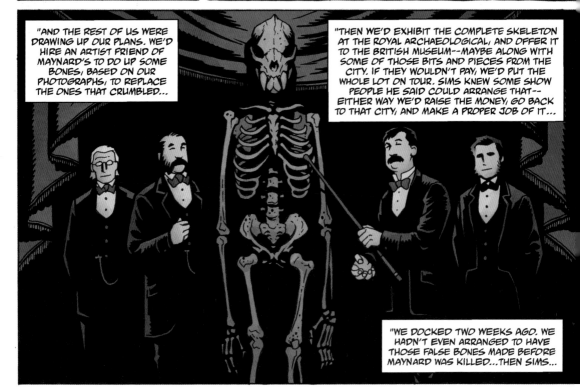

"AND THE REST OF US WERE DRAWING UP OUR PLANS. WE'D HIRE AN ARTIST FRIEND OF MAYNARD'S TO DO UP SOME BONES, BASED ON OUR PHOTOGRAPHS, TO REPLACE THE ONES THAT CRUMBLED..."

"THEN WE'D EXHIBIT THE COMPLETE SKELETON AT THE ROYAL ARCHAEOLOGICAL, AND OFFER IT TO THE BRITISH MUSEUM--MAYBE ALONG WITH SOME OF THOSE BITS AND PIECES FROM THE CITY. IF THEY WOULDN'T PAY, WE'D PUT THE WHOLE LOT ON TOUR. SIMS KNEW SOME SHOW PEOPLE HE SAID COULD ARRANGE THAT-- EITHER WAY WE'D RAISE THE MONEY, GO BACK TO THAT CITY, AND MAKE A PROPER JOB OF IT..."

"WE DOCKED TWO WEEKS AGO. WE HADN'T EVEN ARRANGED TO HAVE THOSE FALSE BONES MADE BEFORE MAYNARD WAS KILLED...THEN SIMS..."

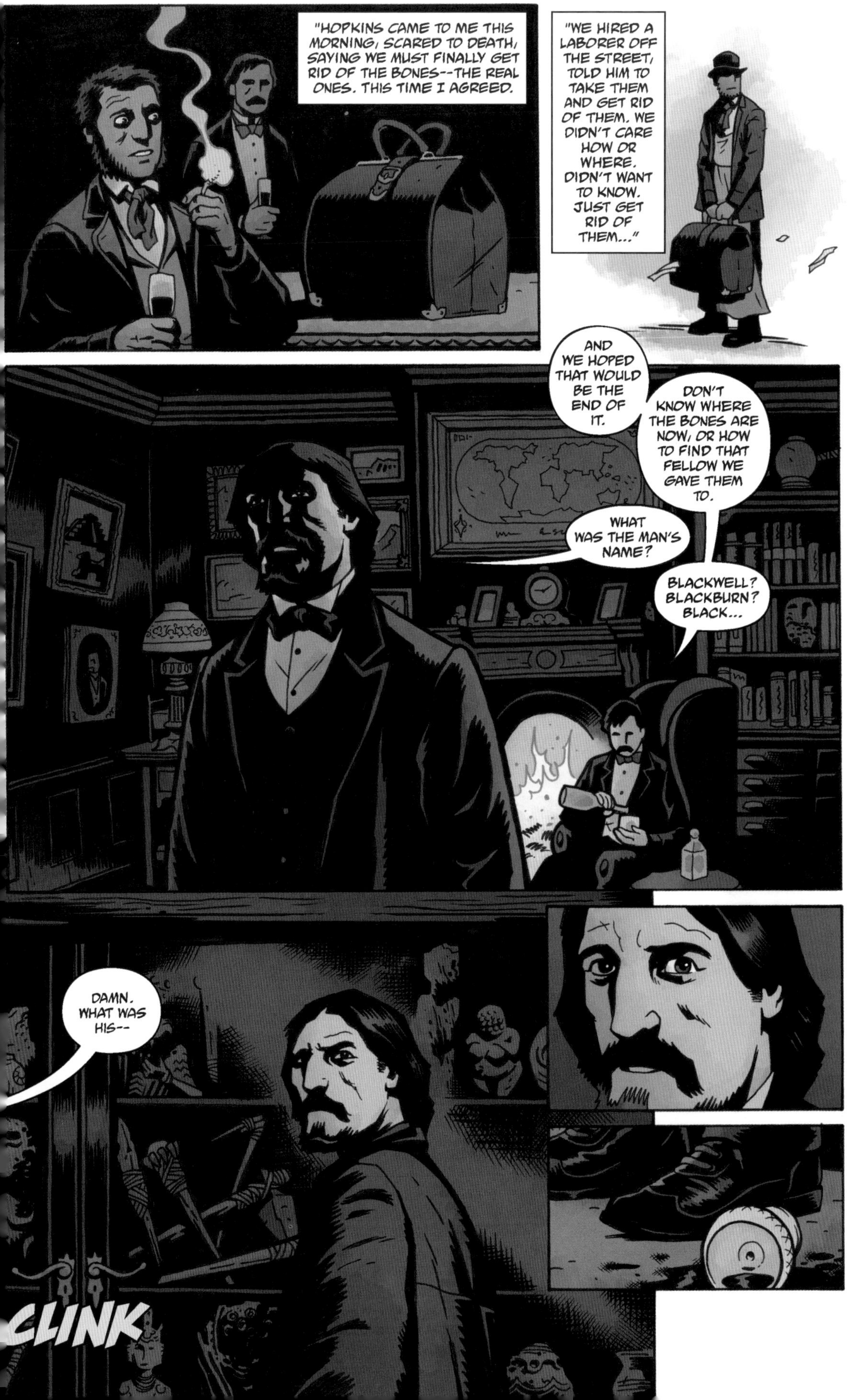
"HOPKINS CAME TO ME THIS MORNING, SCARED TO DEATH, SAYING WE MUST FINALLY GET RID OF THE BONES--THE REAL ONES. THIS TIME I AGREED.
"WE HIRED A LABORER OFF THE STREET, TOLD HIM TO TAKE THEM AND GET RID OF THEM. WE DIDN'T CARE HOW OR WHERE. DIDN'T WANT TO KNOW. JUST GET RID OF THEM..."
AND WE HOPED THAT WOULD BE THE END OF IT.
DON'T KNOW WHERE THE BONES ARE NOW, OR HOW TO FIND THAT FELLOW WE GAVE THEM TO.
WHAT WAS THE MAN'S NAME?
BLACKWELL? BLACKBURN? BLACK...
DAMN. WHAT WAS HIS--
CLINK

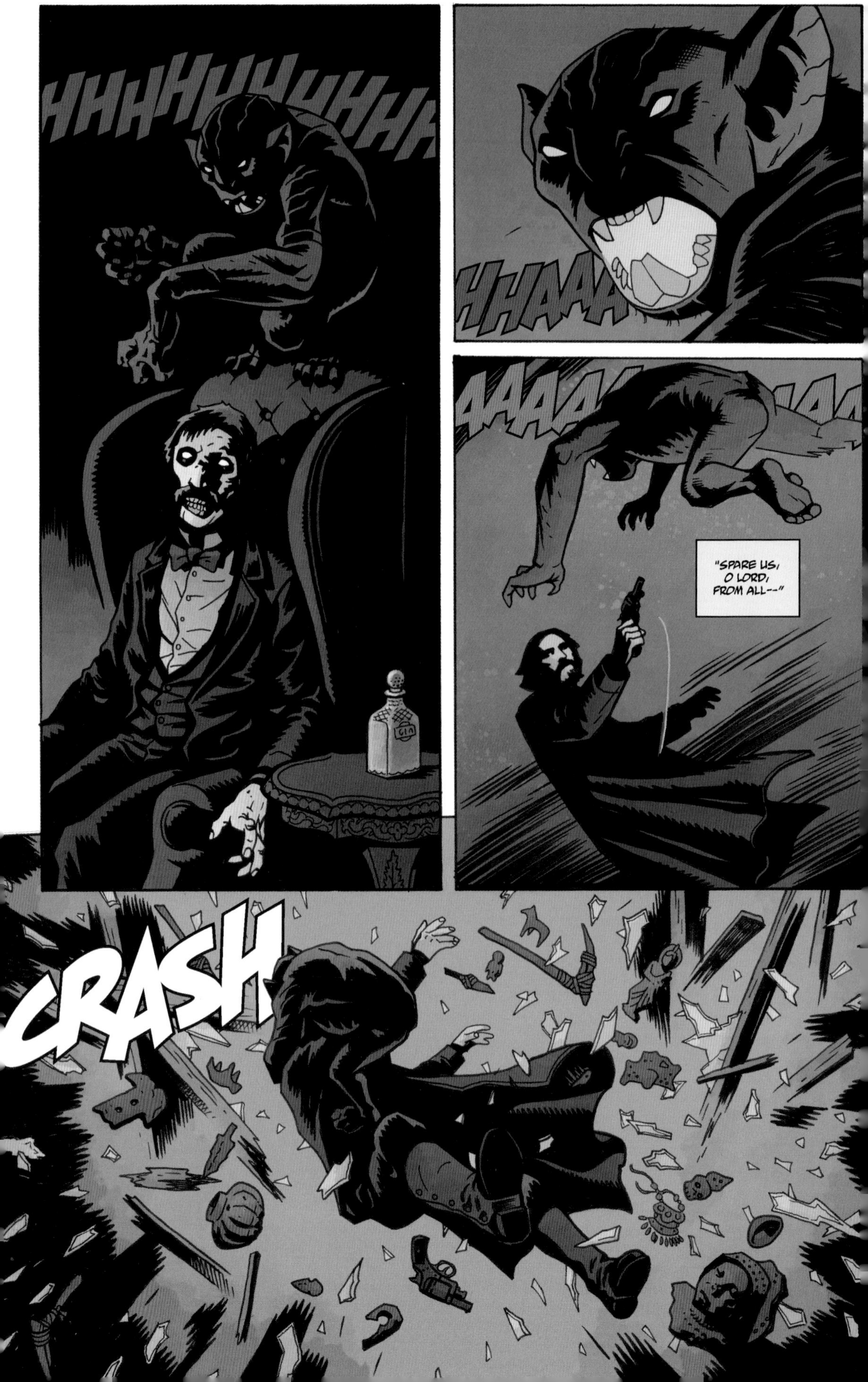
HHHHHUUUUUHHHHH
HHAAA
AAAAAAAA
"SPARE US, O LORD, FROM ALL--"
CRASH

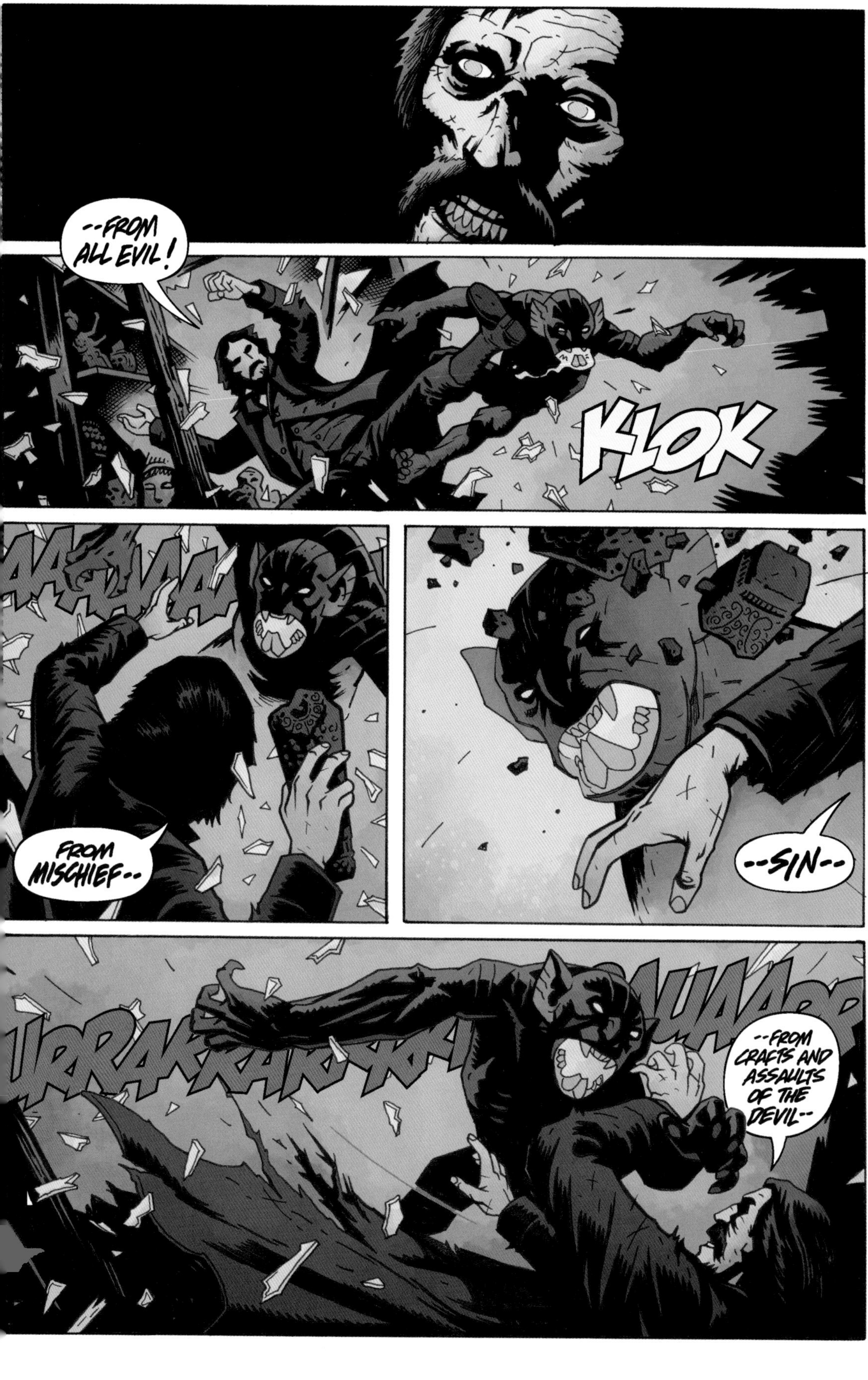
--FROM ALL EVIL!
KLOK
FROM MISCHIEF--
--SIN--
--FROM CRAFTS AND ASSAULTS OF THE DEVIL--

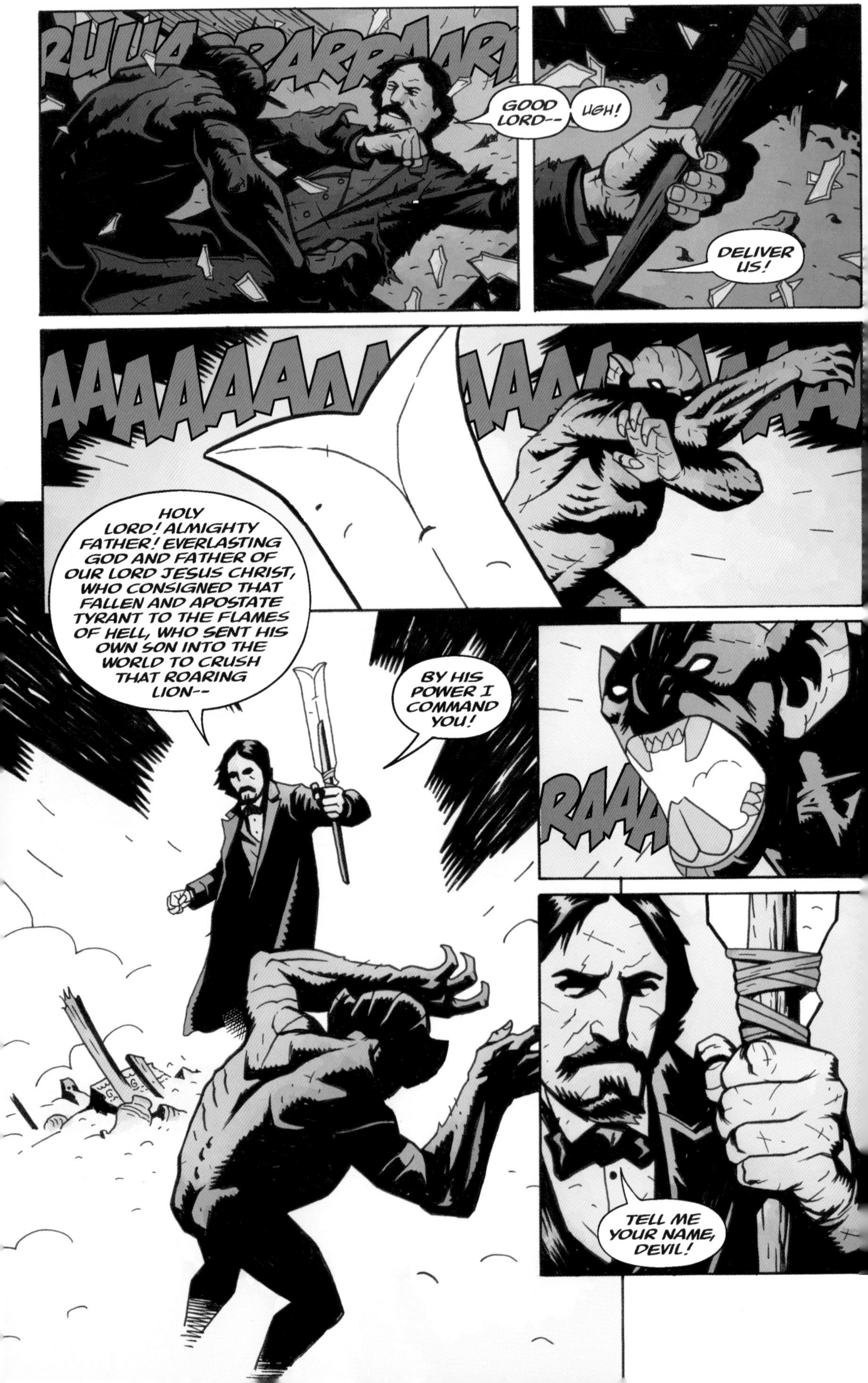
RULLARRARRAARR
GOOD LORD--
UGH!
DELIVER US!
AAAAAAAAAAAAAAAAAAAA
HOLY LORD! ALMIGHTY FATHER! EVERLASTING GOD AND FATHER OF OUR LORD JESUS CHRIST, WHO CONSIGNED THAT FALLEN AND APOSTATE TYRANT TO THE FLAMES OF HELL, WHO SENT HIS OWN SON INTO THE WORLD TO CRUSH THAT ROARING LION--
BY HIS POWER I COMMAND YOU!
RAAA
TELL ME YOUR NAME, DEVIL!

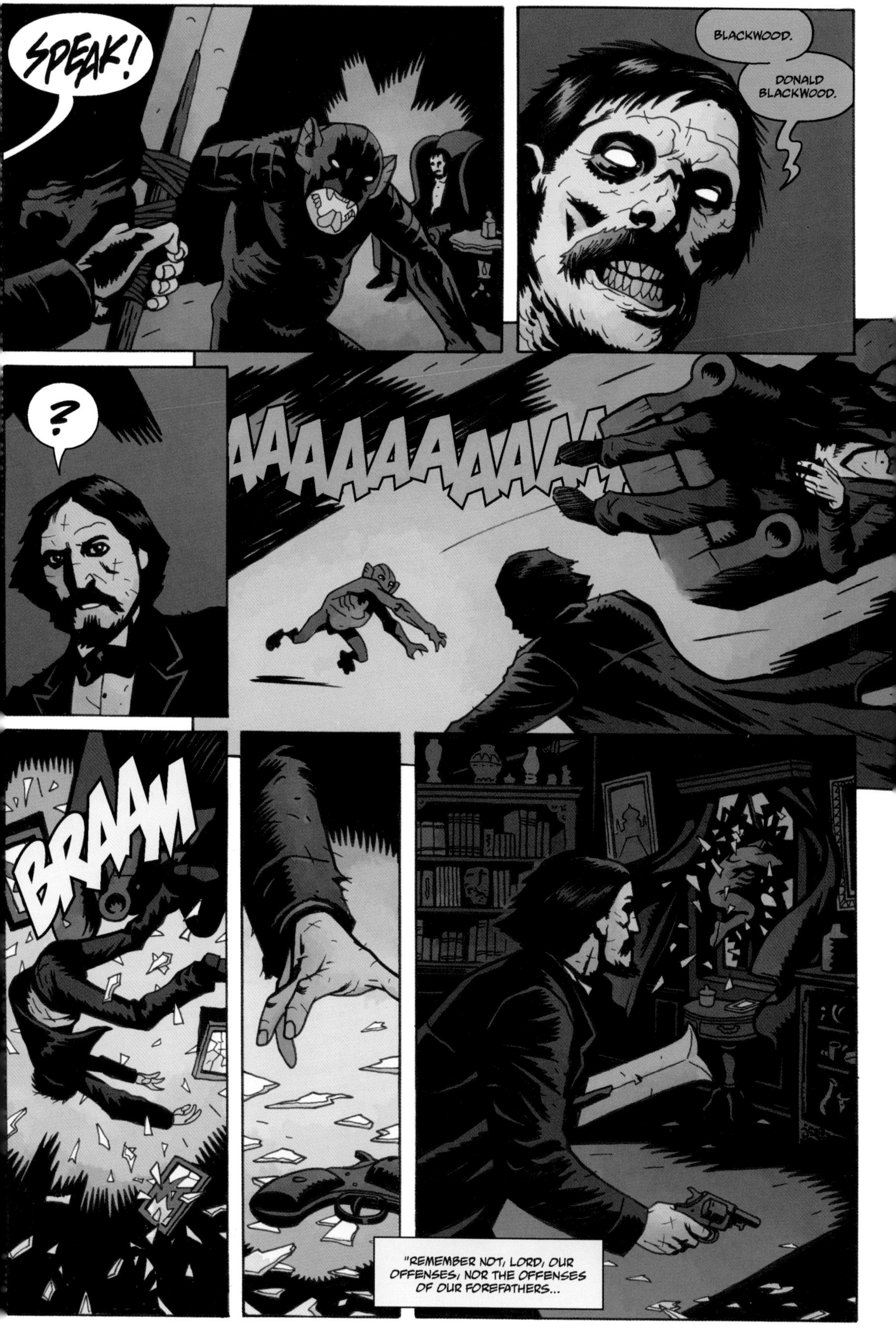
SPEAK!
BLACKWOOD.
DONALD BLACKWOOD.
?
AAAAAAAAAA
BRAAM
"REMEMBER NOT, LORD, OUR OFFENSES, NOR THE OFFENSES OF OUR FOREFATHERS...

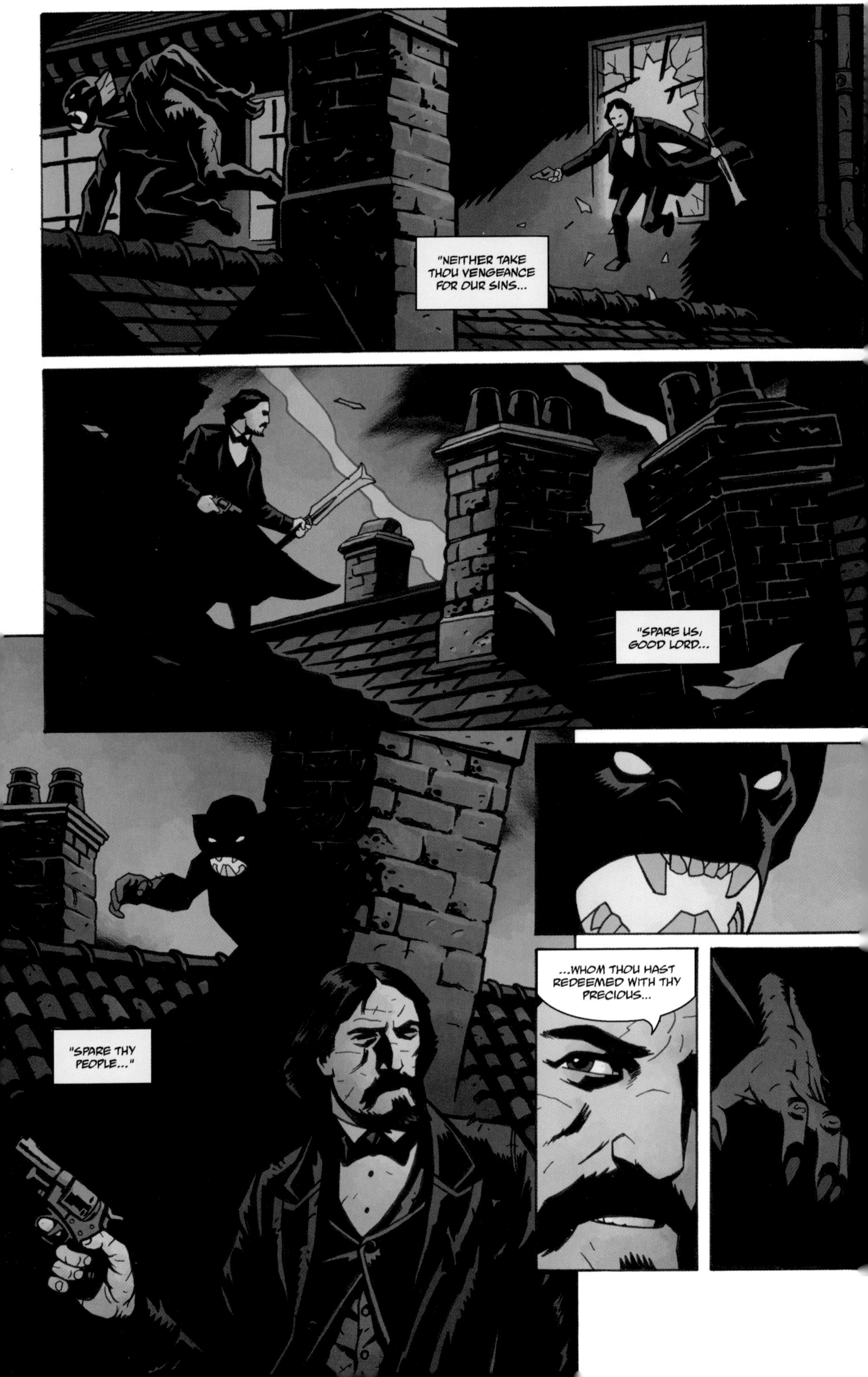
"NEITHER TAKE THOU VENGEANCE FOR OUR SINS...
"SPARE US, GOOD LORD...
"SPARE THY PEOPLE..."
...WHOM THOU HAST REDEEMED WITH THY PRECIOUS...

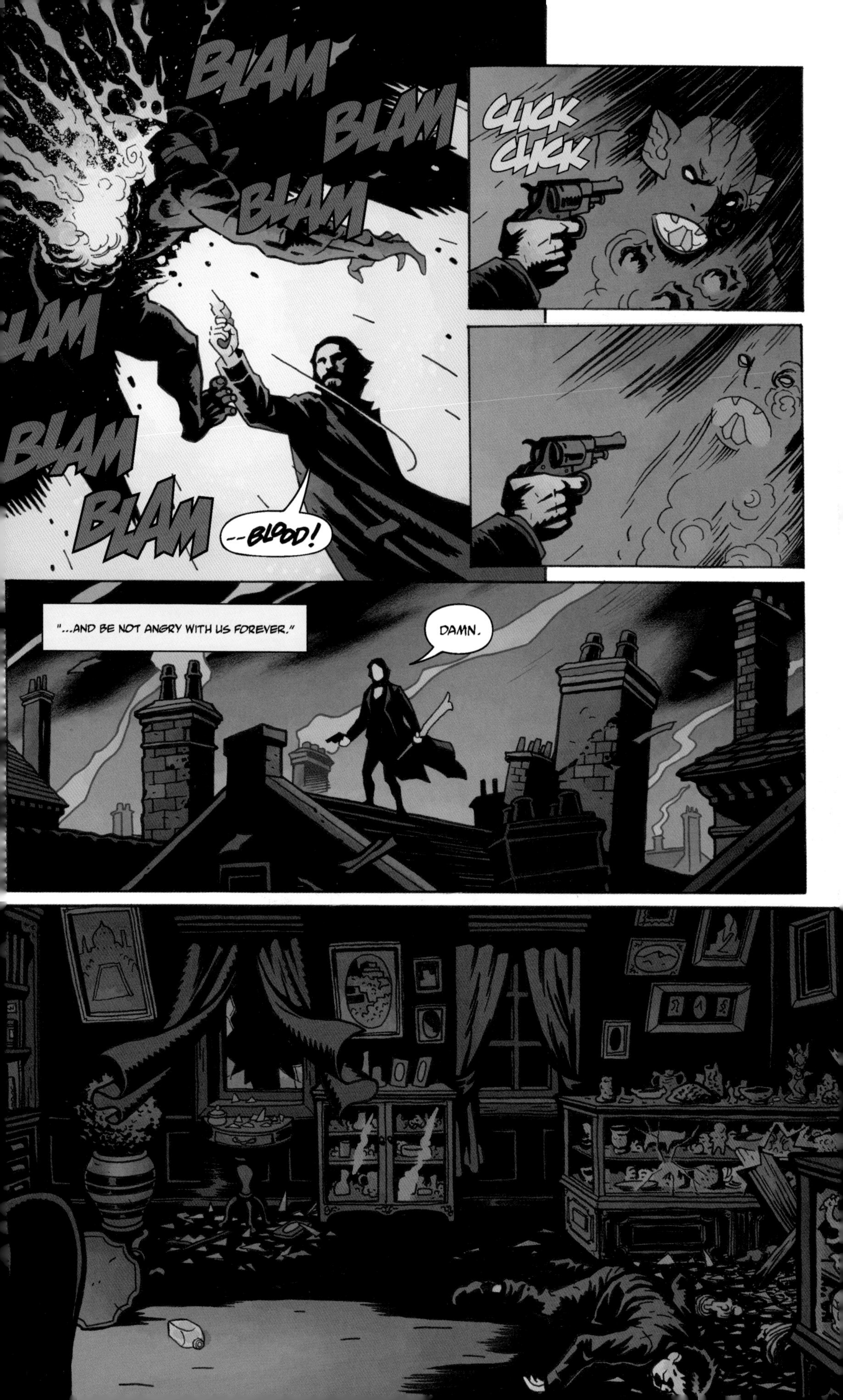
BLAM
BLAM
BLAM
BLAM
BLAM
BLAM
--BLOOD!
CLICK
CLICK
"...AND BE NOT ANGRY WITH US FOREVER."
DAMN.

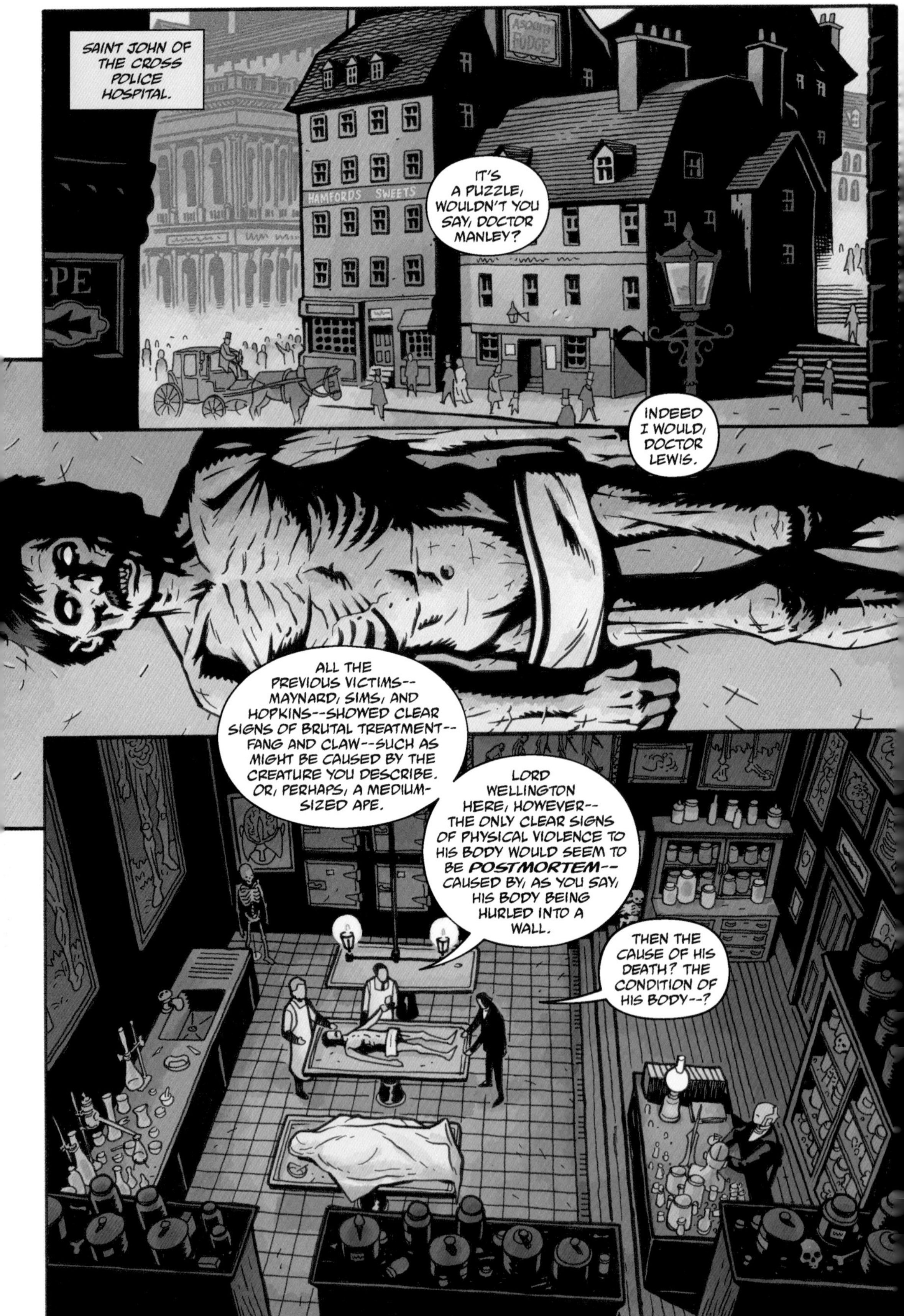
SAINT JOHN OF THE CROSS POLICE HOSPITAL.
ASQUITH FUDGE
HAMFORDS SWEETS
IT'S A PUZZLE, WOULDN'T YOU SAY, DOCTOR MANLEY?
INDEED I WOULD, DOCTOR LEWIS.
ALL THE PREVIOUS VICTIMS--MAYNARD, SIMS, AND HOPKINS--SHOWED CLEAR SIGNS OF BRUTAL TREATMENT--FANG AND CLAW--SUCH AS MIGHT BE CAUSED BY THE CREATURE YOU DESCRIBE. OR, PERHAPS, A MEDIUM-SIZED APE.
LORD WELLINGTON HERE, HOWEVER--THE ONLY CLEAR SIGNS OF PHYSICAL VIOLENCE TO HIS BODY WOULD SEEM TO BE *POSTMORTEM*--CAUSED BY, AS YOU SAY, HIS BODY BEING HURLED INTO A WALL.
THEN THE CAUSE OF HIS DEATH? THE CONDITION OF HIS BODY--?

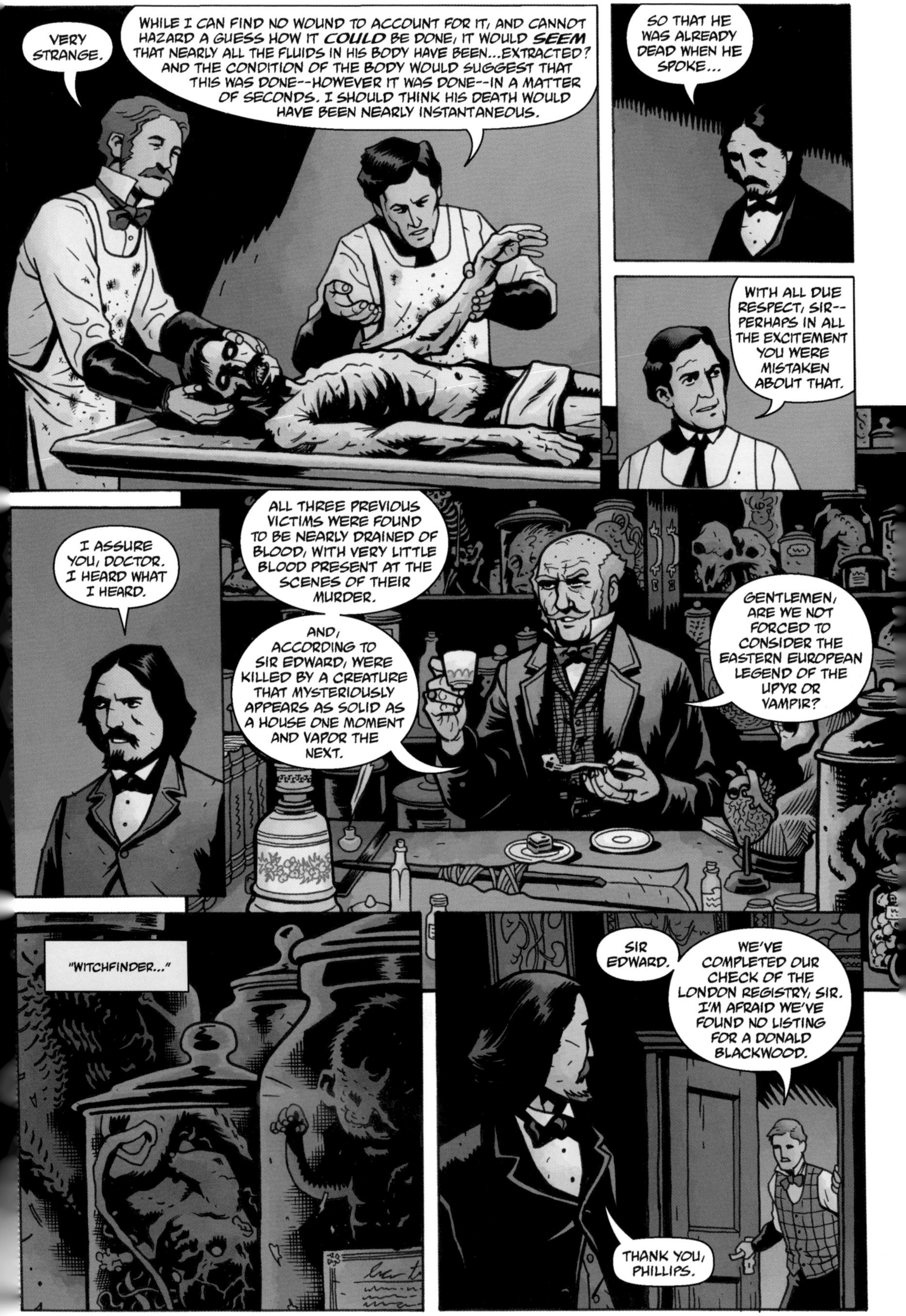
VERY STRANGE.
WHILE I CAN FIND NO WOUND TO ACCOUNT FOR IT, AND CANNOT HAZARD A GUESS HOW IT *COULD* BE DONE, IT WOULD *SEEM* THAT NEARLY ALL THE FLUIDS IN HIS BODY HAVE BEEN...EXTRACTED? AND THE CONDITION OF THE BODY WOULD SUGGEST THAT THIS WAS DONE--HOWEVER IT WAS DONE--IN A MATTER OF SECONDS. I SHOULD THINK HIS DEATH WOULD HAVE BEEN NEARLY INSTANTANEOUS.
SO THAT HE WAS ALREADY DEAD WHEN HE SPOKE...
WITH ALL DUE RESPECT, SIR--PERHAPS IN ALL THE EXCITEMENT YOU WERE MISTAKEN ABOUT THAT.
I ASSURE YOU, DOCTOR. I HEARD WHAT I HEARD.
ALL THREE PREVIOUS VICTIMS WERE FOUND TO BE NEARLY DRAINED OF BLOOD, WITH VERY LITTLE BLOOD PRESENT AT THE SCENES OF THEIR MURDER.
AND, ACCORDING TO SIR EDWARD, WERE KILLED BY A CREATURE THAT MYSTERIOUSLY APPEARS AS SOLID AS A HOUSE ONE MOMENT AND VAPOR THE NEXT.
GENTLEMEN, ARE WE NOT FORCED TO CONSIDER THE EASTERN EUROPEAN LEGEND OF THE UPYR OR VAMPIR?
"WITCHFINDER..."
SIR EDWARD.
WE'VE COMPLETED OUR CHECK OF THE LONDON REGISTRY, SIR. I'M AFRAID WE'VE FOUND NO LISTING FOR A DONALD BLACKWOOD.
THANK YOU, PHILLIPS.

VERY DIFFICULT GETTING RELIABLE INFORMATION FROM THESE DEAD FELLOWS.

DAMNED UNRELIABLE.

DOCTOR LEWIS, AS YOU HAVE *ENTIRELY FAILED* TO PROVIDE A MEDICAL OR SCIENTIFIC EXPLANATION FOR THE CONDITION OF HIS LORDSHIP, WHAT SHALL WE DO? IF THE NATURAL WORLD WILL NOT SERVE, ARE WE NOT FORCED TO CONSIDER THE *SUPER*-NATURAL?

SIR EDWARD?

I SHOT IT AND IT VANISHED, BUT IT WAS MY IMPRESSION THAT THE BULLETS DID IT NO HARM AT ALL.

AND IT WAS ALSO YOUR IMPRESSION THAT THE CREATURE WAS AFRAID OF *THIS?*

YES.

AND HAVE YOU ANY IDEA WHAT THIS IS?

"WITCHFINDER..."

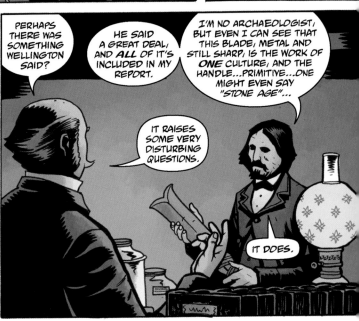

PERHAPS THERE WAS SOMETHING WELLINGTON SAID?

HE SAID A GREAT DEAL, AND *ALL* OF IT'S INCLUDED IN MY REPORT.

I'M NO ARCHAEOLOGIST, BUT EVEN I CAN SEE THAT THIS BLADE, METAL AND STILL SHARP, IS THE WORK OF *ONE* CULTURE, AND THE HANDLE...PRIMITIVE...ONE MIGHT EVEN SAY "STONE AGE"...

IT RAISES SOME VERY DISTURBING QUESTIONS.

IT DOES.

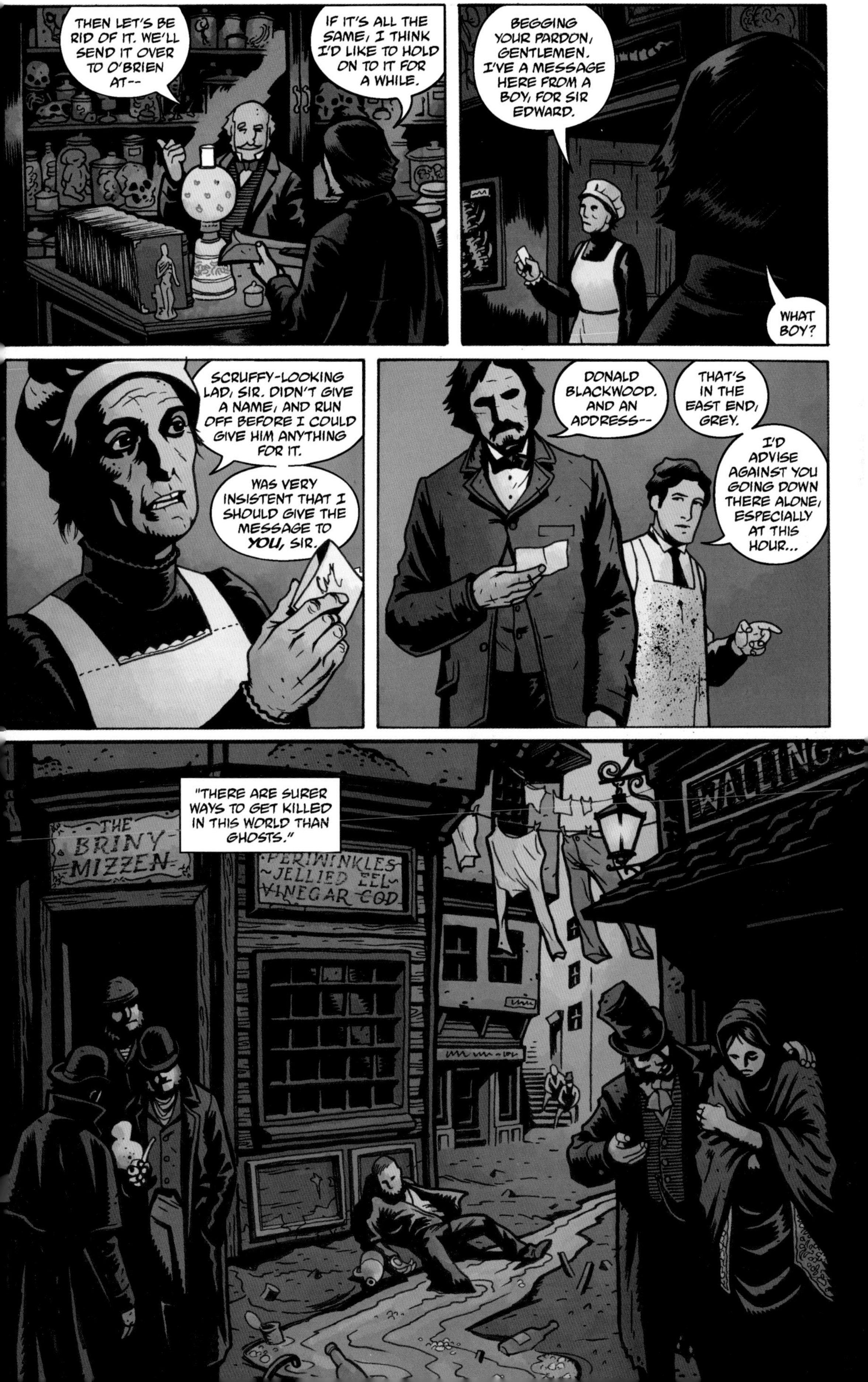
THEN LET'S BE RID OF IT. WE'LL SEND IT OVER TO O'BRIEN AT--
IF IT'S ALL THE SAME, I THINK I'D LIKE TO HOLD ON TO IT FOR A WHILE.
BEGGING YOUR PARDON, GENTLEMEN. I'VE A MESSAGE HERE FROM A BOY, FOR SIR EDWARD.
WHAT BOY?
SCRUFFY-LOOKING LAD, SIR. DIDN'T GIVE A NAME, AND RUN OFF BEFORE I COULD GIVE HIM ANYTHING FOR IT.
WAS VERY INSISTENT THAT I SHOULD GIVE THE MESSAGE TO YOU, SIR.
DONALD BLACKWOOD. AND AN ADDRESS--
THAT'S IN THE EAST END, GREY.
I'D ADVISE AGAINST YOU GOING DOWN THERE ALONE, ESPECIALLY AT THIS HOUR...
"THERE ARE SURER WAYS TO GET KILLED IN THIS WORLD THAN GHOSTS."
THE BRINY MIZZEN
PERIWINKLES ~JELLIED EEL~ VINEGAR COD

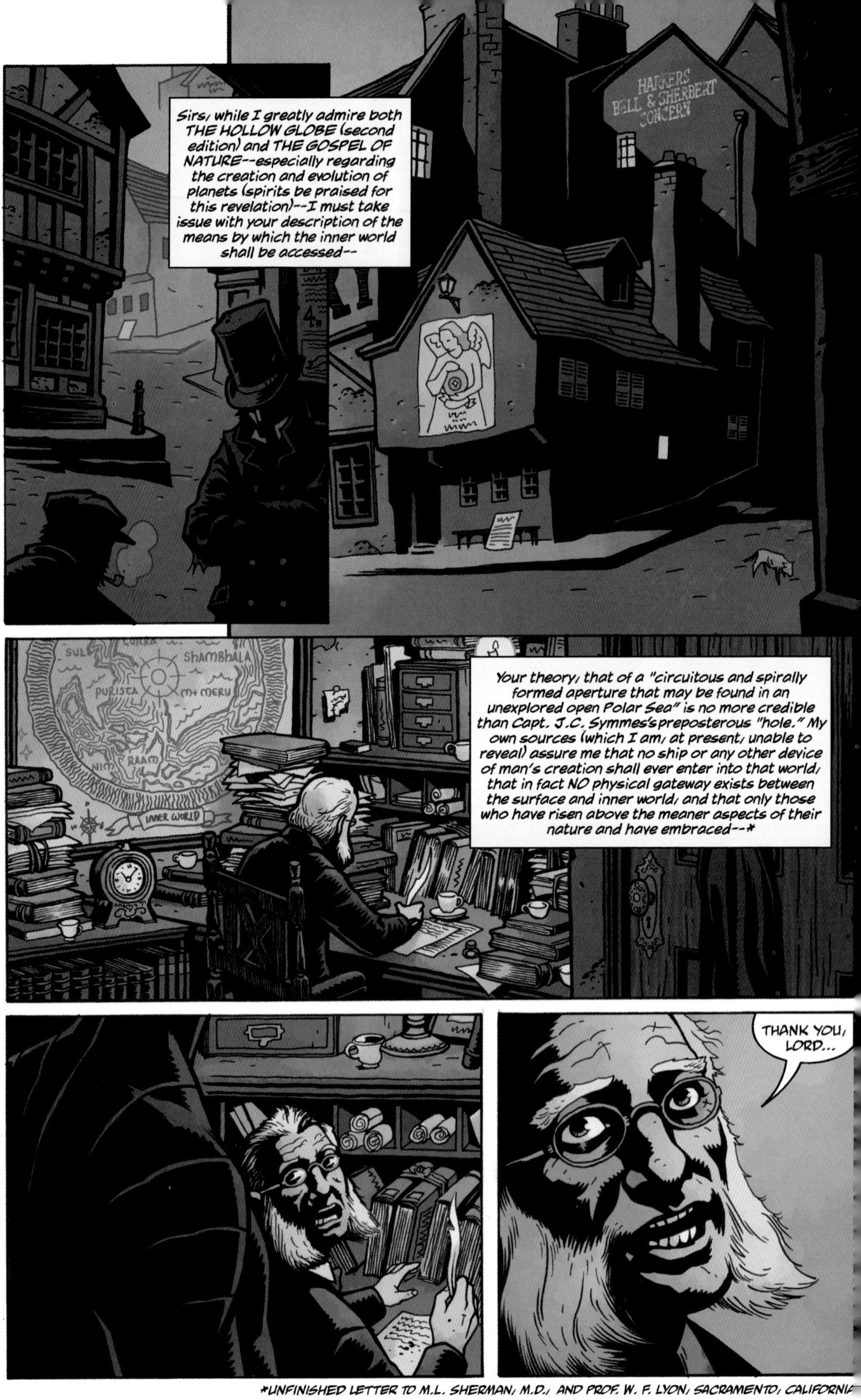
Sirs, while I greatly admire both THE HOLLOW GLOBE (second edition) and THE GOSPEL OF NATURE--especially regarding the creation and evolution of planets (spirits be praised for this revelation)--I must take issue with your description of the means by which the inner world shall be accessed--
HARKERS
BELL & SHERBERT
CONCERN
SUL
SHAMBHALA
PURISTA
MT MERU
RAAM
NIM
INNER WORLD
Your theory, that of a "circuitous and spirally formed aperture that may be found in an unexplored open Polar Sea" is no more credible than Capt. J.C. Symmes's preposterous "hole." My own sources (which I am, at present, unable to reveal) assure me that no ship or any other device of man's creation shall ever enter into that world, that in fact NO physical gateway exists between the surface and inner world, and that only those who have risen above the meaner aspects of their nature and have embraced--*
THANK YOU, LORD...

*UNFINISHED LETTER TO M.L. SHERMAN, M.D., AND PROF. W. F. LYON, SACRAMENTO, CALIFORNIA

RRRRRR

RUFF
RUFF

ZZZZZZ

IT'LL BE THAT WAY, SIR.

MIND YOUR STEP NOW, AND SEE YOU STAY CLOSE TO THESE OFFICERS.

DAMN IT, GREY--

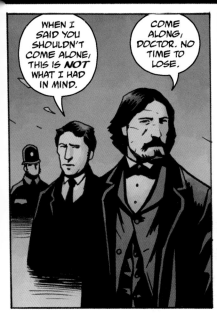

WHEN I SAID YOU SHOULDN'T COME ALONE, THIS IS *NOT* WHAT I HAD IN MIND.

COME ALONG, DOCTOR. NO TIME TO LOSE.

WOULD THAT BE IT, SIR?

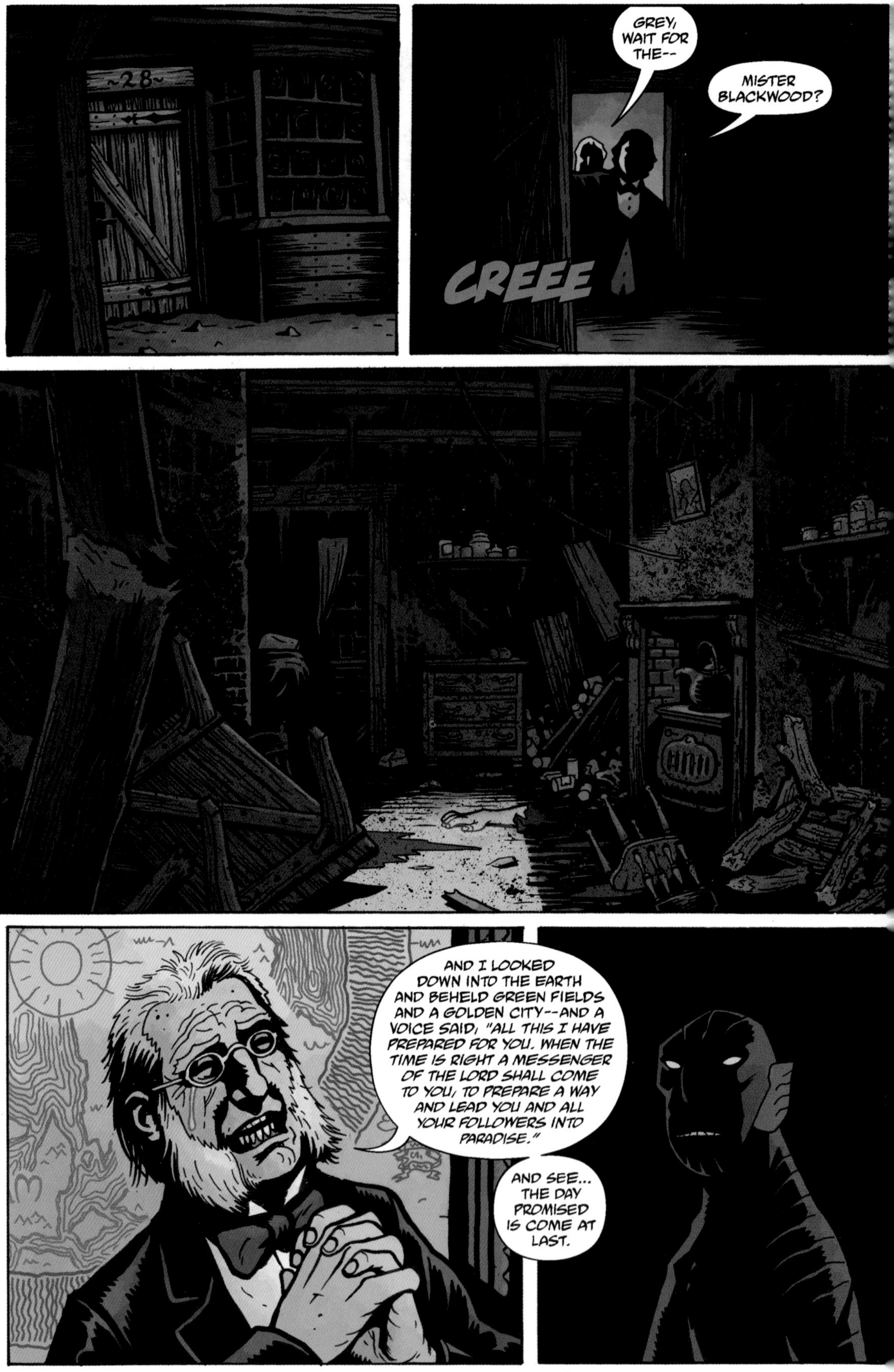
~28~
GREY, WAIT FOR THE--
MISTER BLACKWOOD?
CREEE
AND I LOOKED DOWN INTO THE EARTH AND BEHELD GREEN FIELDS AND A GOLDEN CITY--AND A VOICE SAID, "ALL THIS I HAVE PREPARED FOR YOU. WHEN THE TIME IS RIGHT A MESSENGER OF THE LORD SHALL COME TO YOU, TO PREPARE A WAY AND LEAD YOU AND ALL YOUR FOLLOWERS INTO PARADISE."
AND SEE... THE DAY PROMISED IS COME AT LAST.

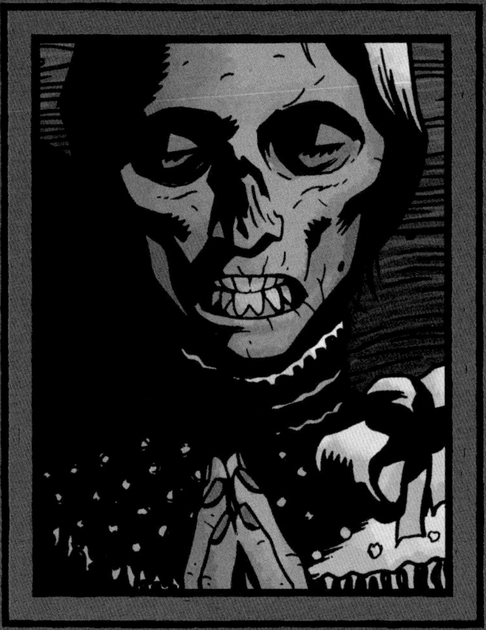

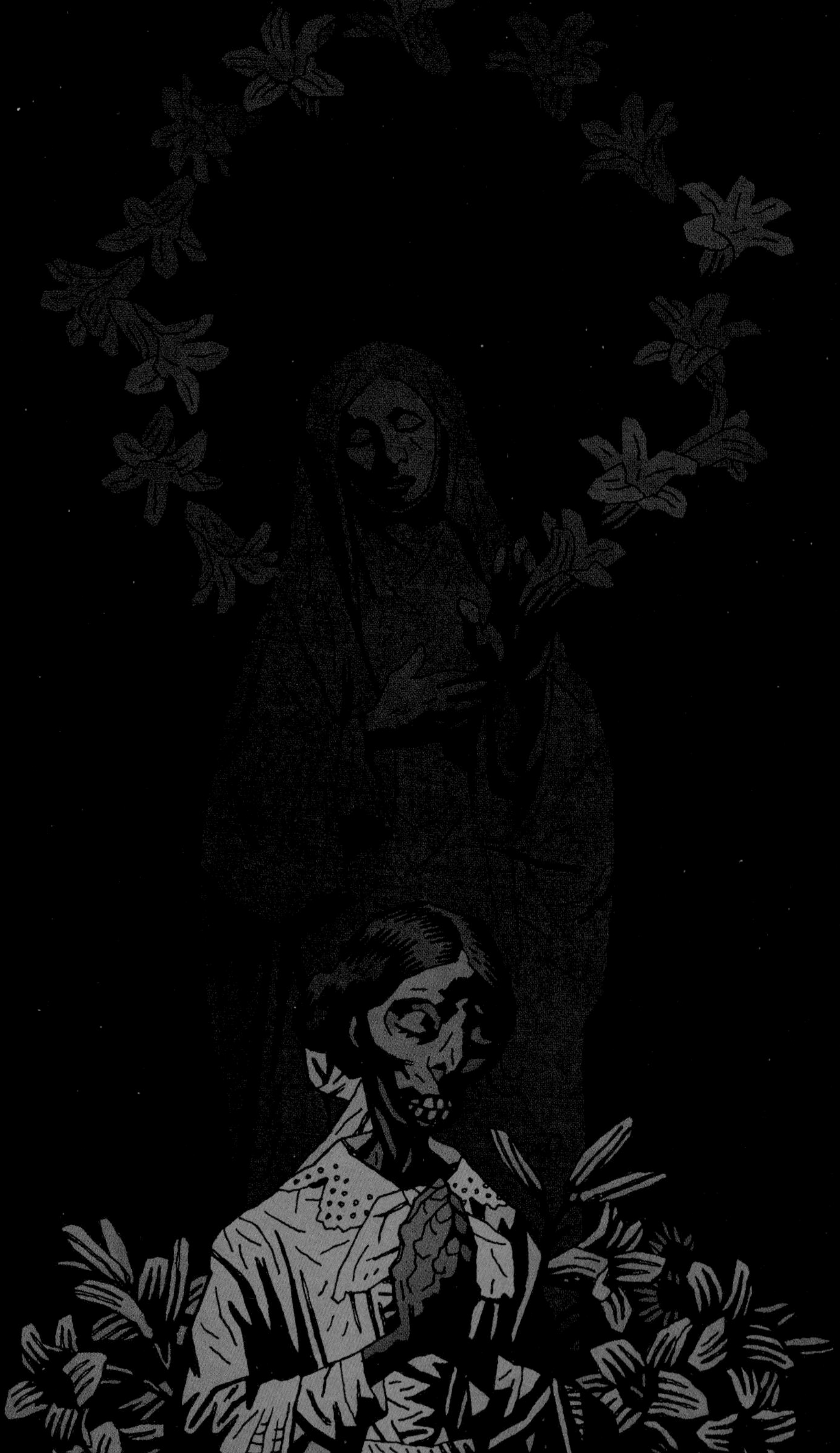

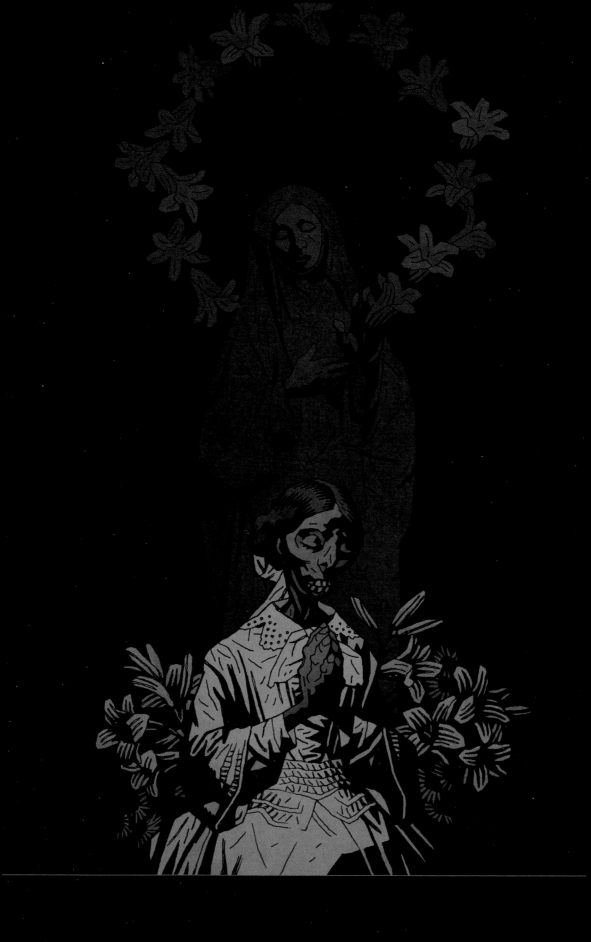

MY GOD.

HORRIBLE.

THERE'S MORE OVER HERE.

IS THAT HIS HEAD?

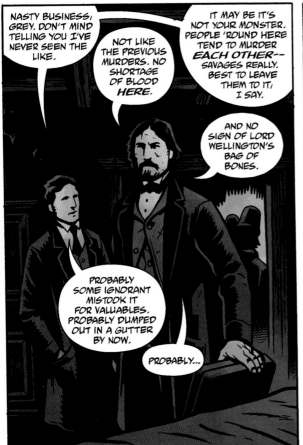

NASTY BUSINESS, GREY. DON'T MIND TELLING YOU I'VE NEVER SEEN THE LIKE.

NOT LIKE THE PREVIOUS MURDERS. NO SHORTAGE OF BLOOD HERE.

IT MAY BE IT'S NOT YOUR MONSTER. PEOPLE 'ROUND HERE TEND TO MURDER EACH OTHER-- SAVAGES REALLY. BEST TO LEAVE THEM TO IT, I SAY.

AND NO SIGN OF LORD WELLINGTON'S BAG OF BONES.

PROBABLY SOME IGNORANT MISTOOK IT FOR VALUABLES. PROBABLY DUMPED OUT IN A GUTTER BY NOW.

PROBABLY...

LEWIS, WHY DON'T YOU HELP THE OFFICERS SEARCH THOSE GUTTERS.

I'M A DOCTOR, SIR. NOT A RAGMAN.

"WITCHFINDER..."

SOME-ONE THERE?

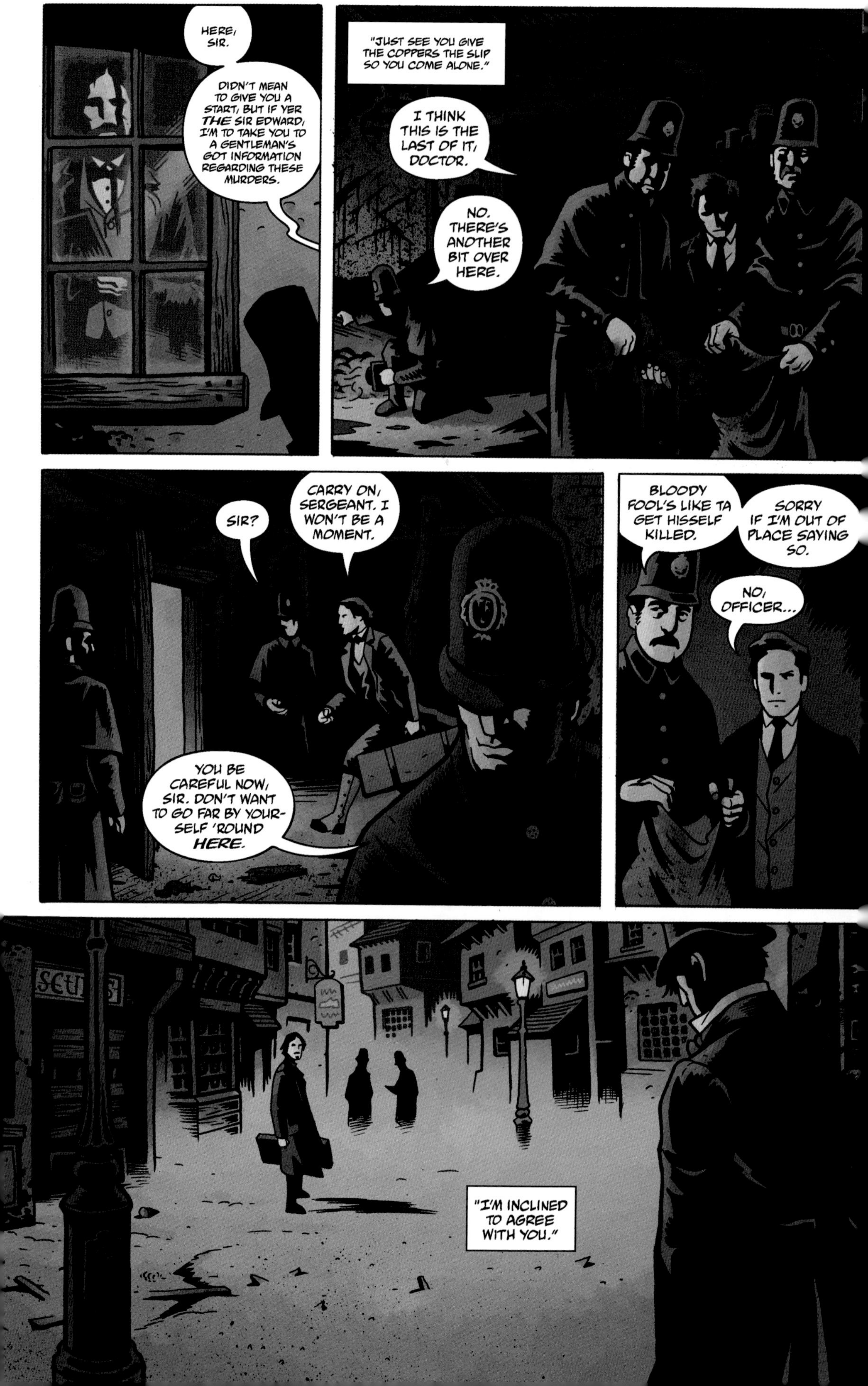
HERE, SIR.
DIDN'T MEAN TO GIVE YOU A START, BUT IF YER THE SIR EDWARD, I'M TO TAKE YOU TO A GENTLEMAN'S GOT INFORMATION REGARDING THESE MURDERS.
"JUST SEE YOU GIVE THE COPPERS THE SLIP SO YOU COME ALONE."
I THINK THIS IS THE LAST OF IT, DOCTOR.
NO. THERE'S ANOTHER BIT OVER HERE.
SIR?
CARRY ON, SERGEANT. I WON'T BE A MOMENT.
YOU BE CAREFUL NOW, SIR. DON'T WANT TO GO FAR BY YOUR-SELF 'ROUND HERE.
BLOODY FOOL'S LIKE TA GET HISSELF KILLED.
SORRY IF I'M OUT OF PLACE SAYING SO.
NO, OFFICER...
"I'M INCLINED TO AGREE WITH YOU."

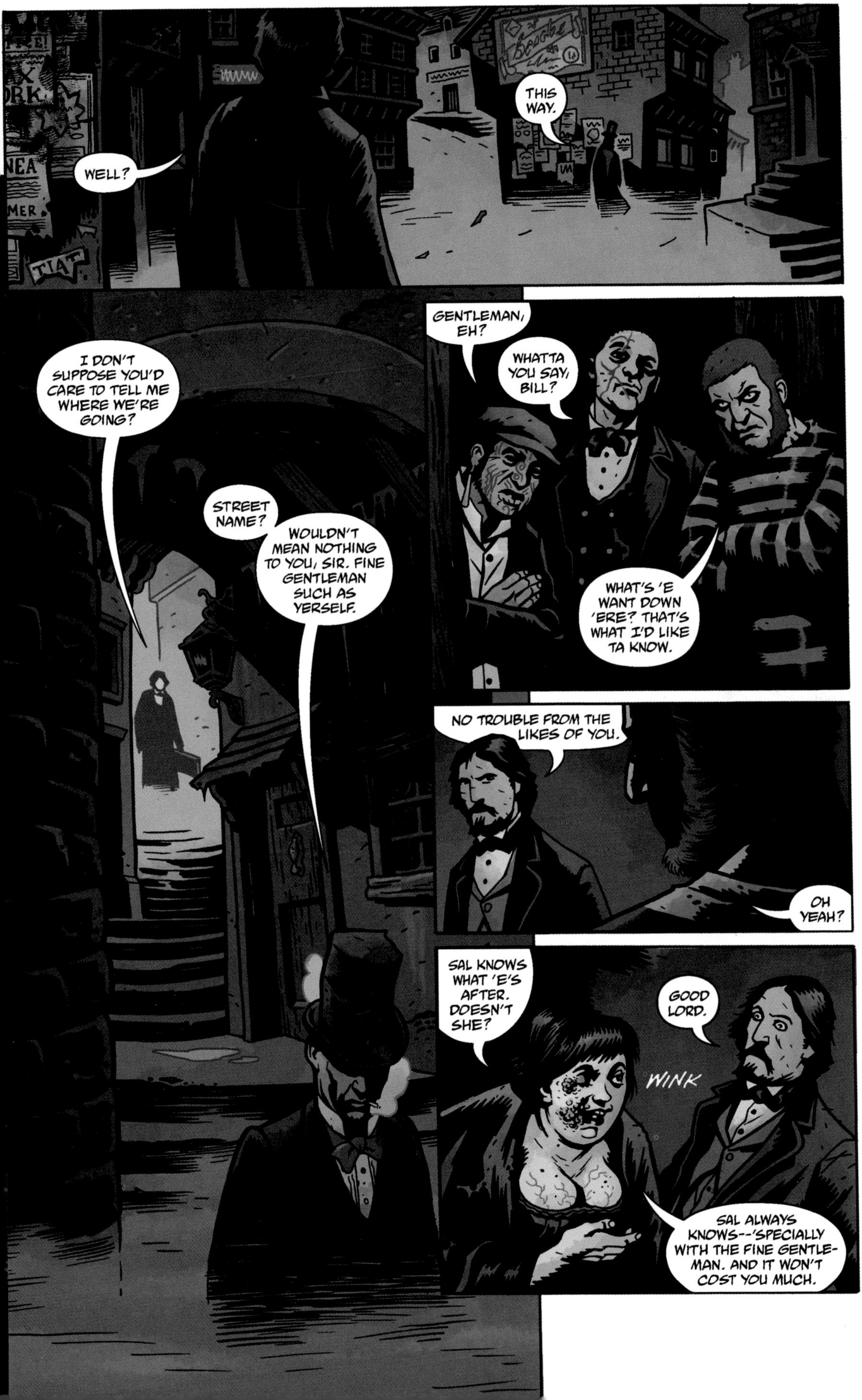
WELL?
THIS WAY.
I DON'T SUPPOSE YOU'D CARE TO TELL ME WHERE WE'RE GOING?
STREET NAME?
WOULDN'T MEAN NOTHING TO YOU, SIR. FINE GENTLEMAN SUCH AS YERSELF.
GENTLEMAN, EH?
WHATTA YOU SAY, BILL?
WHAT'S 'E WANT DOWN 'ERE? THAT'S WHAT I'D LIKE TA KNOW.
NO TROUBLE FROM THE LIKES OF YOU.
OH YEAH?
SAL KNOWS WHAT 'E'S AFTER. DOESN'T SHE?
GOOD LORD.
WINK
SAL ALWAYS KNOWS--'SPECIALLY WITH THE FINE GENTLE-MAN. AND IT WON'T COST YOU MUCH.

NO, DEARIE, YA DON'T WANT 'ER. I CAN DO FER YA.
NO, ME!
PLEASE!!
YOU LADIES, YOU LEAVE HIM BE. HE'S HERE FOR THE CAPTAIN.
OOH. CAPTAIN. VERY NICE.
WELL, DEAR. SOME OTHER TIME PERHAPS.
I DOUBT IT.
SIR?
THIS WAY.
SORRY IF THOSE LADIES GAVE YOU A START. CAN'T HARDLY BLAME 'EM TAKIN' YOU FER A CUSTOMER. NO OFFENSE.
WHAT'S YOUR NAME, BOY?
ROBERT W. SALT, ESQUIRE, SIR. LATE OF RAT'S CASTLE, AND BOUND FOR PRISON TILL I HAD PROPER MANNERS BEAT INTO ME.
NOW IF YOU'LL COME RIGHT THIS WAY.
MIND YER HEAD.

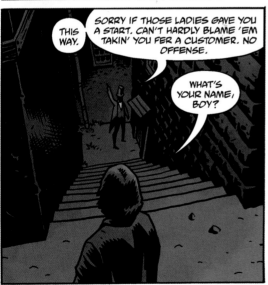

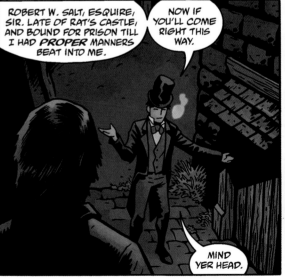

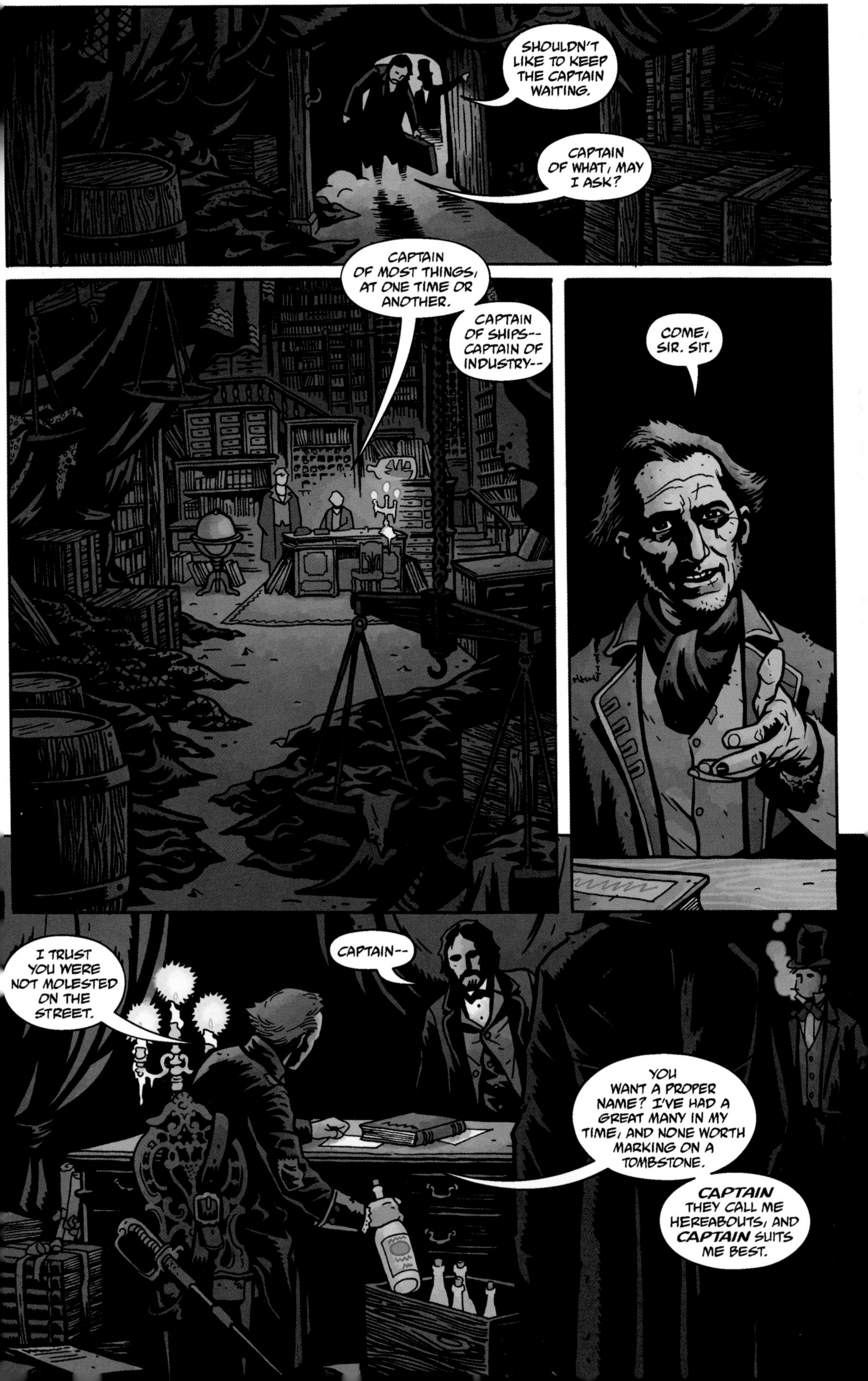
SHOULDN'T LIKE TO KEEP THE CAPTAIN WAITING.
CAPTAIN OF WHAT, MAY I ASK?
CAPTAIN OF MOST THINGS, AT ONE TIME OR ANOTHER.
CAPTAIN OF SHIPS-- CAPTAIN OF INDUSTRY--
COME, SIR. SIT.
I TRUST YOU WERE NOT MOLESTED ON THE STREET.
CAPTAIN--
YOU WANT A PROPER NAME? I'VE HAD A GREAT MANY IN MY TIME, AND NONE WORTH MARKING ON A TOMBSTONE.
CAPTAIN THEY CALL ME HEREABOUTS, AND CAPTAIN SUITS ME BEST.

YOU KNOW MISTER SALT ALREADY. HERE'S HIS TWIN, MISTER BACON.

LIKE BOOKENDS, DON'T YOU THINK?

GRUNT

EXACTLY ALIKE.

AND GOOD LADS SO LONG AS THEY STEER CLEAR OF THE BOTTLE.

CLINK CLINK

YOU'LL JOIN ME?

OF COURSE.

BY GOD, SIR. I LIKE YOU!

YOU'RE JUST THE MAN I HOPED YOU'D BE!

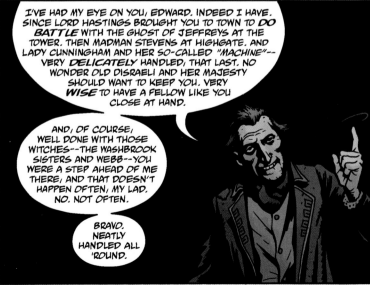

I'VE HAD MY EYE ON YOU, EDWARD. INDEED I HAVE. SINCE LORD HASTINGS BROUGHT YOU TO TOWN TO DO BATTLE WITH THE GHOST OF JEFFREYS AT THE TOWER. THEN MADMAN STEVENS AT HIGHGATE. AND LADY CUNNINGHAM AND HER SO-CALLED "MACHINE"-- VERY DELICATELY HANDLED, THAT LAST. NO WONDER OLD DISRAELI AND HER MAJESTY SHOULD WANT TO KEEP YOU. VERY WISE TO HAVE A FELLOW LIKE YOU CLOSE AT HAND.

AND, OF COURSE, WELL DONE WITH THOSE WITCHES--THE WASHBROOK SISTERS AND WEBB--YOU WERE A STEP AHEAD OF ME THERE, AND THAT DOESN'T HAPPEN OFTEN, MY LAD. NO. NOT OFTEN.

BRAVO. NEATLY HANDLED ALL 'ROUND.

YOU KNOW THINGS YOU SHOULDN'T, CAPTAIN.

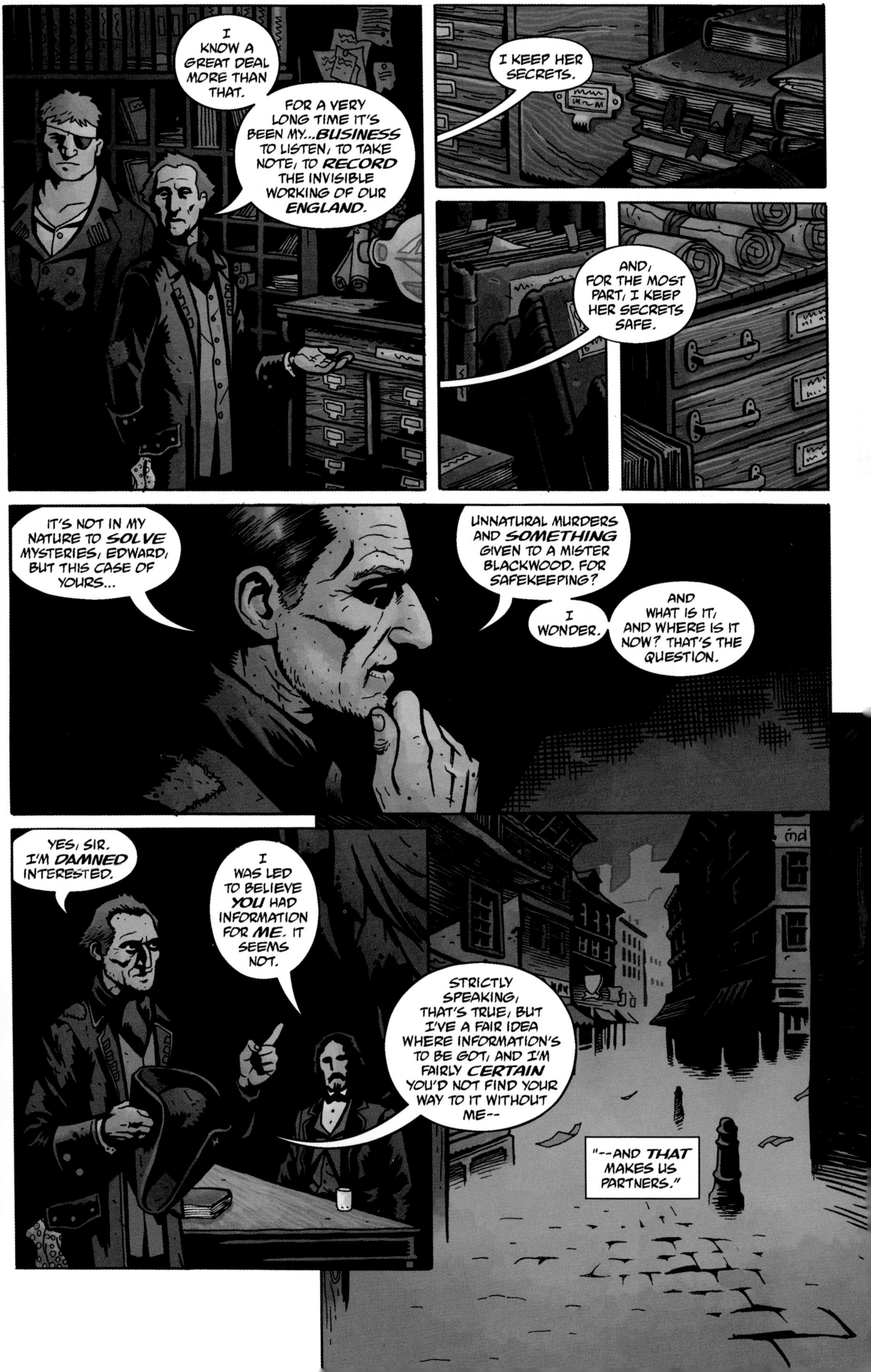
I KNOW A GREAT DEAL MORE THAN THAT.
FOR A VERY LONG TIME IT'S BEEN MY...BUSINESS TO LISTEN, TO TAKE NOTE, TO RECORD THE INVISIBLE WORKING OF OUR ENGLAND.
I KEEP HER SECRETS.
AND, FOR THE MOST PART, I KEEP HER SECRETS SAFE.
IT'S NOT IN MY NATURE TO SOLVE MYSTERIES, EDWARD, BUT THIS CASE OF YOURS...
UNNATURAL MURDERS AND SOMETHING GIVEN TO A MISTER BLACKWOOD. FOR SAFEKEEPING?
I WONDER.
AND WHAT IS IT, AND WHERE IS IT NOW? THAT'S THE QUESTION.
YES, SIR. I'M DAMNED INTERESTED.
I WAS LED TO BELIEVE YOU HAD INFORMATION FOR ME. IT SEEMS NOT.
STRICTLY SPEAKING, THAT'S TRUE, BUT I'VE A FAIR IDEA WHERE INFORMATION'S TO BE GOT, AND I'M FAIRLY CERTAIN YOU'D NOT FIND YOUR WAY TO IT WITHOUT ME--
"--AND THAT MAKES US PARTNERS."

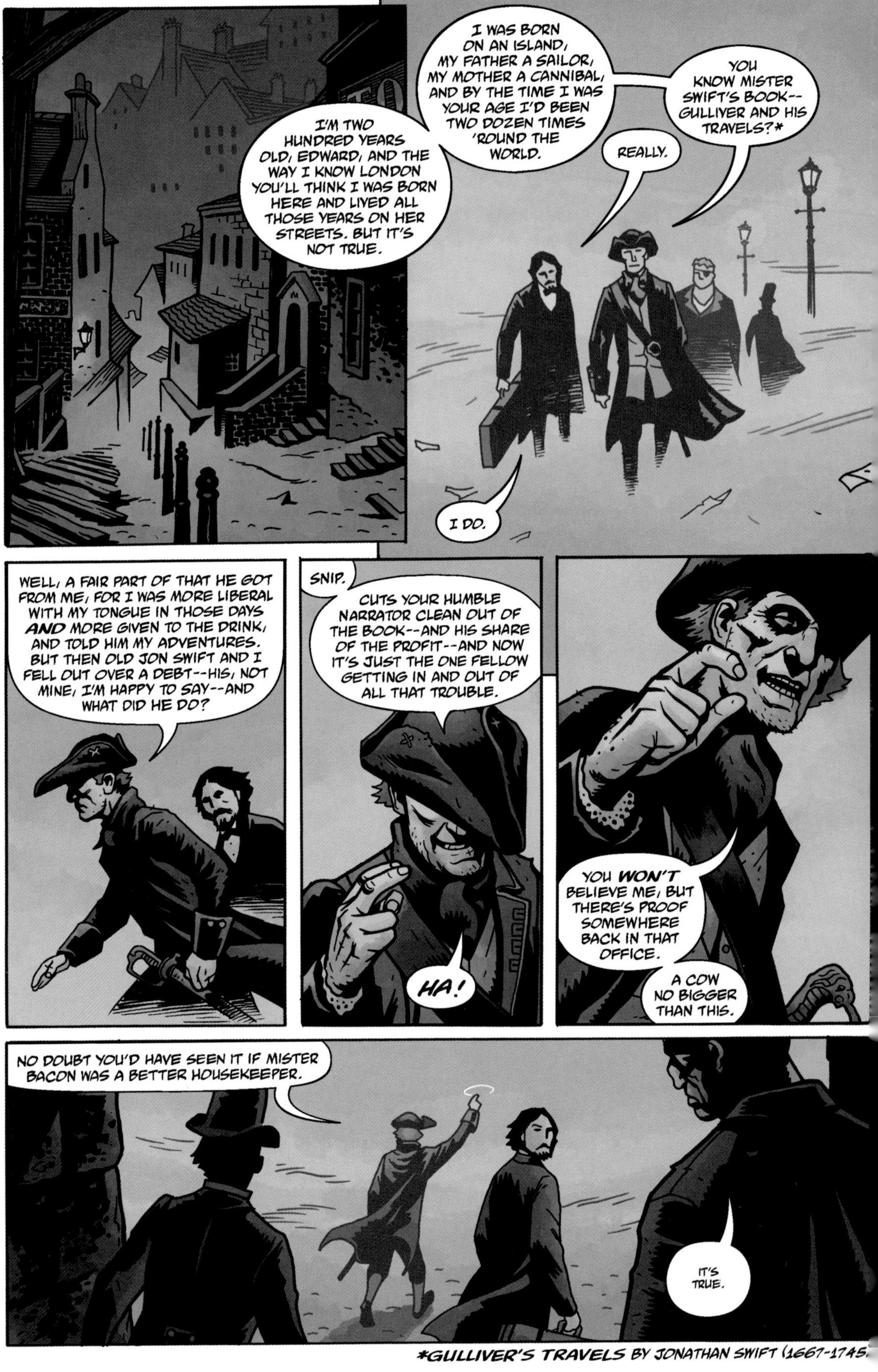
I'M TWO HUNDRED YEARS OLD, EDWARD, AND THE WAY I KNOW LONDON YOU'LL THINK I WAS BORN HERE AND LIVED ALL THOSE YEARS ON HER STREETS. BUT IT'S NOT TRUE.
I WAS BORN ON AN ISLAND, MY FATHER A SAILOR, MY MOTHER A CANNIBAL, AND BY THE TIME I WAS YOUR AGE I'D BEEN TWO DOZEN TIMES 'ROUND THE WORLD.
REALLY.
YOU KNOW MISTER SWIFT'S BOOK--GULLIVER AND HIS TRAVELS?*
I DO.
WELL, A FAIR PART OF THAT HE GOT FROM ME, FOR I WAS MORE LIBERAL WITH MY TONGUE IN THOSE DAYS AND MORE GIVEN TO THE DRINK, AND TOLD HIM MY ADVENTURES. BUT THEN OLD JON SWIFT AND I FELL OUT OVER A DEBT--HIS, NOT MINE, I'M HAPPY TO SAY--AND WHAT DID HE DO?
SNIP.
CUTS YOUR HUMBLE NARRATOR CLEAN OUT OF THE BOOK--AND HIS SHARE OF THE PROFIT--AND NOW IT'S JUST THE ONE FELLOW GETTING IN AND OUT OF ALL THAT TROUBLE.
HA!
YOU WON'T BELIEVE ME, BUT THERE'S PROOF SOMEWHERE BACK IN THAT OFFICE.
A COW NO BIGGER THAN THIS.
NO DOUBT YOU'D HAVE SEEN IT IF MISTER BACON WAS A BETTER HOUSEKEEPER.
IT'S TRUE.

***GULLIVER'S TRAVELS** BY JONATHAN SWIFT (1667-1745)

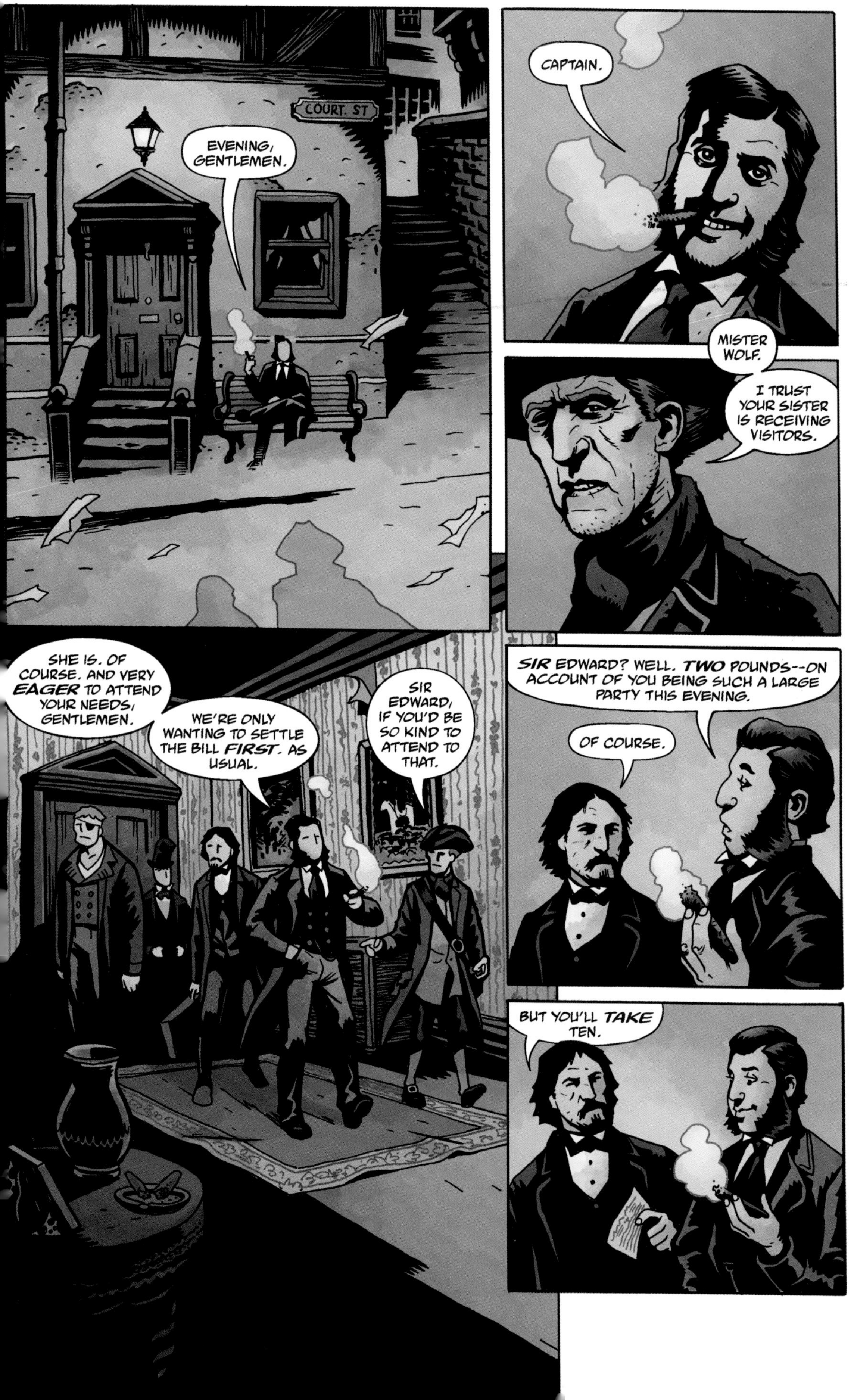
COURT. ST
EVENING, GENTLEMEN.
CAPTAIN.
MISTER WOLF.
I TRUST YOUR SISTER IS RECEIVING VISITORS.
SHE IS. OF COURSE. AND VERY EAGER TO ATTEND YOUR NEEDS, GENTLEMEN.
WE'RE ONLY WANTING TO SETTLE THE BILL FIRST. AS USUAL.
SIR EDWARD, IF YOU'D BE SO KIND TO ATTEND TO THAT.
SIR EDWARD? WELL. TWO POUNDS--ON ACCOUNT OF YOU BEING SUCH A LARGE PARTY THIS EVENING.
OF COURSE.
BUT YOU'LL TAKE TEN.

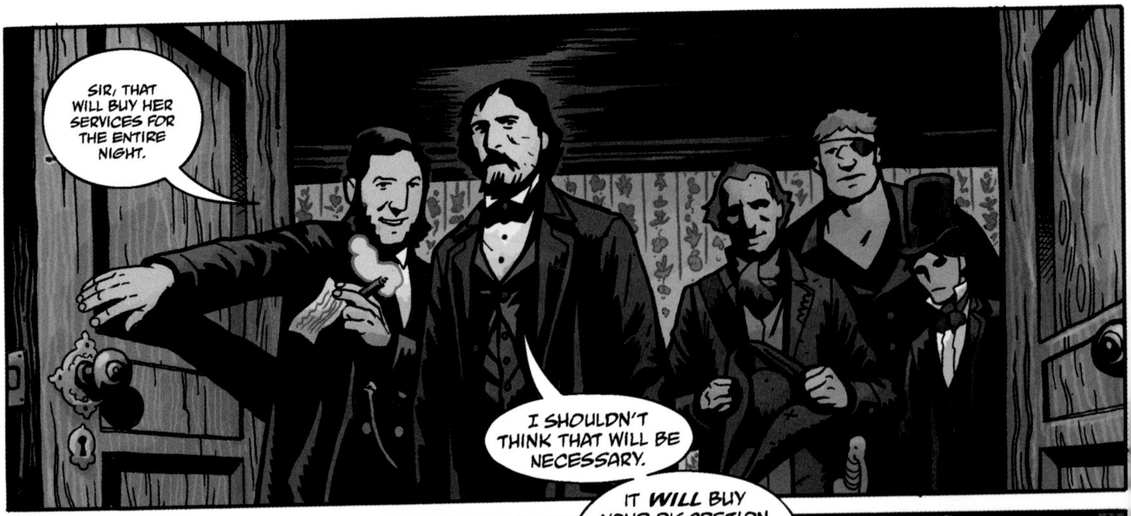
SIR, THAT WILL BUY HER SERVICES FOR THE ENTIRE NIGHT.
I SHOULDN'T THINK THAT WILL BE NECESSARY.

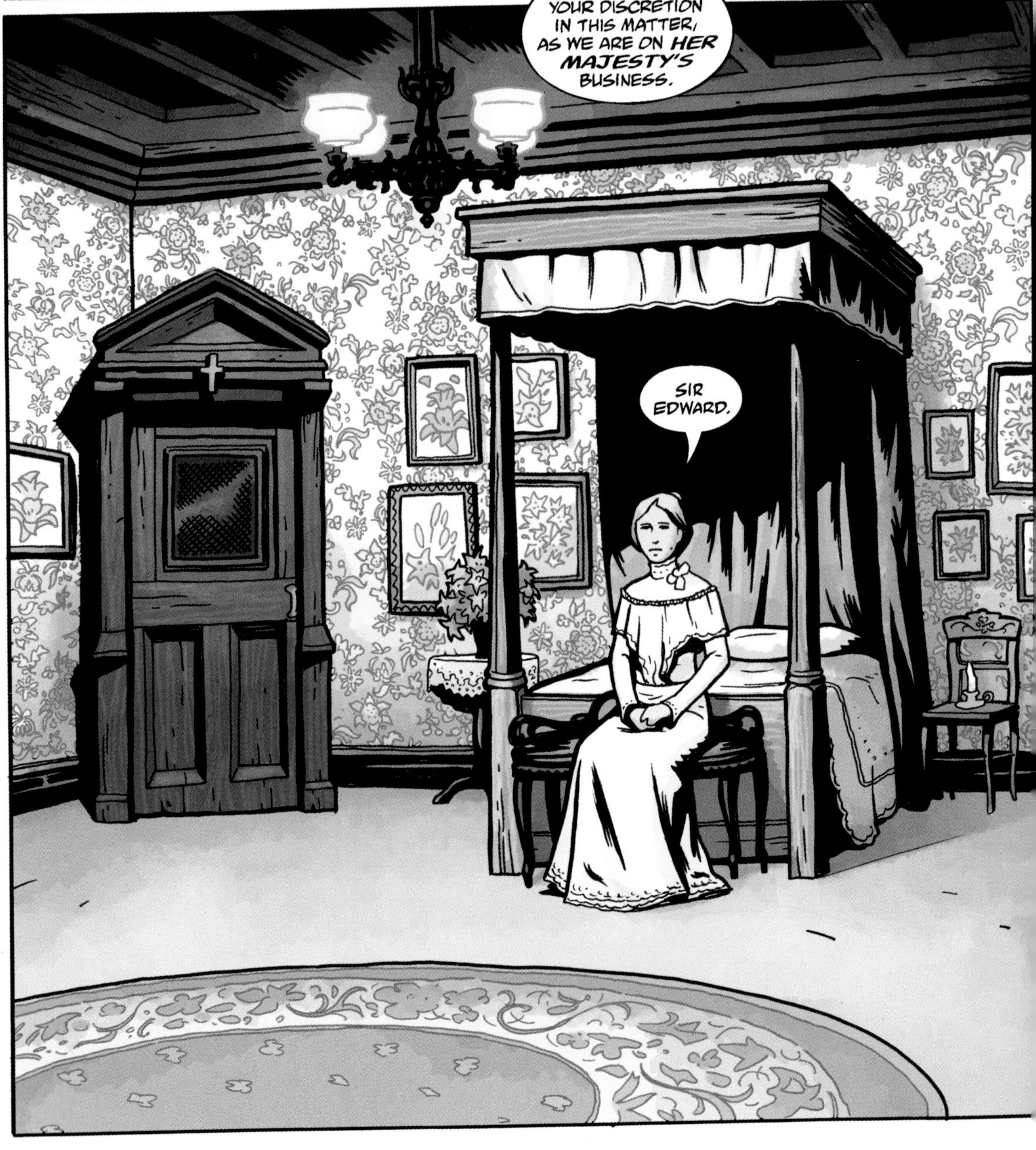
IT WILL BUY YOUR DISCRETION IN THIS MATTER, AS WE ARE ON HER MAJESTY'S BUSINESS.
SIR EDWARD.

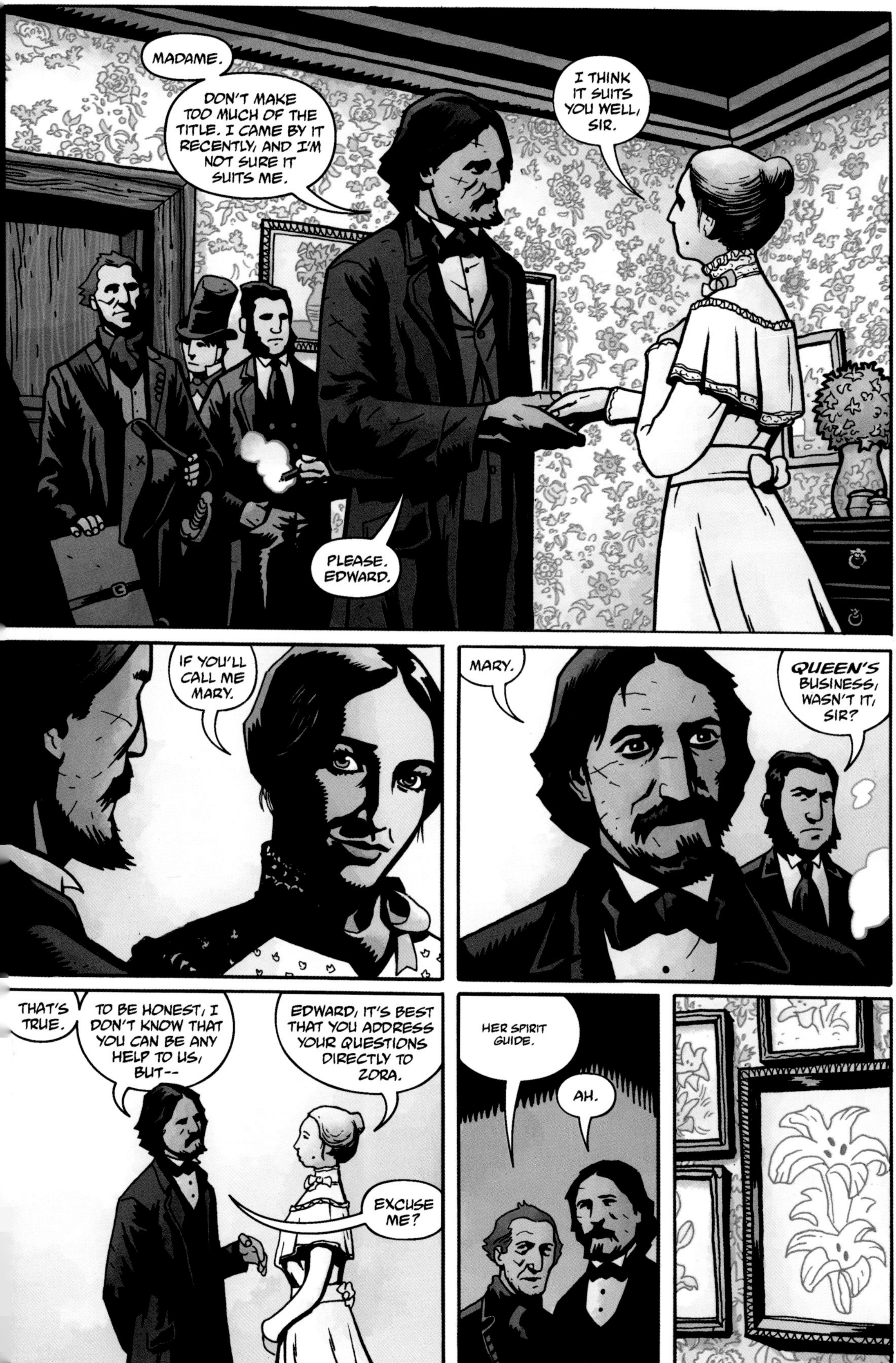
MADAME.
DON'T MAKE TOO MUCH OF THE TITLE. I CAME BY IT RECENTLY, AND I'M NOT SURE IT SUITS ME.
I THINK IT SUITS YOU WELL, SIR.
PLEASE. EDWARD.
IF YOU'LL CALL ME MARY.
MARY.
QUEEN'S BUSINESS, WASN'T IT, SIR?
THAT'S TRUE.
TO BE HONEST, I DON'T KNOW THAT YOU CAN BE ANY HELP TO US, BUT--
EDWARD, IT'S BEST THAT YOU ADDRESS YOUR QUESTIONS DIRECTLY TO ZORA.
EXCUSE ME?
HER SPIRIT GUIDE.
AH.

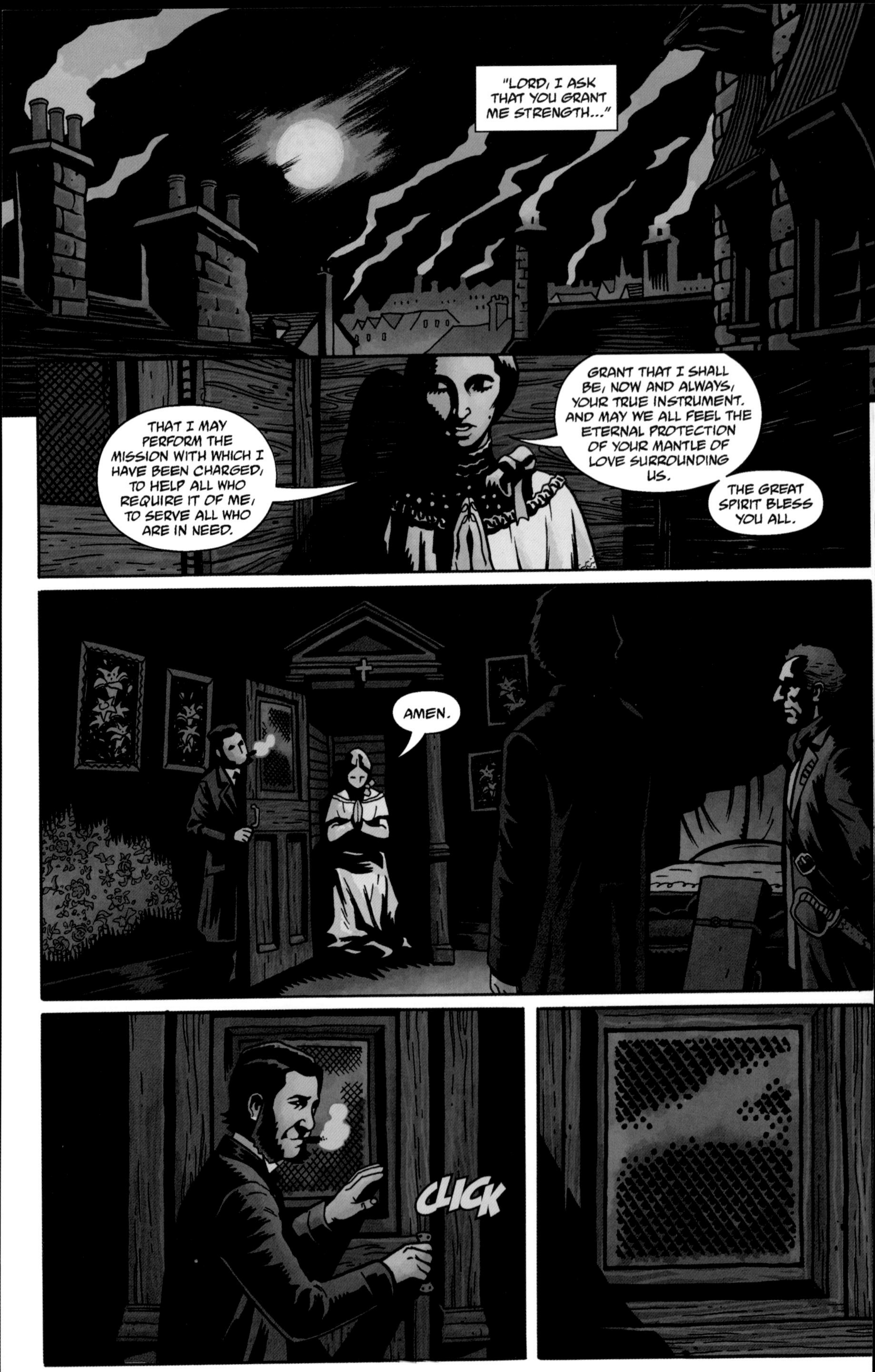
"LORD, I ASK THAT YOU GRANT ME STRENGTH..."
THAT I MAY PERFORM THE MISSION WITH WHICH I HAVE BEEN CHARGED, TO HELP ALL WHO REQUIRE IT OF ME, TO SERVE ALL WHO ARE IN NEED.
GRANT THAT I SHALL BE, NOW AND ALWAYS, YOUR TRUE INSTRUMENT. AND MAY WE ALL FEEL THE ETERNAL PROTECTION OF YOUR MANTLE OF LOVE SURROUNDING US.
THE GREAT SPIRIT BLESS YOU ALL.
AMEN.
CLICK

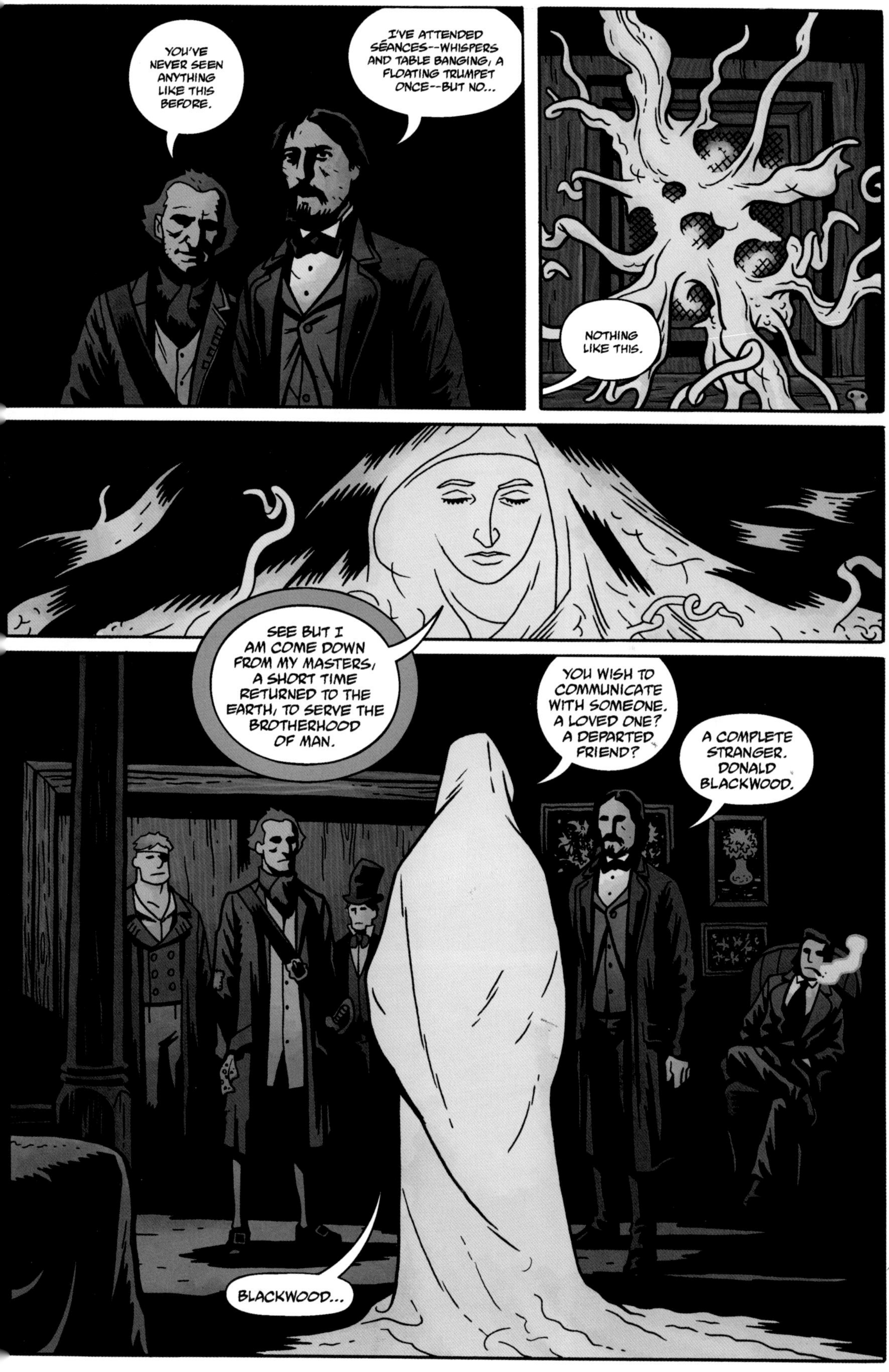
YOU'VE NEVER SEEN ANYTHING LIKE THIS BEFORE.
I'VE ATTENDED SÉANCES--WHISPERS AND TABLE BANGING, A FLOATING TRUMPET ONCE--BUT NO...
NOTHING LIKE THIS.
SEE BUT I AM COME DOWN FROM MY MASTERS, A SHORT TIME RETURNED TO THE EARTH, TO SERVE THE BROTHERHOOD OF MAN.
YOU WISH TO COMMUNICATE WITH SOMEONE. A LOVED ONE? A DEPARTED FRIEND?
A COMPLETE STRANGER. DONALD BLACKWOOD.
BLACKWOOD...

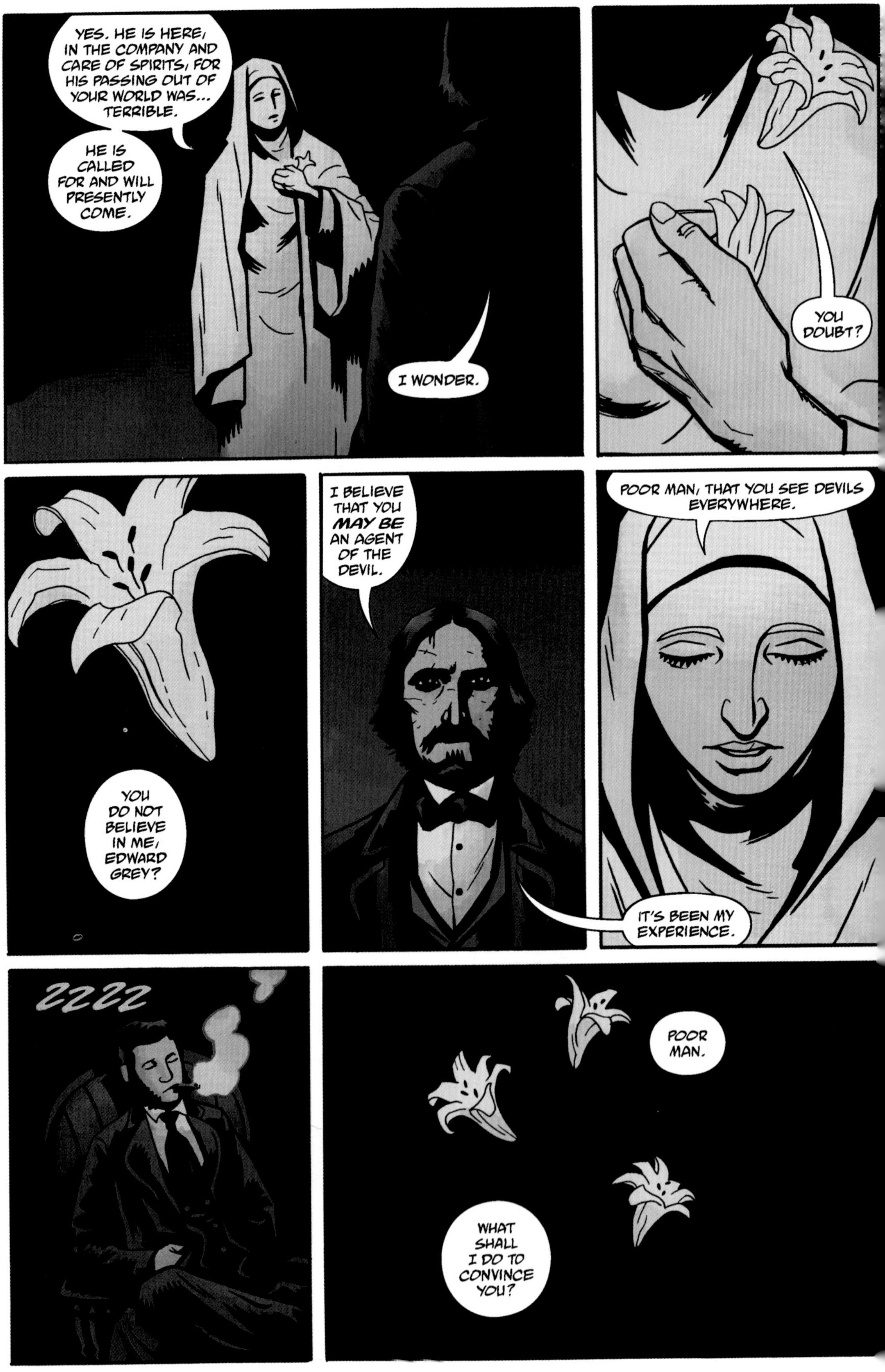
YES. HE IS HERE, IN THE COMPANY AND CARE OF SPIRITS, FOR HIS PASSING OUT OF YOUR WORLD WAS... TERRIBLE.
HE IS CALLED FOR AND WILL PRESENTLY COME.
I WONDER.
YOU DOUBT?
YOU DO NOT BELIEVE IN ME, EDWARD GREY?
I BELIEVE THAT YOU MAY BE AN AGENT OF THE DEVIL.
POOR MAN, THAT YOU SEE DEVILS EVERYWHERE.
IT'S BEEN MY EXPERIENCE.
ZZZZ
POOR MAN.
WHAT SHALL I DO TO CONVINCE YOU?

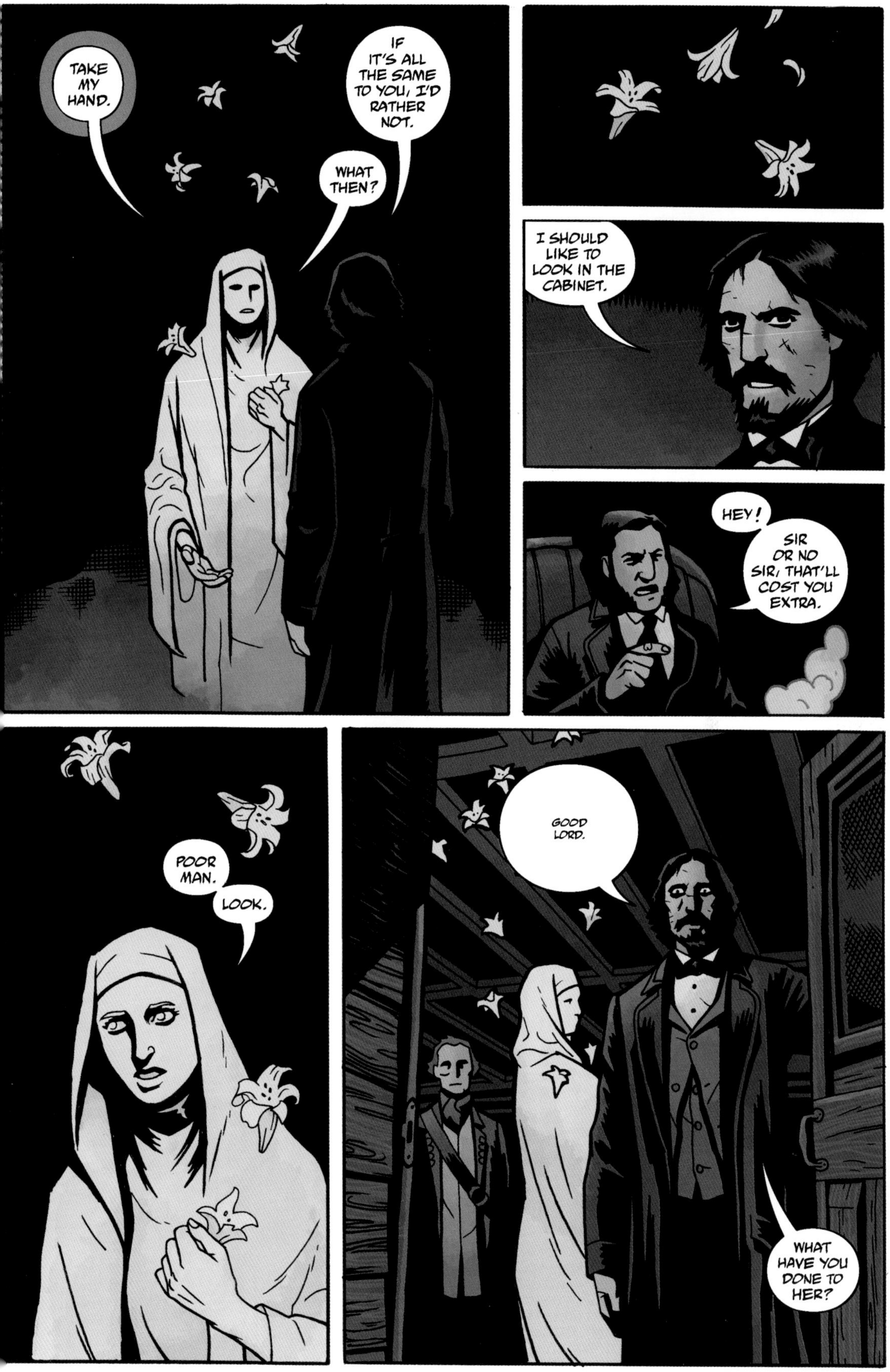
TAKE MY HAND.
IF IT'S ALL THE SAME TO YOU, I'D RATHER NOT.
WHAT THEN?
I SHOULD LIKE TO LOOK IN THE CABINET.
HEY!
SIR OR NO SIR, THAT'LL COST YOU EXTRA.
POOR MAN.
LOOK.
GOOD LORD.
WHAT HAVE YOU DONE TO HER?

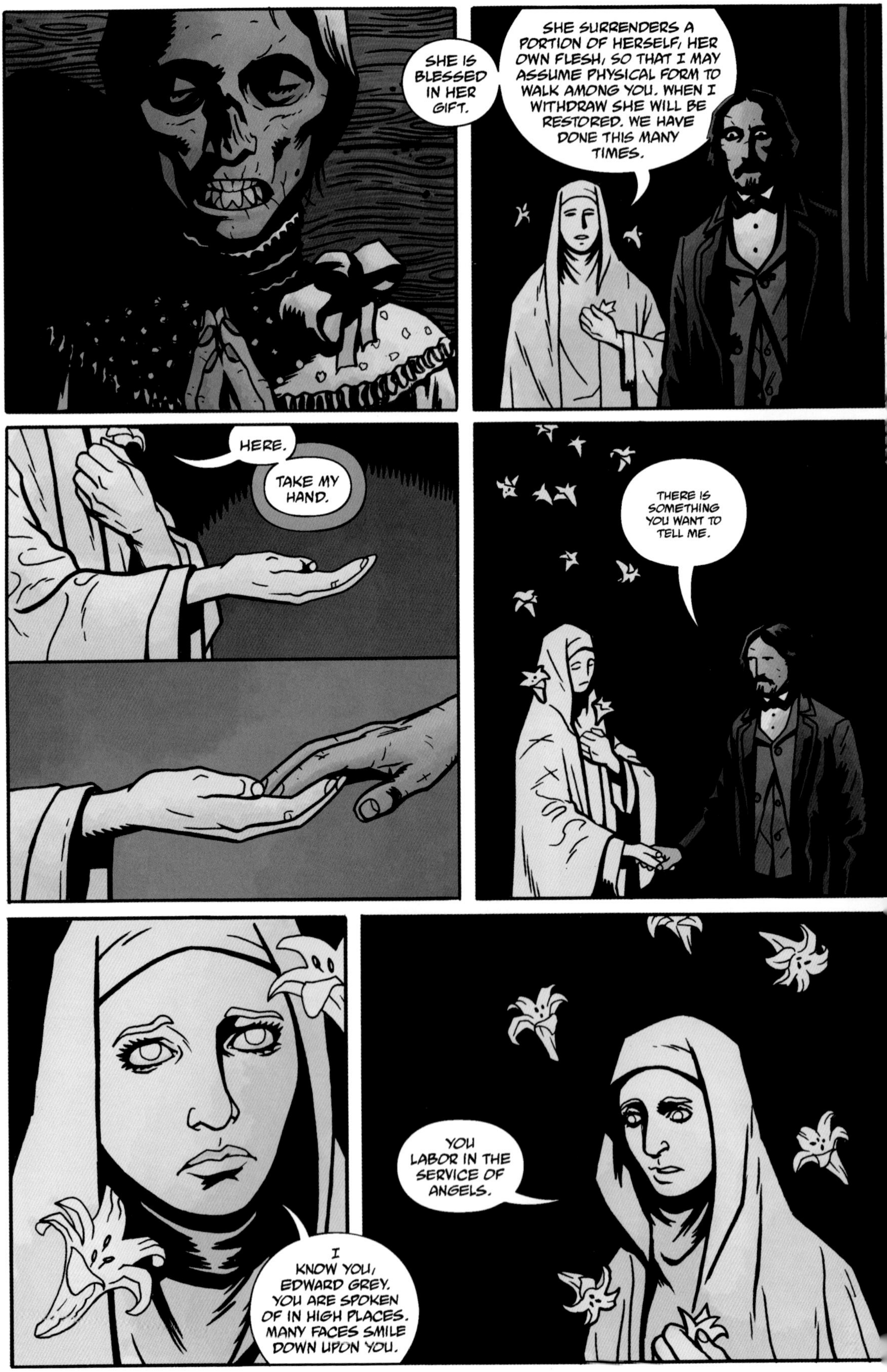
SHE IS BLESSED IN HER GIFT.
SHE SURRENDERS A PORTION OF HERSELF, HER OWN FLESH, SO THAT I MAY ASSUME PHYSICAL FORM TO WALK AMONG YOU. WHEN I WITHDRAW SHE WILL BE RESTORED. WE HAVE DONE THIS MANY TIMES.
HERE.
TAKE MY HAND.
THERE IS SOMETHING YOU WANT TO TELL ME.
I KNOW YOU, EDWARD GREY. YOU ARE SPOKEN OF IN HIGH PLACES. MANY FACES SMILE DOWN UPON YOU.
YOU LABOR IN THE SERVICE OF ANGELS.

WELL, THAT'S A COMFORT TO KNOW.

DO NOT BE TOO QUICK TO THANK ME FOR THE NEWS...

"REMEMBER THE FATE OF SO MANY IN THAT SERVICE."

POOR MAN.

WHAT IS IT?

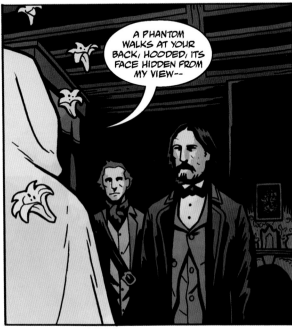

A PHANTOM WALKS AT YOUR BACK, HOODED, ITS FACE HIDDEN FROM MY VIEW--

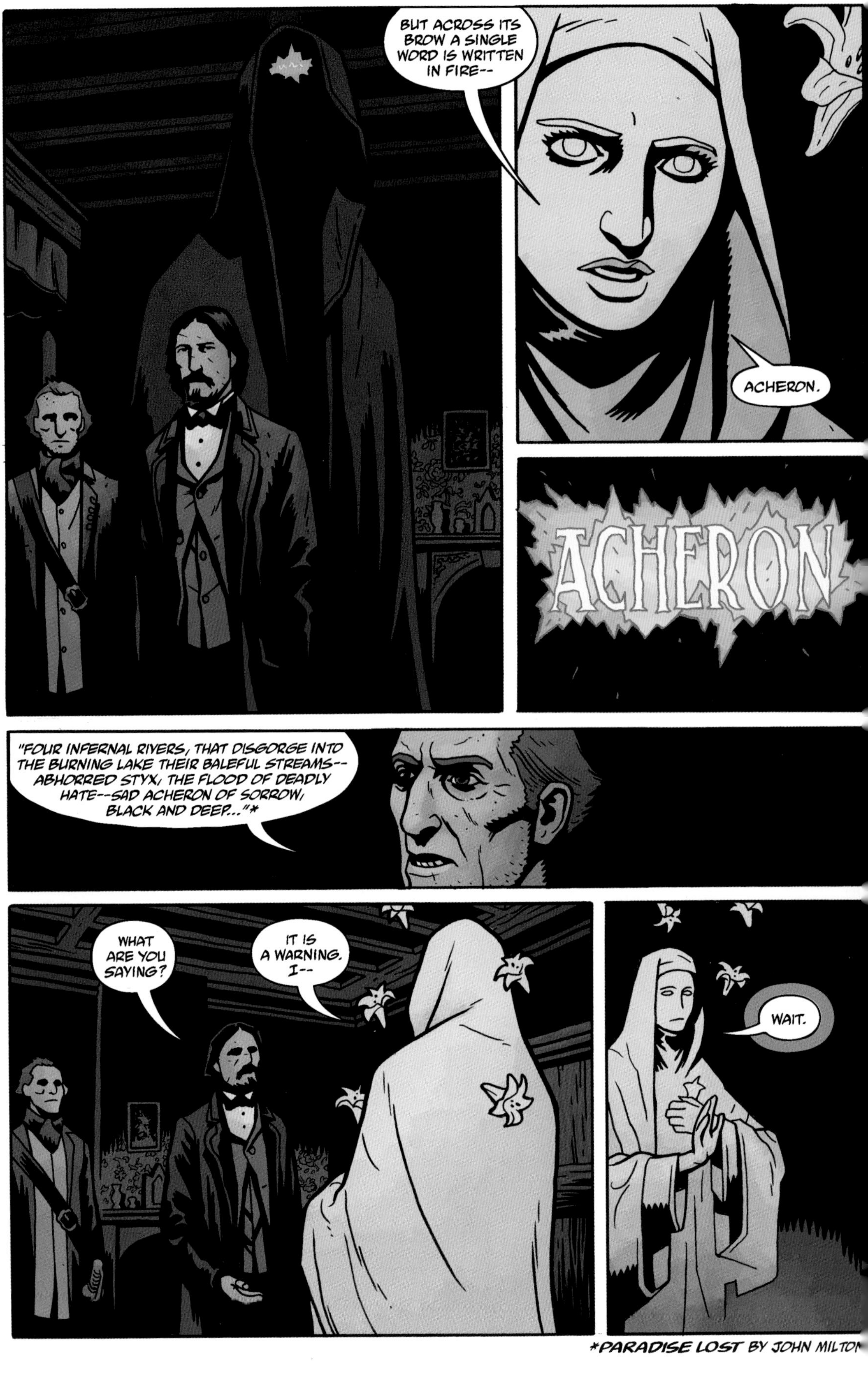
BUT ACROSS ITS BROW A SINGLE WORD IS WRITTEN IN FIRE--
ACHERON.
ACHERON
"FOUR INFERNAL RIVERS, THAT DISGORGE INTO THE BURNING LAKE THEIR BALEFUL STREAMS--ABHORRED STYX, THE FLOOD OF DEADLY HATE--SAD ACHERON OF SORROW, BLACK AND DEEP..."*
WHAT ARE YOU SAYING?
IT IS A WARNING. I--
WAIT.

***PARADISE LOST** BY JOHN MILTO

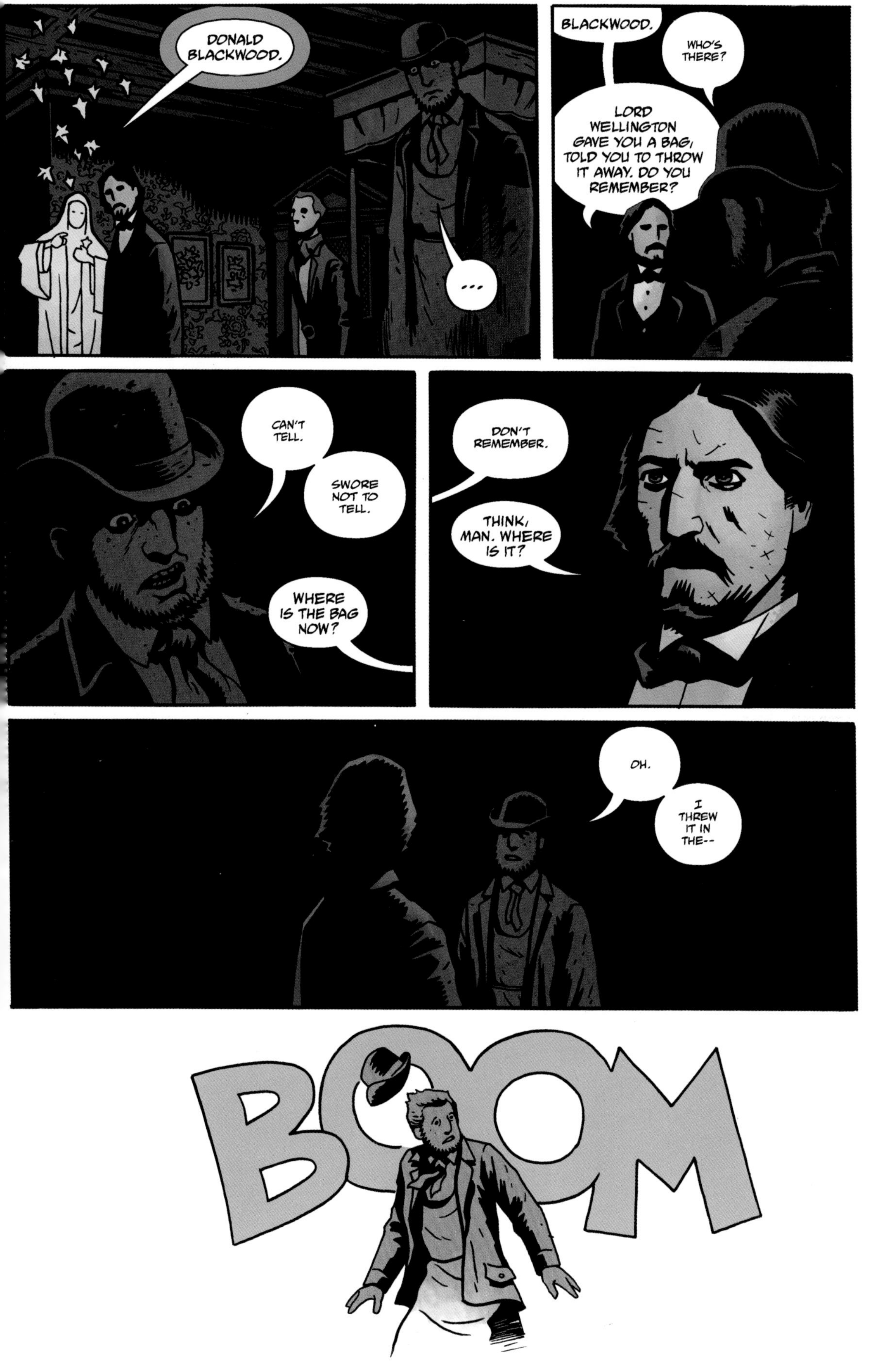
DONALD BLACKWOOD.
...
BLACKWOOD.
WHO'S THERE?
LORD WELLINGTON GAVE YOU A BAG, TOLD YOU TO THROW IT AWAY. DO YOU REMEMBER?
CAN'T TELL.
SWORE NOT TO TELL.
WHERE IS THE BAG NOW?
DON'T REMEMBER.
THINK, MAN. WHERE IS IT?
OH.
I THREW IT IN THE--
BOOM

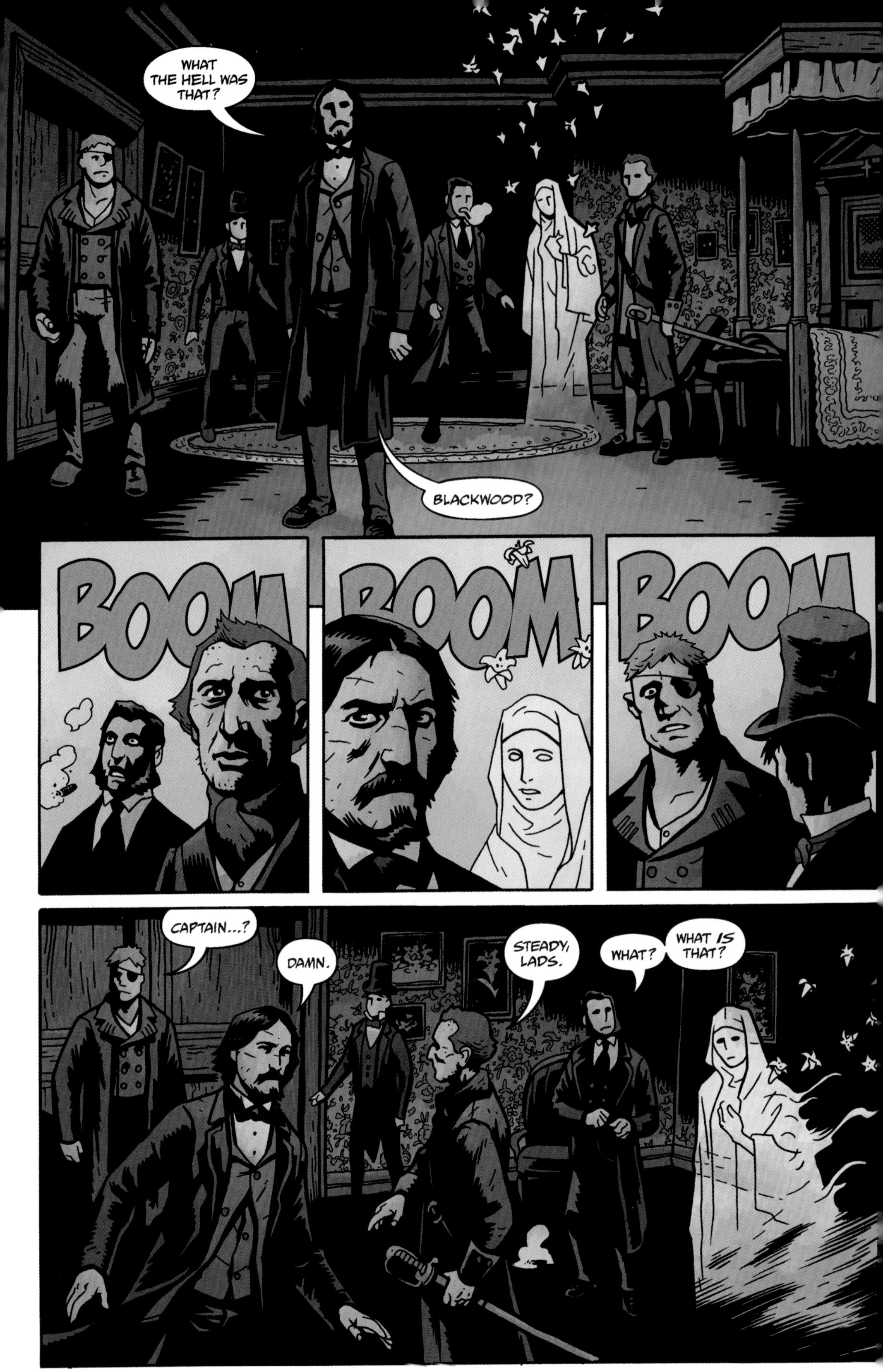
WHAT THE HELL WAS THAT?
BLACKWOOD?
BOOM
BOOM
BOOM
CAPTAIN...?
DAMN.
STEADY, LADS.
WHAT?
WHAT IS THAT?

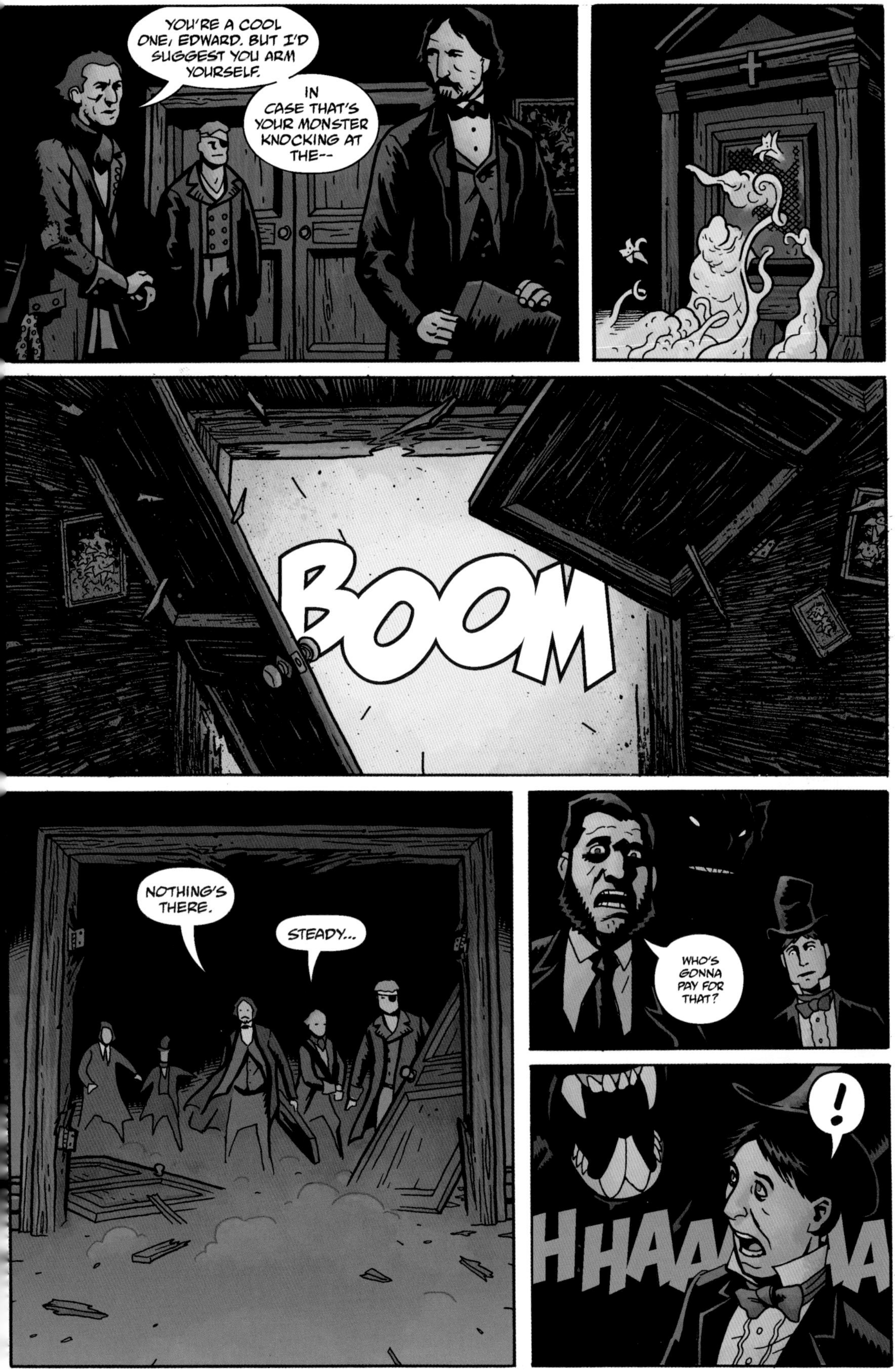
YOU'RE A COOL ONE, EDWARD. BUT I'D SUGGEST YOU ARM YOURSELF.
IN CASE THAT'S YOUR MONSTER KNOCKING AT THE--
BOOM
NOTHING'S THERE.
STEADY...
WHO'S GONNA PAY FOR THAT?
!

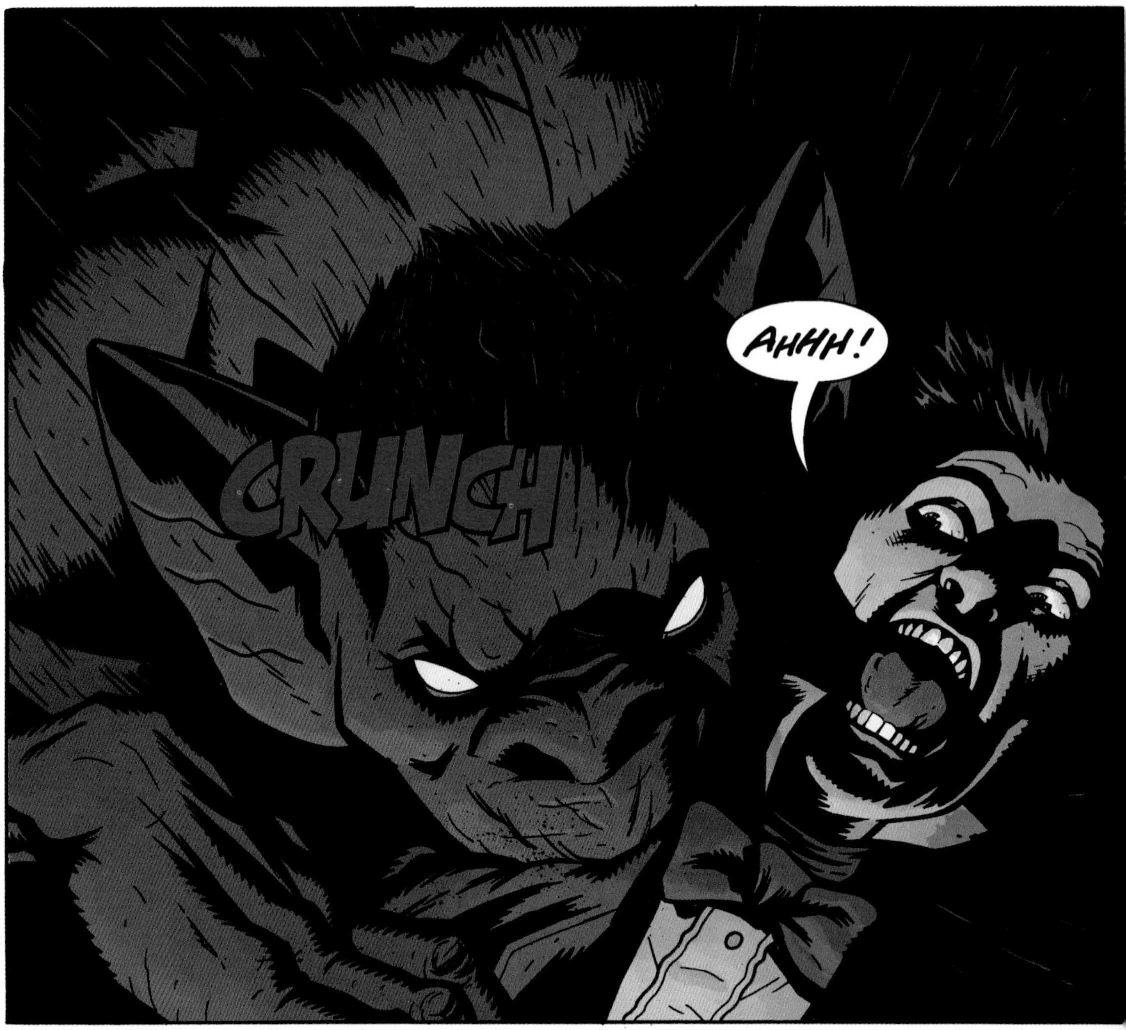
CRUNCH
AHHH!
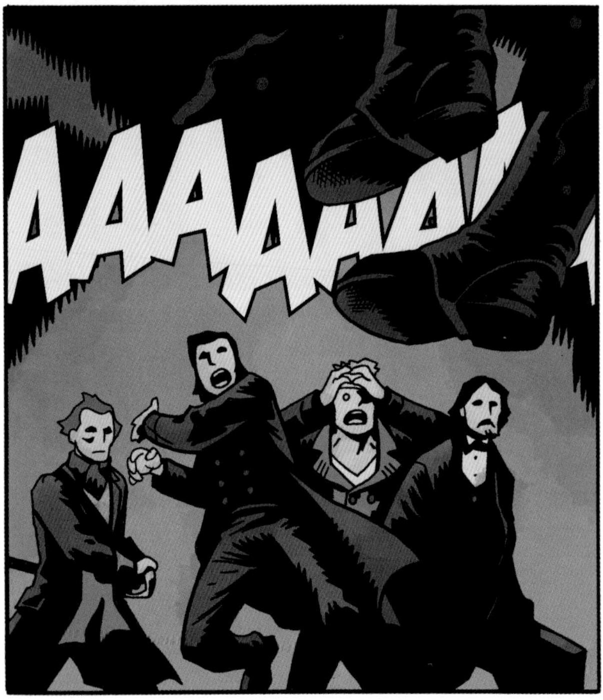
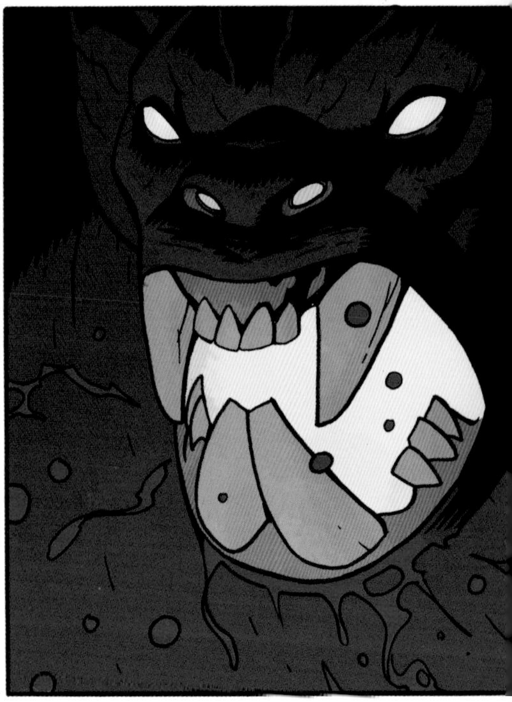

CHAPTER THREE

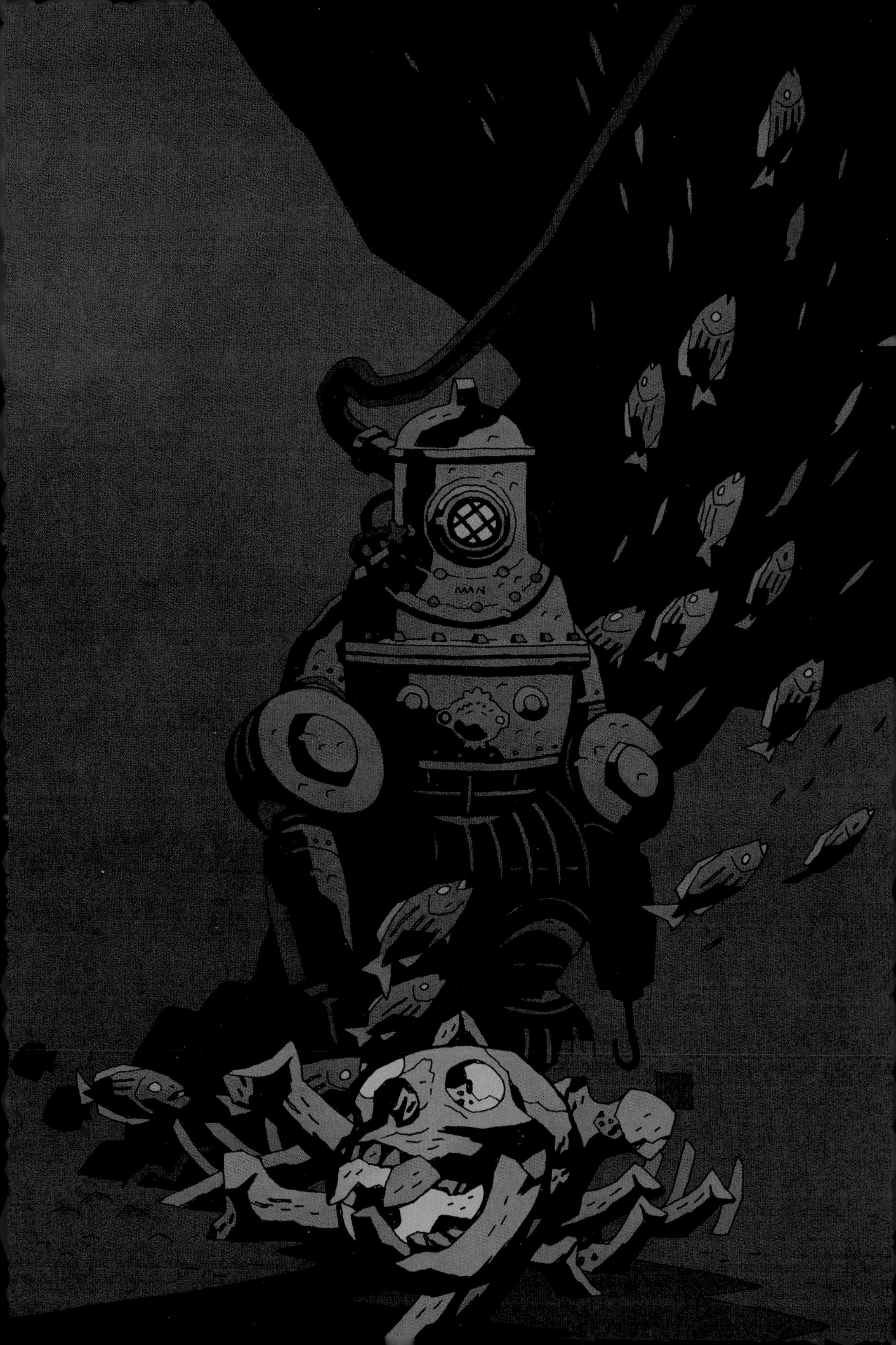

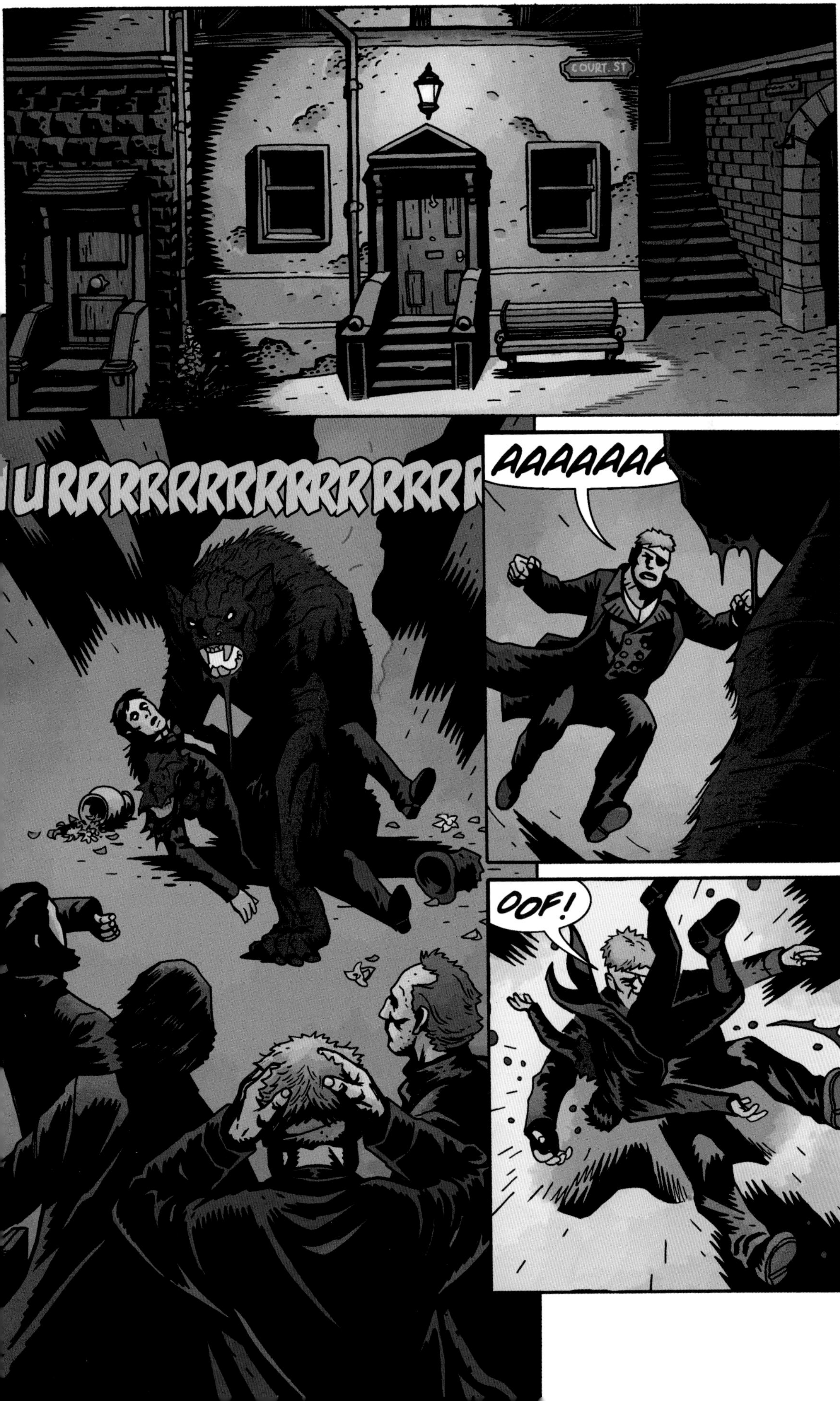
COURT. ST
URRRRRRRRRRRRRRR
AAAAAAA
OOF!

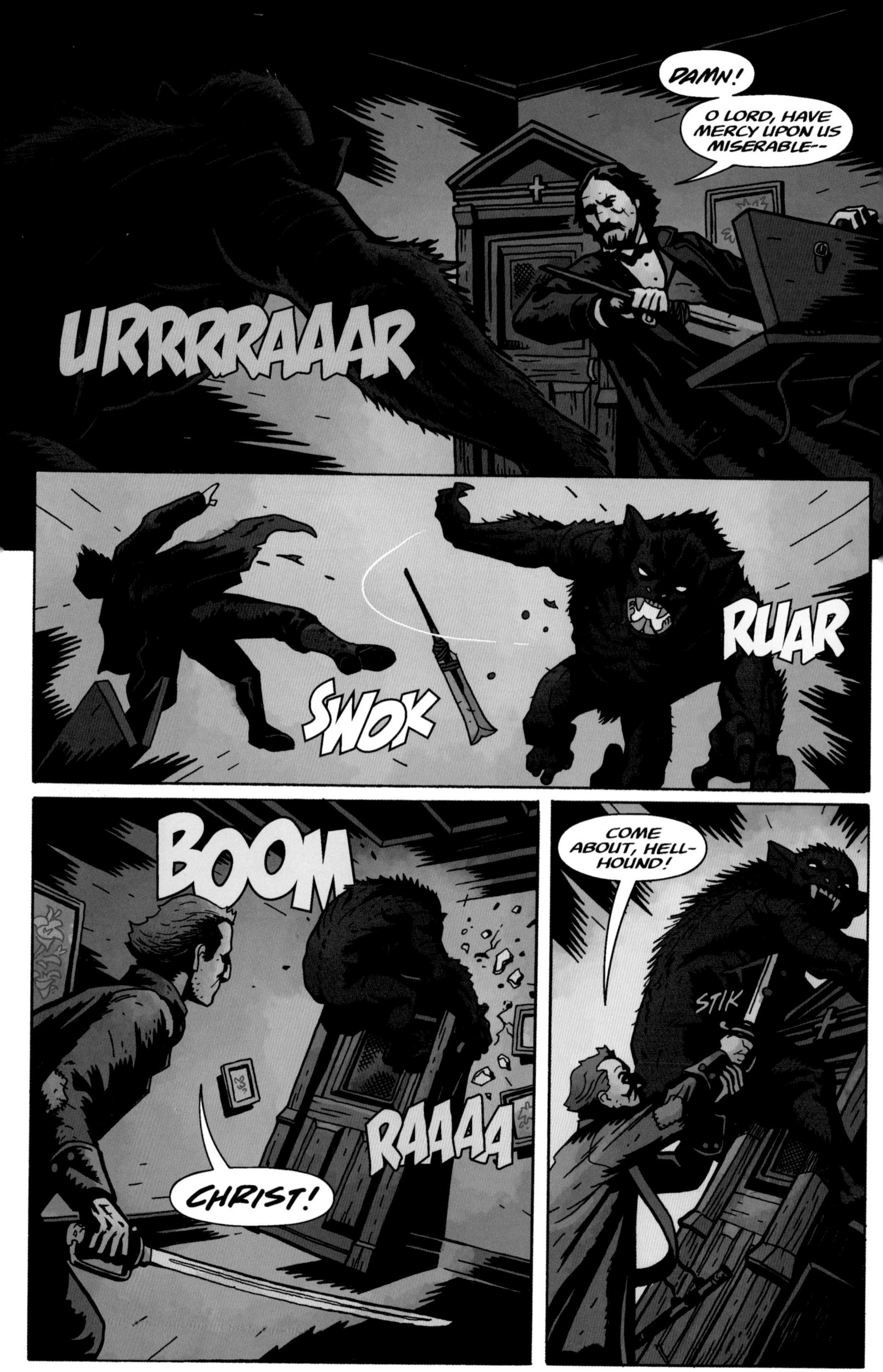
DAMN!
O LORD, HAVE MERCY UPON US MISERABLE--
URRRRAAAR
RUAR
SWOK
BOOM
RAAAA
CHRIST!
COME ABOUT, HELL-HOUND!
STIK

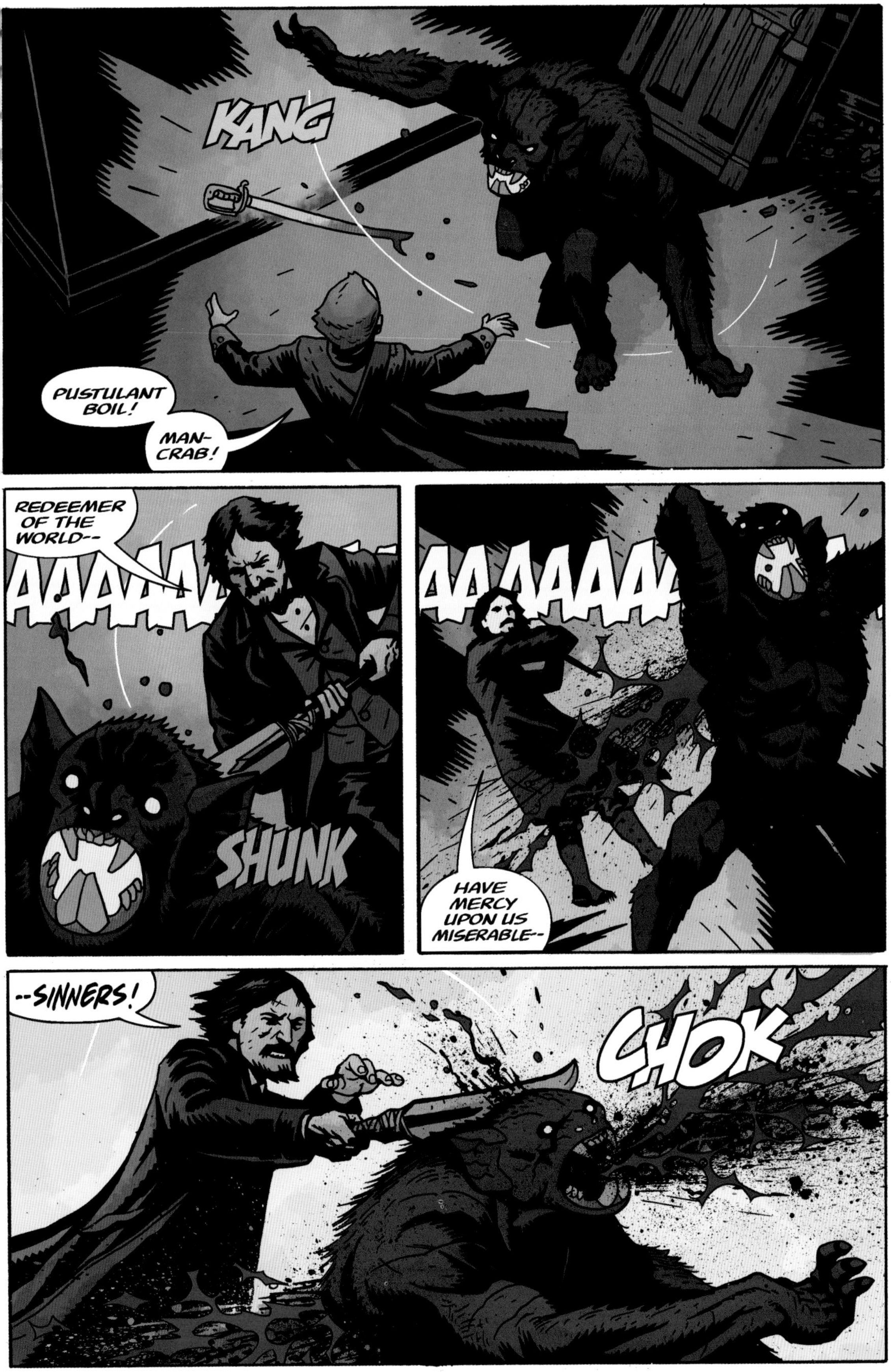
KANG
PUSTULANT BOIL!
MAN-CRAB!
REDEEMER OF THE WORLD--
SHUNK
HAVE MERCY UPON US MISERABLE--
--SINNERS!
CHOK

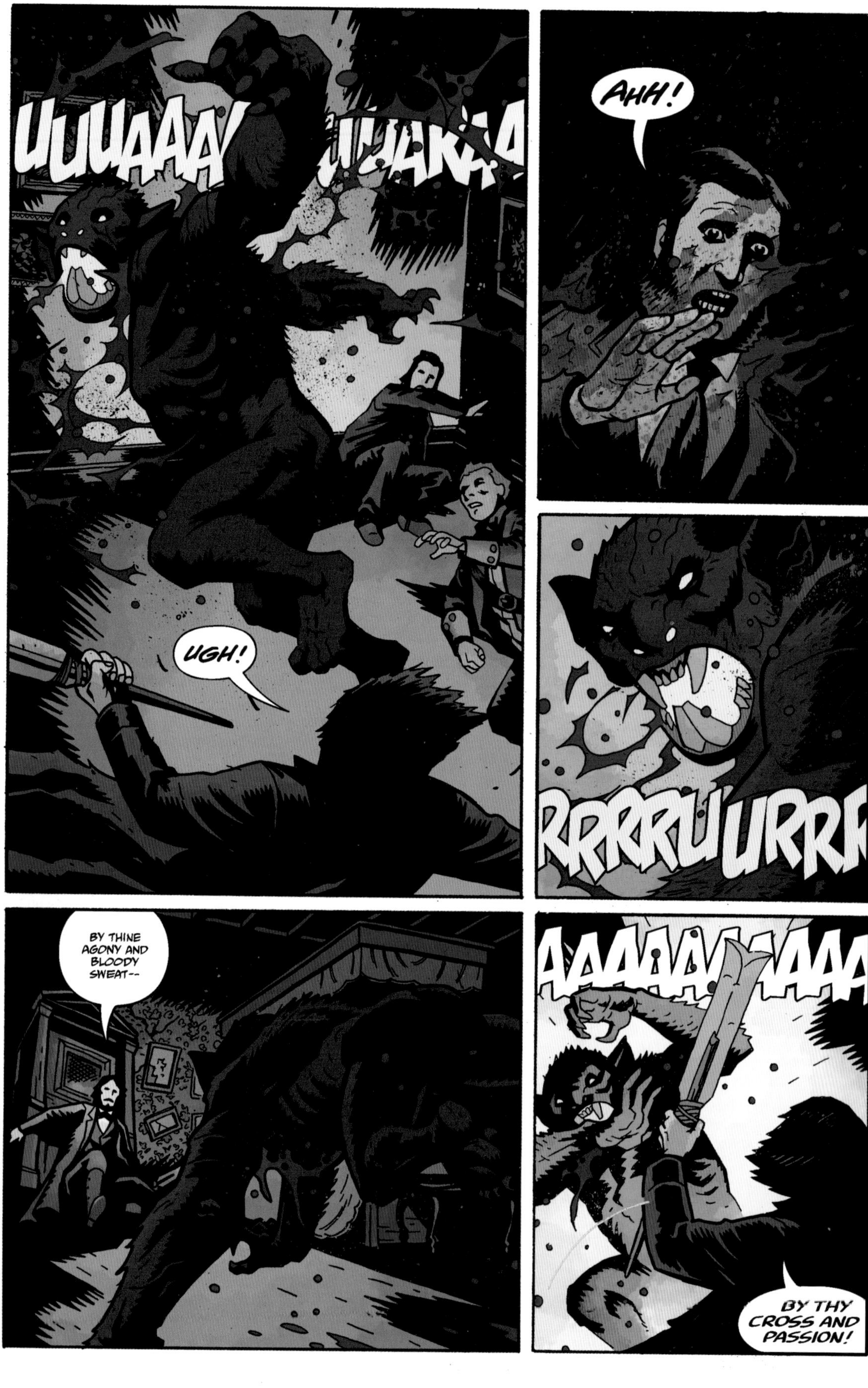
UUUAAA! UUAKAA
UGH!
AHH!
RRRRU URRR
BY THINE AGONY AND BLOODY SWEAT--
AAAAAAAAA
BY THY CROSS AND PASSION!

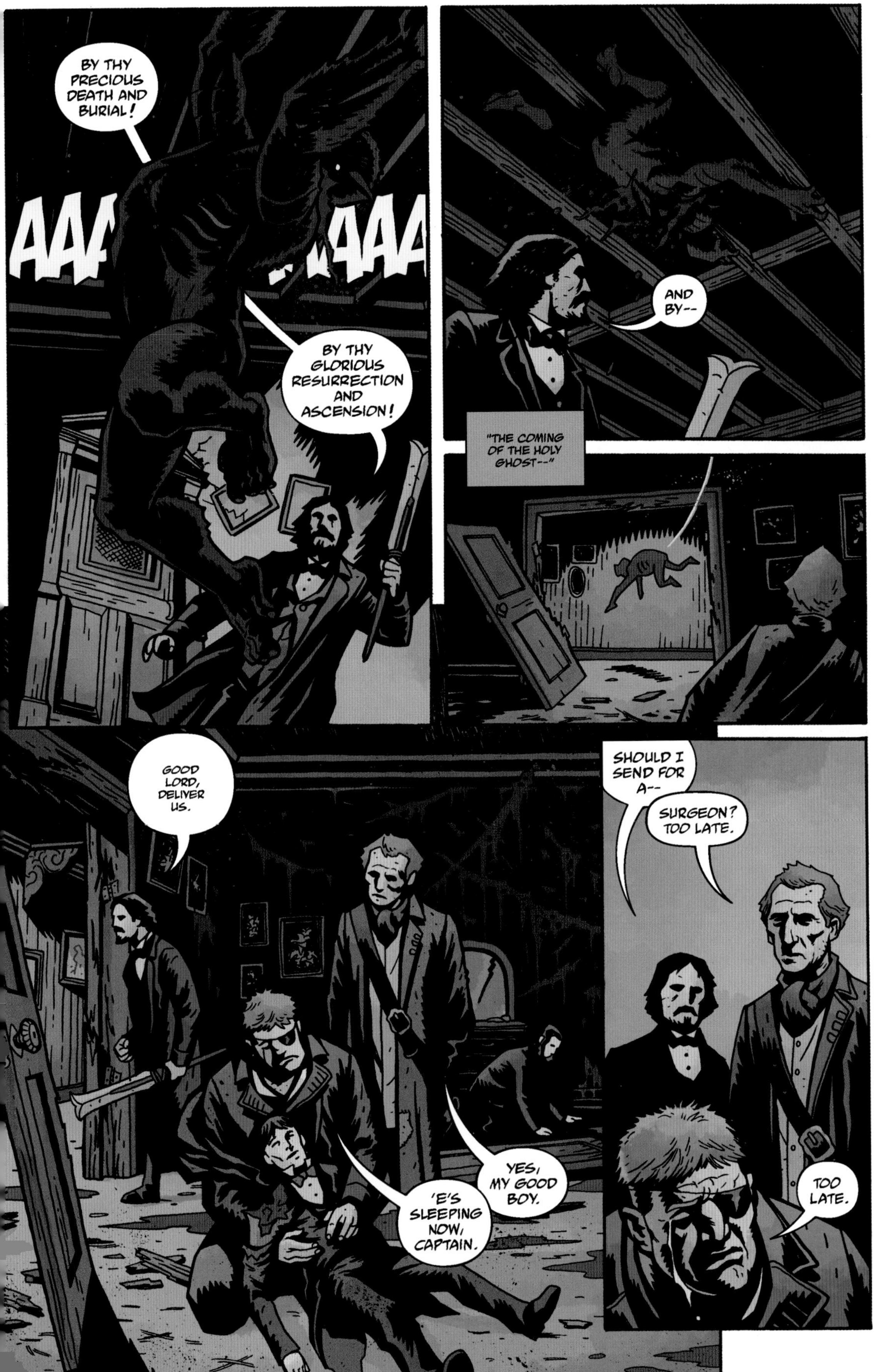
BY THY PRECIOUS DEATH AND BURIAL!
AAA... AAAA
BY THY GLORIOUS RESURRECTION AND ASCENSION!
AND BY--
"THE COMING OF THE HOLY GHOST--"
GOOD LORD, DELIVER US.
'E'S SLEEPING NOW, CAPTAIN.
YES, MY GOOD BOY.
SHOULD I SEND FOR A--
SURGEON? TOO LATE.
TOO LATE.

MISS WOLF?

MARY.

'E WAS GOOD.

IT'S TRUE. AND YOU'RE A GOOD FELLOW YOURSELF, DAN. AND A BRAVER LAD I NEVER SAW.

SOB

YOU'RE NOT HURT?

A LITTLE SHAKEN.

THE CREATURE--

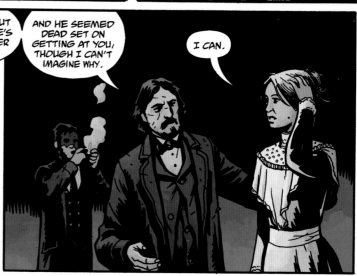

GONE NOW, BUT I'M AFRAID HE'S KILLED MISTER SALT.

AND HE SEEMED DEAD SET ON GETTING AT YOU, THOUGH I CAN'T IMAGINE WHY.

I CAN.

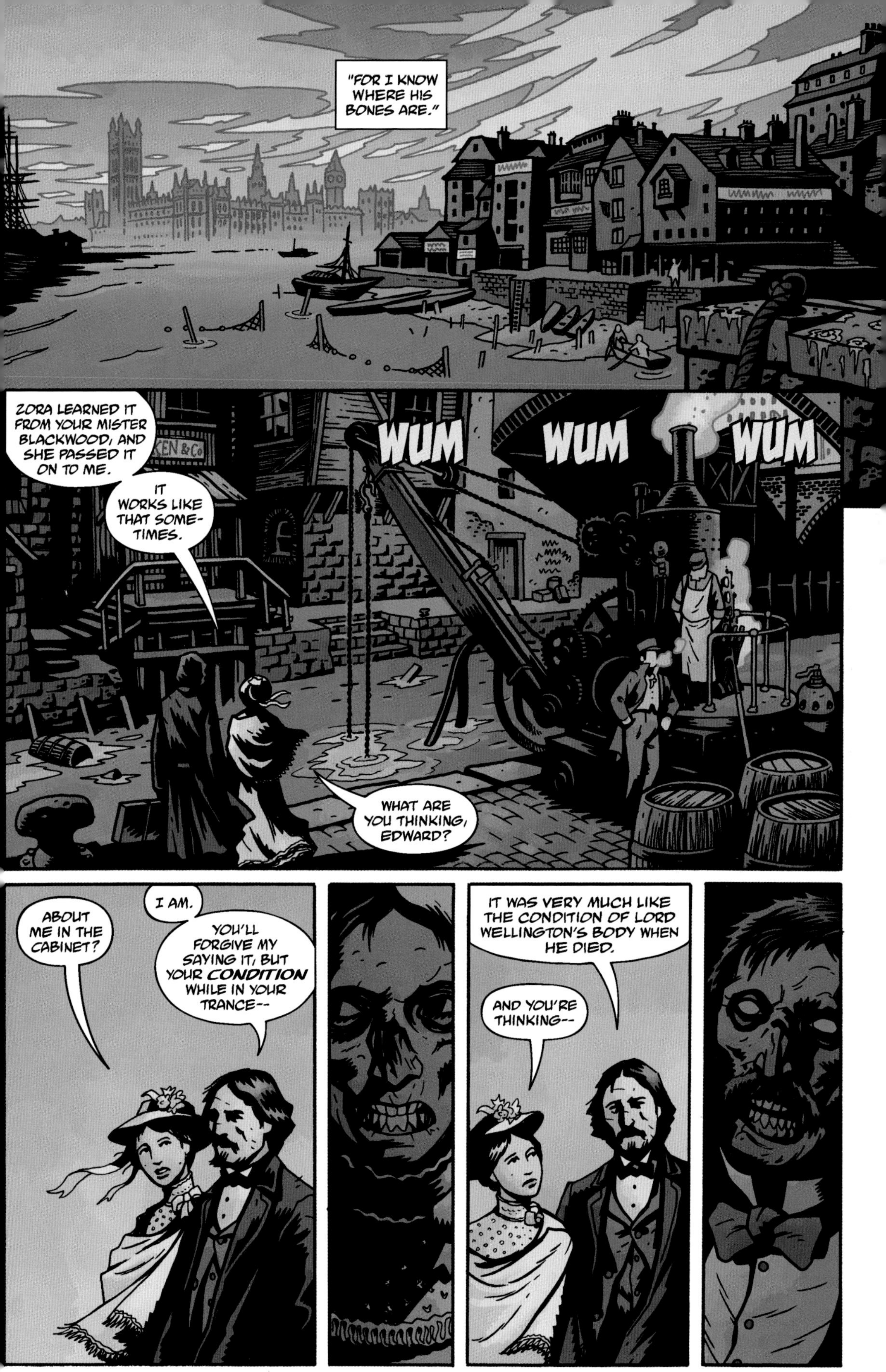
"FOR I KNOW WHERE HIS BONES ARE."
ZORA LEARNED IT FROM YOUR MISTER BLACKWOOD, AND SHE PASSED IT ON TO ME.
IT WORKS LIKE THAT SOME-TIMES.
WUM WUM WUM
WHAT ARE YOU THINKING, EDWARD?
ABOUT ME IN THE CABINET?
I AM.
YOU'LL FORGIVE MY SAYING IT, BUT YOUR CONDITION WHILE IN YOUR TRANCE--
IT WAS VERY MUCH LIKE THE CONDITION OF LORD WELLINGTON'S BODY WHEN HE DIED.
AND YOU'RE THINKING--

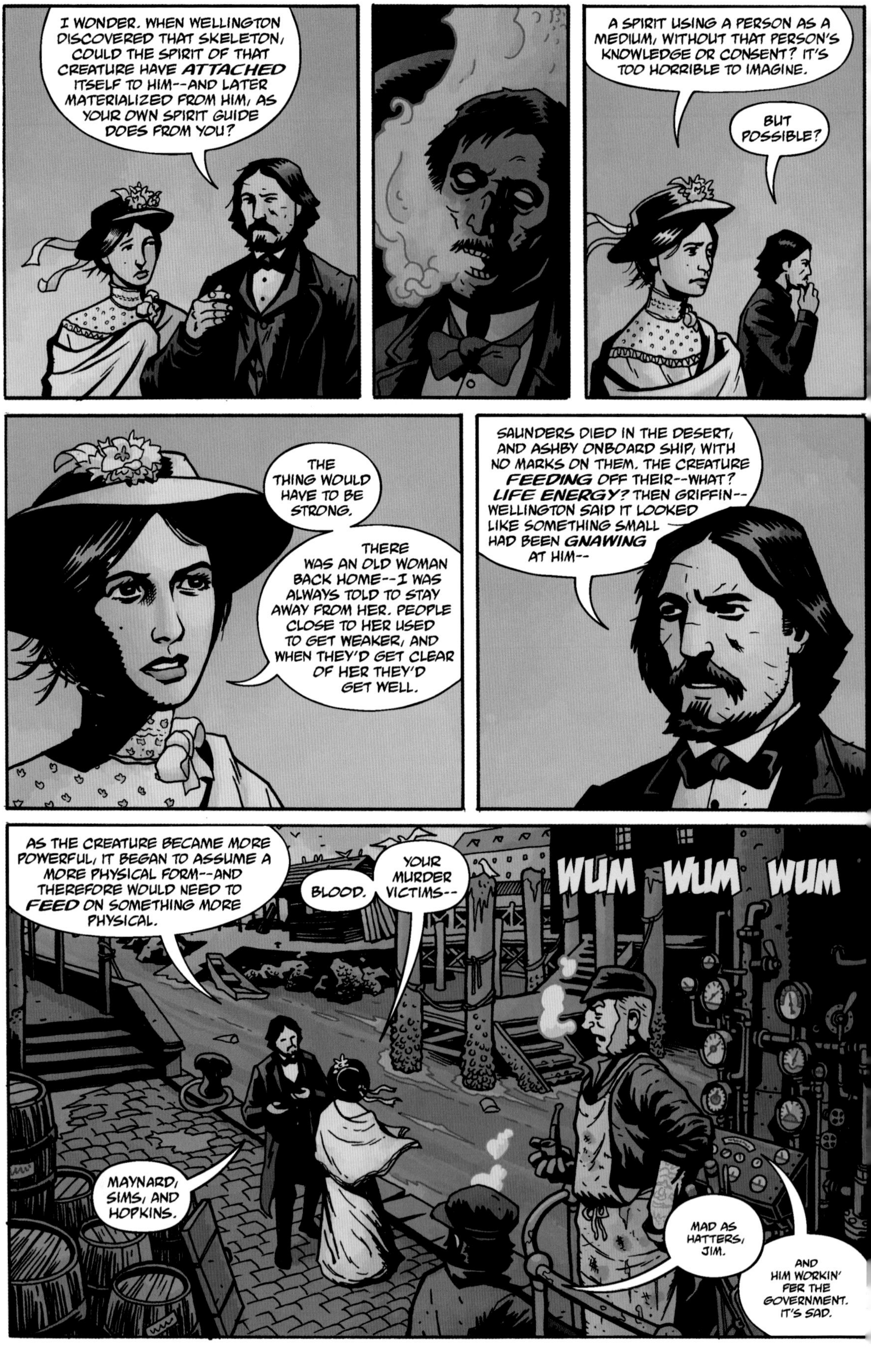

I WONDER. WHEN WELLINGTON DISCOVERED THAT SKELETON, COULD THE SPIRIT OF THAT CREATURE HAVE *ATTACHED* ITSELF TO HIM--AND LATER MATERIALIZED FROM HIM, AS YOUR OWN SPIRIT GUIDE DOES FROM YOU?
A SPIRIT USING A PERSON AS A MEDIUM, WITHOUT THAT PERSON'S KNOWLEDGE OR CONSENT? IT'S TOO HORRIBLE TO IMAGINE.
BUT POSSIBLE?
THE THING WOULD HAVE TO BE STRONG.
THERE WAS AN OLD WOMAN BACK HOME--I WAS ALWAYS TOLD TO STAY AWAY FROM HER. PEOPLE CLOSE TO HER USED TO GET WEAKER, AND WHEN THEY'D GET CLEAR OF HER THEY'D GET WELL.
SAUNDERS DIED IN THE DESERT, AND ASHBY ONBOARD SHIP, WITH NO MARKS ON THEM. THE CREATURE *FEEDING* OFF THEIR--WHAT? *LIFE ENERGY?* THEN GRIFFIN--WELLINGTON SAID IT LOOKED LIKE SOMETHING SMALL HAD BEEN *GNAWING* AT HIM--
AS THE CREATURE BECAME MORE POWERFUL, IT BEGAN TO ASSUME A MORE PHYSICAL FORM--AND THEREFORE WOULD NEED TO *FEED* ON SOMETHING MORE PHYSICAL.
BLOOD.
YOUR MURDER VICTIMS--
MAYNARD, SIMS, AND HOPKINS.
WUM WUM WUM
MAD AS HATTERS, JIM.
AND HIM WORKIN' FER THE GOVERNMENT. IT'S SAD.

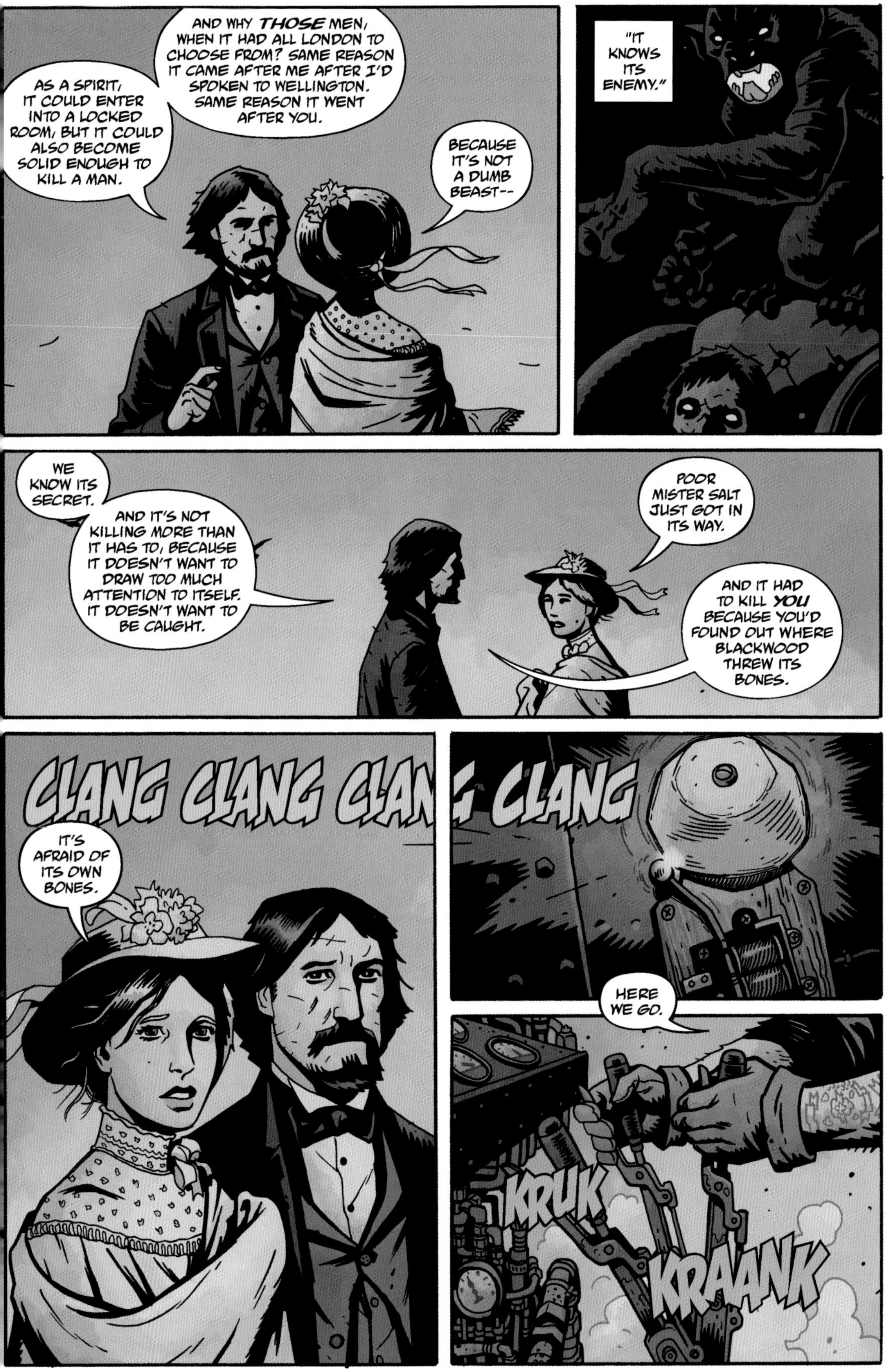

AS A SPIRIT, IT COULD ENTER INTO A LOCKED ROOM, BUT IT COULD ALSO BECOME SOLID ENOUGH TO KILL A MAN.
AND WHY THOSE MEN, WHEN IT HAD ALL LONDON TO CHOOSE FROM? SAME REASON IT CAME AFTER ME AFTER I'D SPOKEN TO WELLINGTON. SAME REASON IT WENT AFTER YOU.
BECAUSE IT'S NOT A DUMB BEAST--
"IT KNOWS ITS ENEMY."
WE KNOW ITS SECRET.
AND IT'S NOT KILLING MORE THAN IT HAS TO, BECAUSE IT DOESN'T WANT TO DRAW TOO MUCH ATTENTION TO ITSELF. IT DOESN'T WANT TO BE CAUGHT.
POOR MISTER SALT JUST GOT IN ITS WAY.
AND IT HAD TO KILL YOU BECAUSE YOU'D FOUND OUT WHERE BLACKWOOD THREW ITS BONES.
CLANG CLANG CLANG CLANG
IT'S AFRAID OF ITS OWN BONES.
HERE WE GO.
KRUK
KRAANK

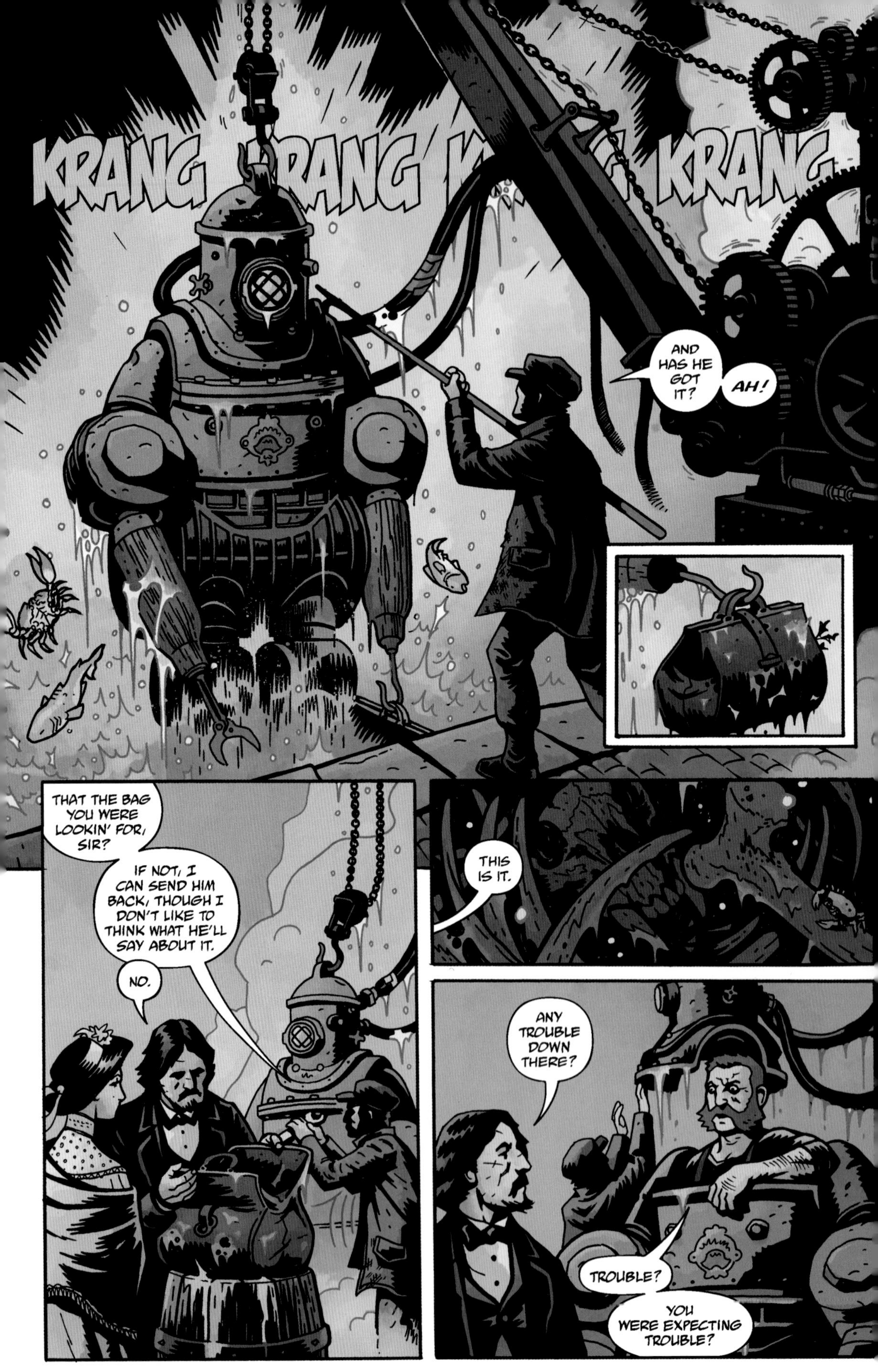
KRANG KRANG KRANG KRANG
AND HAS HE GOT IT?
AH!
THAT THE BAG YOU WERE LOOKIN' FOR, SIR?
IF NOT, I CAN SEND HIM BACK, THOUGH I DON'T LIKE TO THINK WHAT HE'LL SAY ABOUT IT.
NO.
THIS IS IT.
ANY TROUBLE DOWN THERE?
TROUBLE?
YOU WERE EXPECTING TROUBLE?

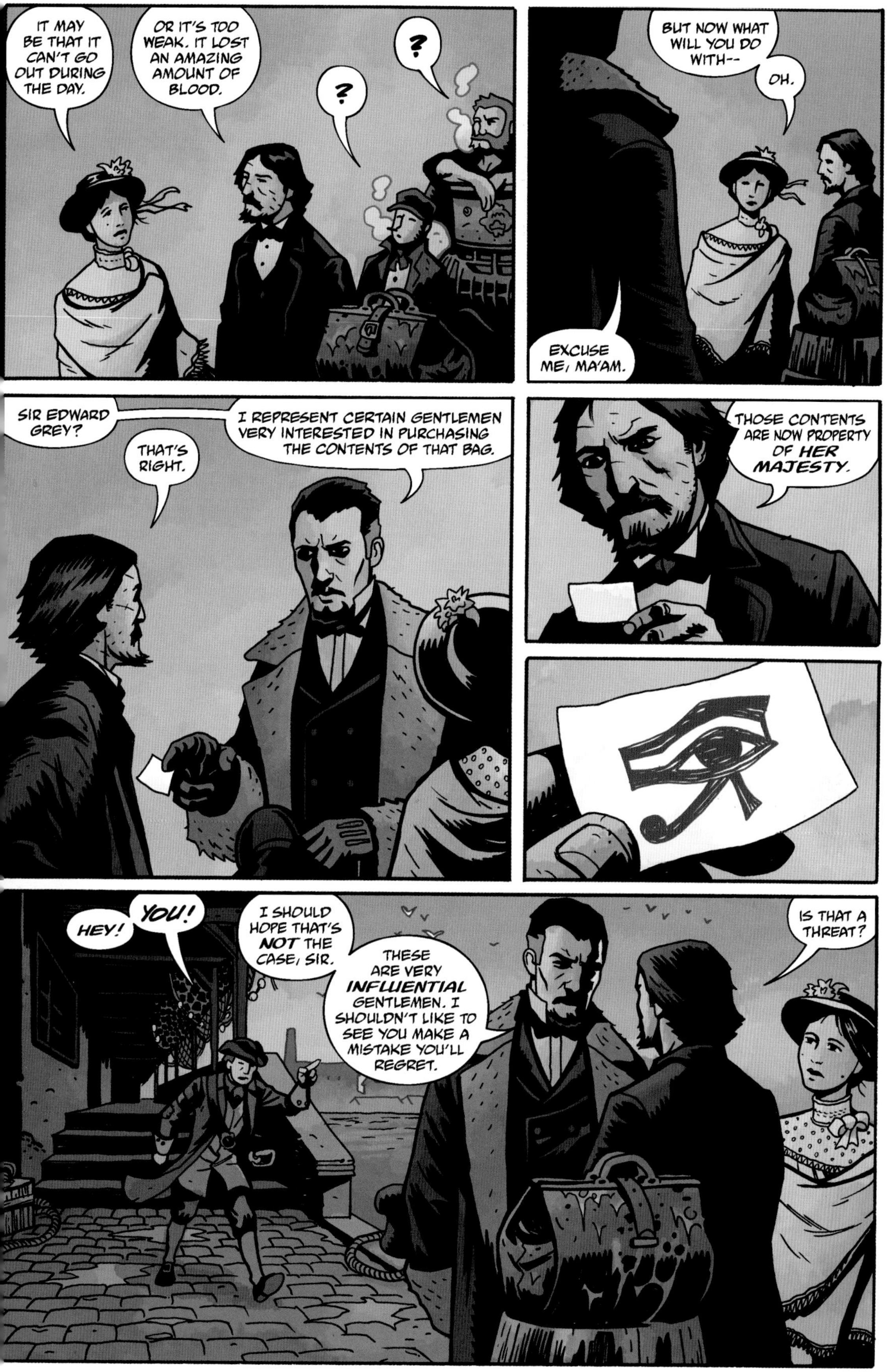
IT MAY BE THAT IT CAN'T GO OUT DURING THE DAY.
OR IT'S TOO WEAK. IT LOST AN AMAZING AMOUNT OF BLOOD.
?
?
BUT NOW WHAT WILL YOU DO WITH--
OH.
EXCUSE ME, MA'AM.
SIR EDWARD GREY?
THAT'S RIGHT.
I REPRESENT CERTAIN GENTLEMEN VERY INTERESTED IN PURCHASING THE CONTENTS OF THAT BAG.
THOSE CONTENTS ARE NOW PROPERTY OF HER MAJESTY.
HEY!
YOU!
I SHOULD HOPE THAT'S NOT THE CASE, SIR.
THESE ARE VERY INFLUENTIAL GENTLEMEN. I SHOULDN'T LIKE TO SEE YOU MAKE A MISTAKE YOU'LL REGRET.
IS THAT A THREAT?

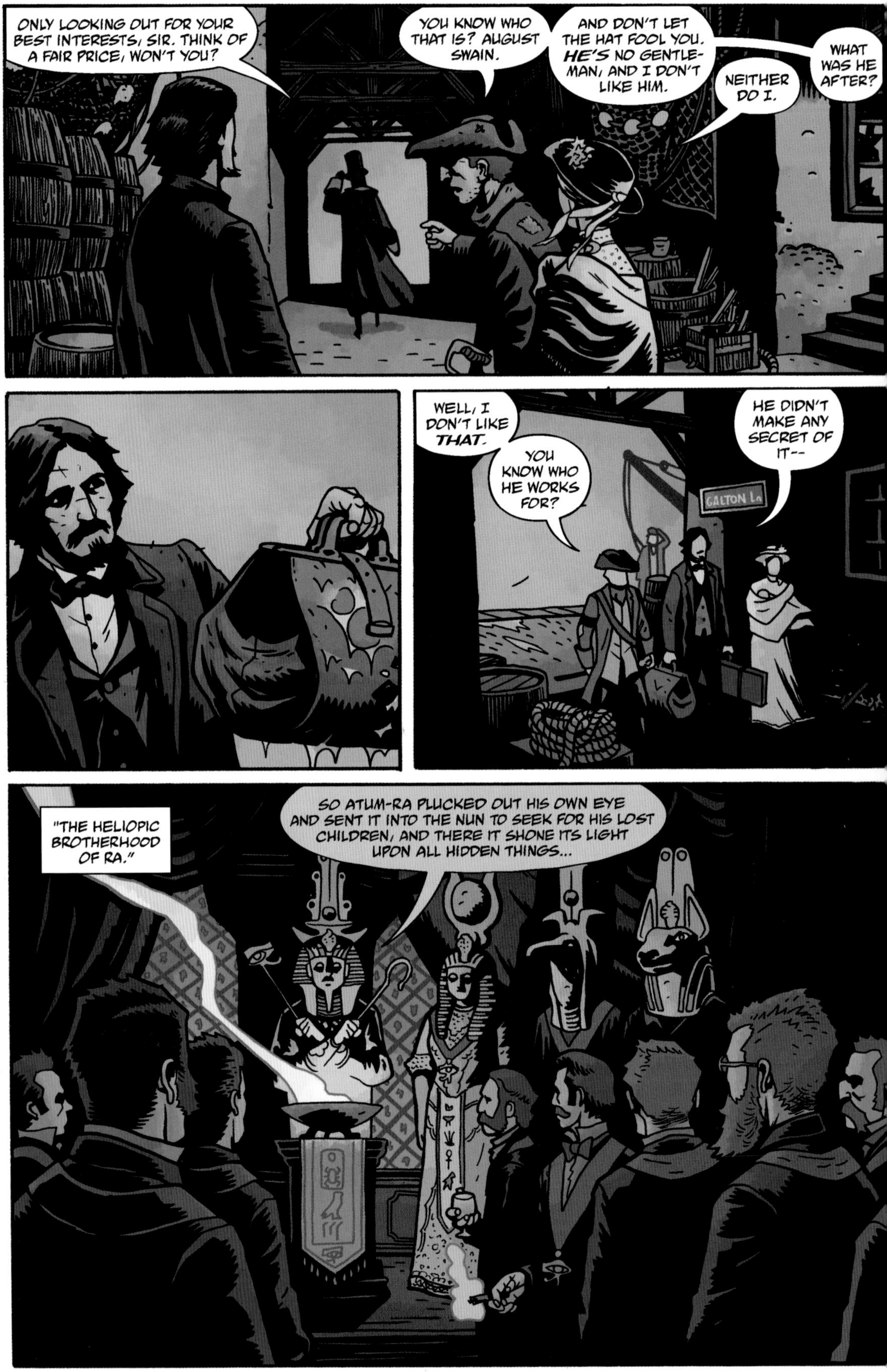
ONLY LOOKING OUT FOR YOUR BEST INTERESTS, SIR. THINK OF A FAIR PRICE, WON'T YOU?
YOU KNOW WHO THAT IS? AUGUST SWAIN.
AND DON'T LET THE HAT FOOL YOU. HE'S NO GENTLE-MAN, AND I DON'T LIKE HIM.
NEITHER DO I.
WHAT WAS HE AFTER?
WELL, I DON'T LIKE THAT.
YOU KNOW WHO HE WORKS FOR?
HE DIDN'T MAKE ANY SECRET OF IT--
GALTON Ln
"THE HELIOPIC BROTHERHOOD OF RA."
SO ATUM-RA PLUCKED OUT HIS OWN EYE AND SENT IT INTO THE NUN TO SEEK FOR HIS LOST CHILDREN, AND THERE IT SHONE ITS LIGHT UPON ALL HIDDEN THINGS...

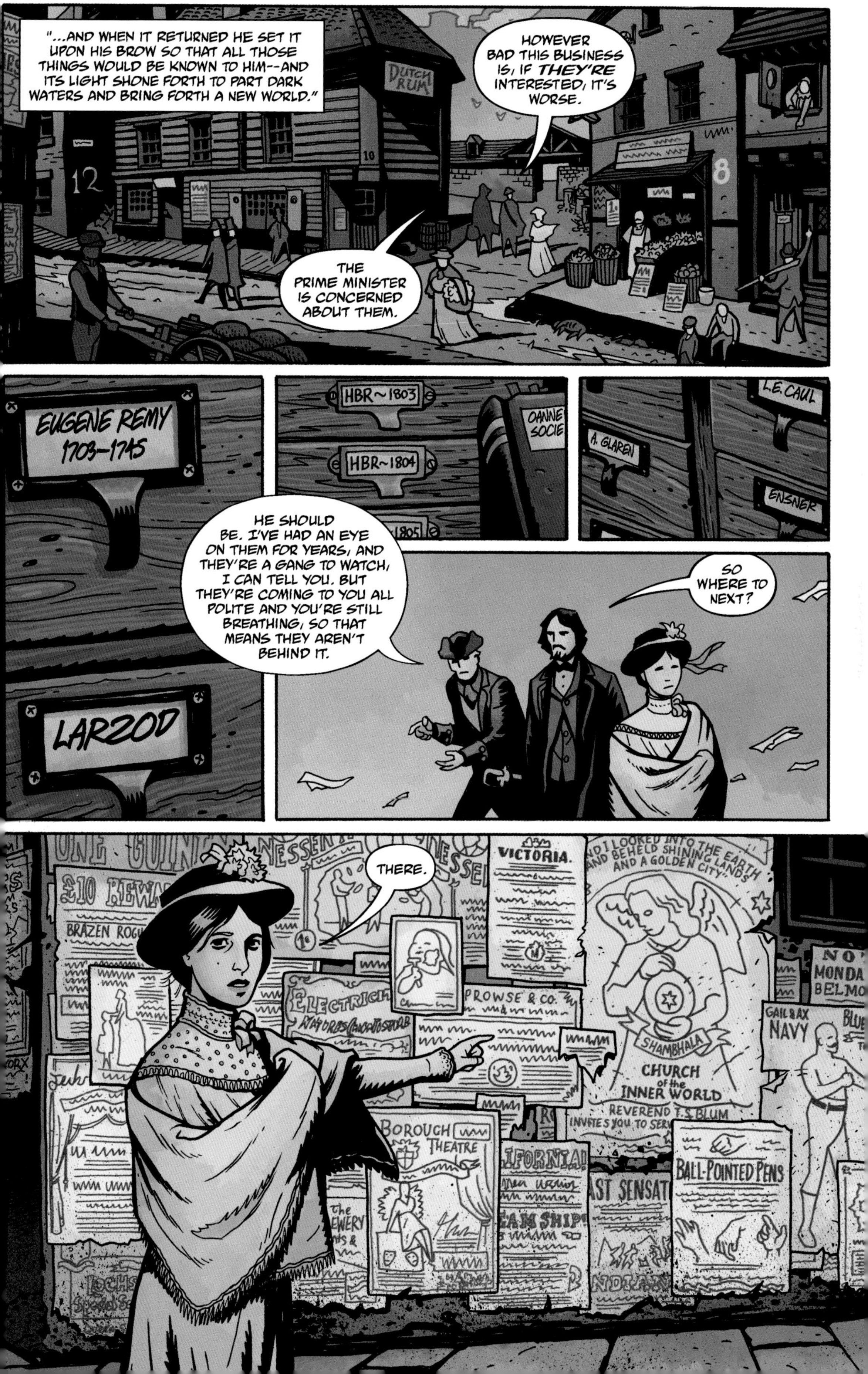
"...AND WHEN IT RETURNED HE SET IT UPON HIS BROW SO THAT ALL THOSE THINGS WOULD BE KNOWN TO HIM--AND ITS LIGHT SHONE FORTH TO PART DARK WATERS AND BRING FORTH A NEW WORLD."
DUTCH RUM
HOWEVER BAD THIS BUSINESS IS, IF *THEY'RE* INTERESTED, IT'S WORSE.
THE PRIME MINISTER IS CONCERNED ABOUT THEM.
EUGENE REMY 1703–1745
HBR~1803
HBR~1804
L.E. CAUL
A. GLAREN
ENSNER
HE SHOULD BE. I'VE HAD AN EYE ON THEM FOR YEARS, AND THEY'RE A GANG TO WATCH, I CAN TELL YOU. BUT THEY'RE COMING TO YOU ALL POLITE AND YOU'RE STILL BREATHING, SO THAT MEANS THEY AREN'T BEHIND IT.
LARZOD
SO WHERE TO NEXT?
THERE.
VICTORIA.
"AND I LOOKED INTO THE EARTH AND BEHELD SHINING LANDS AND A GOLDEN CITY"
SHAMBHALA
CHURCH of the INNER WORLD
REVEREND F.S. BLUM
PROWSE & CO.
BOROUGH THEATRE
BALL-POINTED PENS
GAIL & AX NAVY

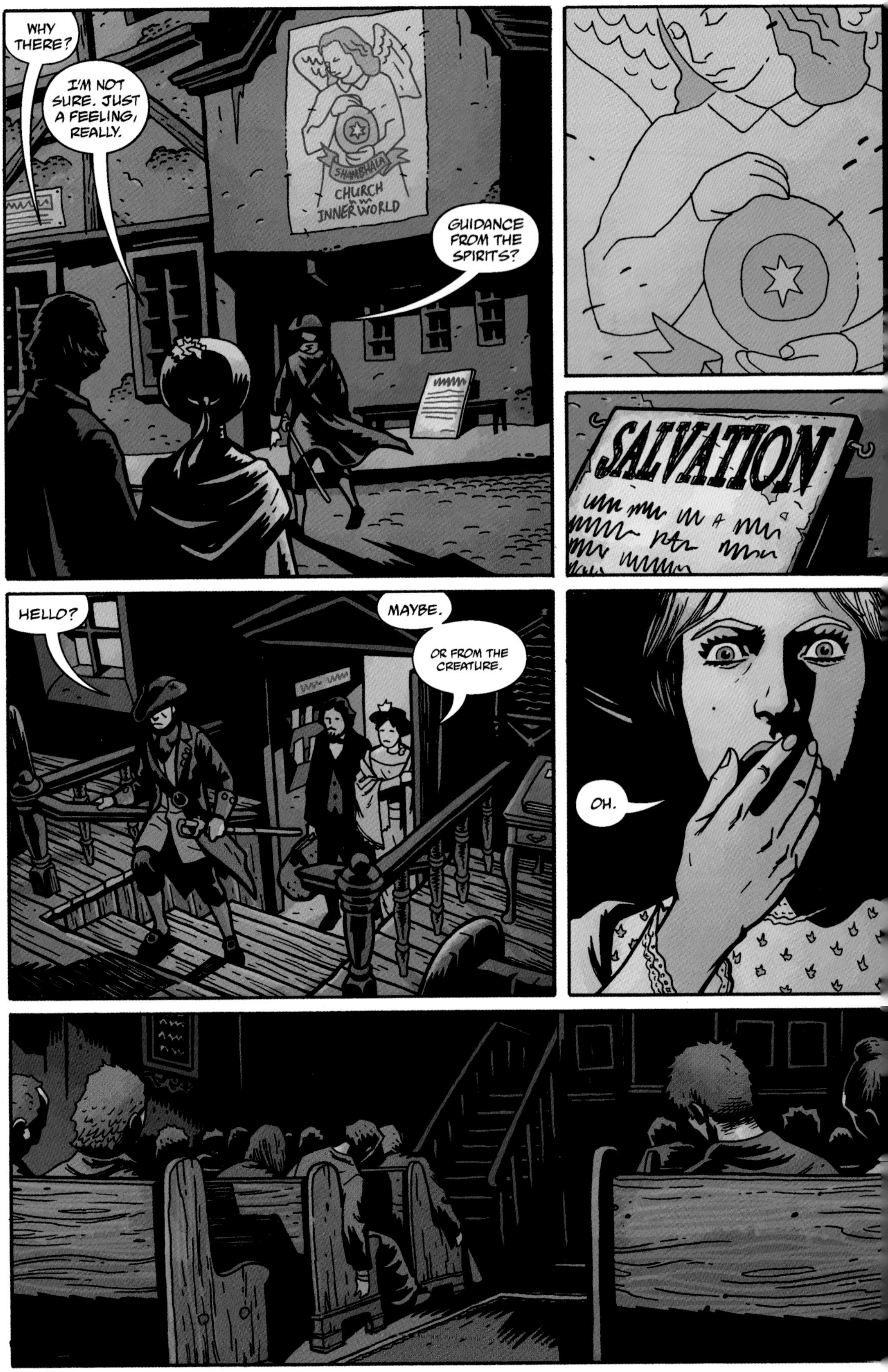
WHY THERE?
I'M NOT SURE. JUST A FEELING, REALLY.
SHAMBHALA
CHURCH
INNER WORLD
GUIDANCE FROM THE SPIRITS?
SALVATION
HELLO?
MAYBE.
OR FROM THE CREATURE.
OH.

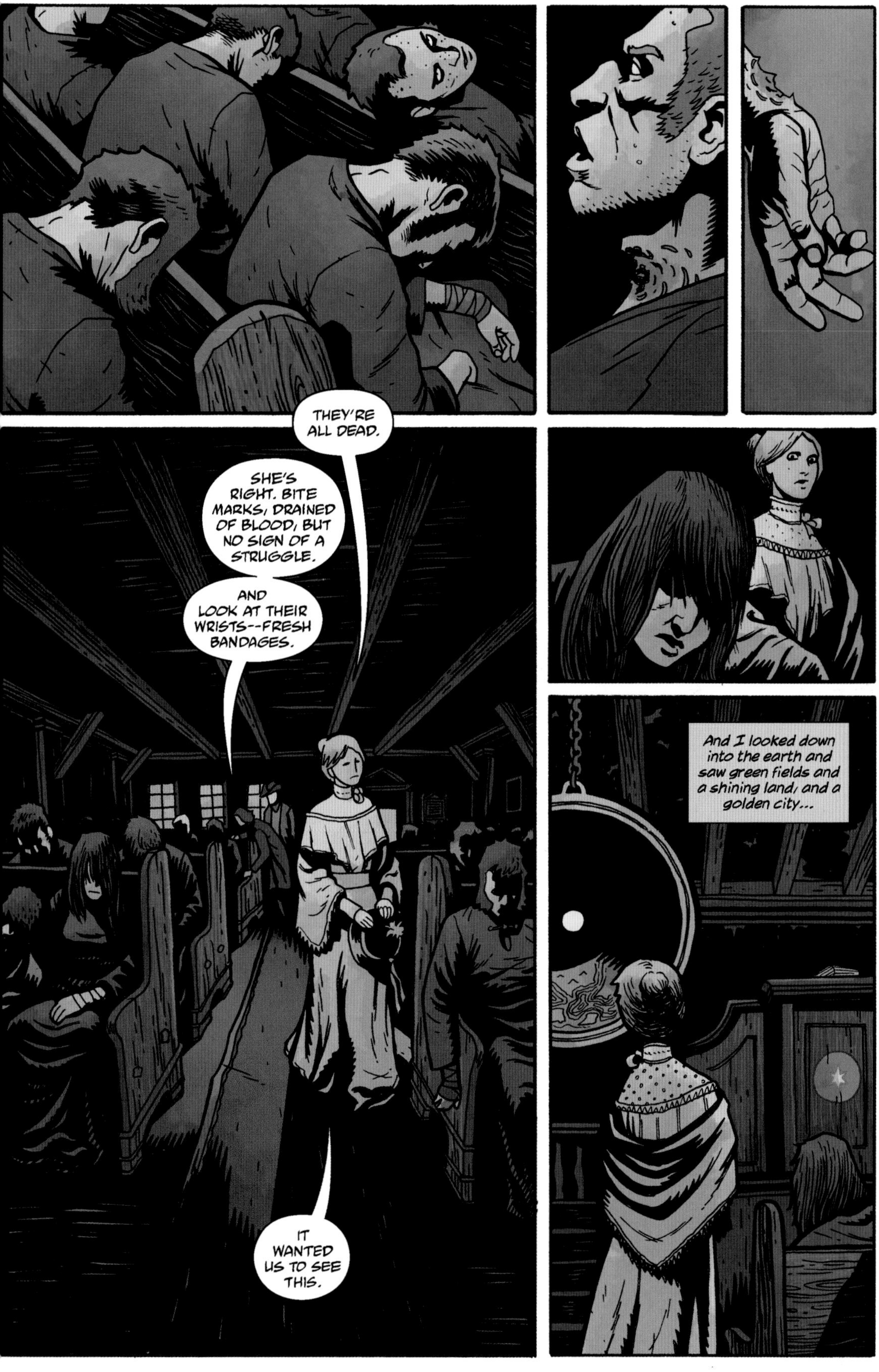
THEY'RE ALL DEAD.
SHE'S RIGHT. BITE MARKS, DRAINED OF BLOOD, BUT NO SIGN OF A STRUGGLE.
AND LOOK AT THEIR WRISTS--FRESH BANDAGES.
IT WANTED US TO SEE THIS.
And I looked down into the earth and saw green fields and a shining land, and a golden city...

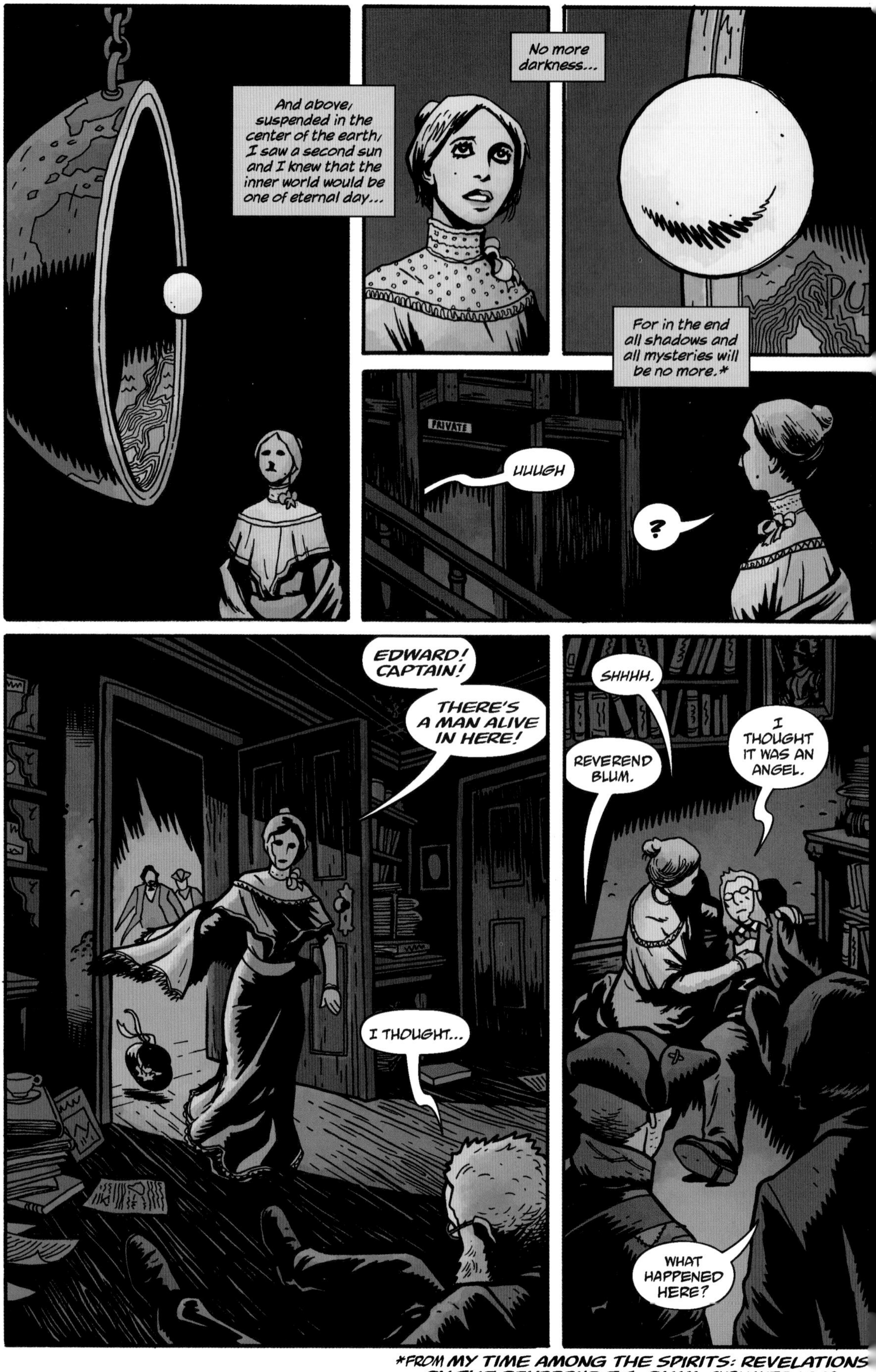
And above, suspended in the center of the earth, I saw a second sun and I knew that the inner world would be one of eternal day...
No more darkness...
For in the end all shadows and all mysteries will be no more.*
PRIVATE
UUUGH
?
EDWARD! CAPTAIN!
THERE'S A MAN ALIVE IN HERE!
I THOUGHT...
SHHHH.
REVEREND BLUM.
I THOUGHT IT WAS AN ANGEL.
WHAT HAPPENED HERE?

*FROM **MY TIME AMONG THE SPIRITS: REVELATIONS BY THE REVEREND T.S. BLUM.** PUBLISHED 1869.

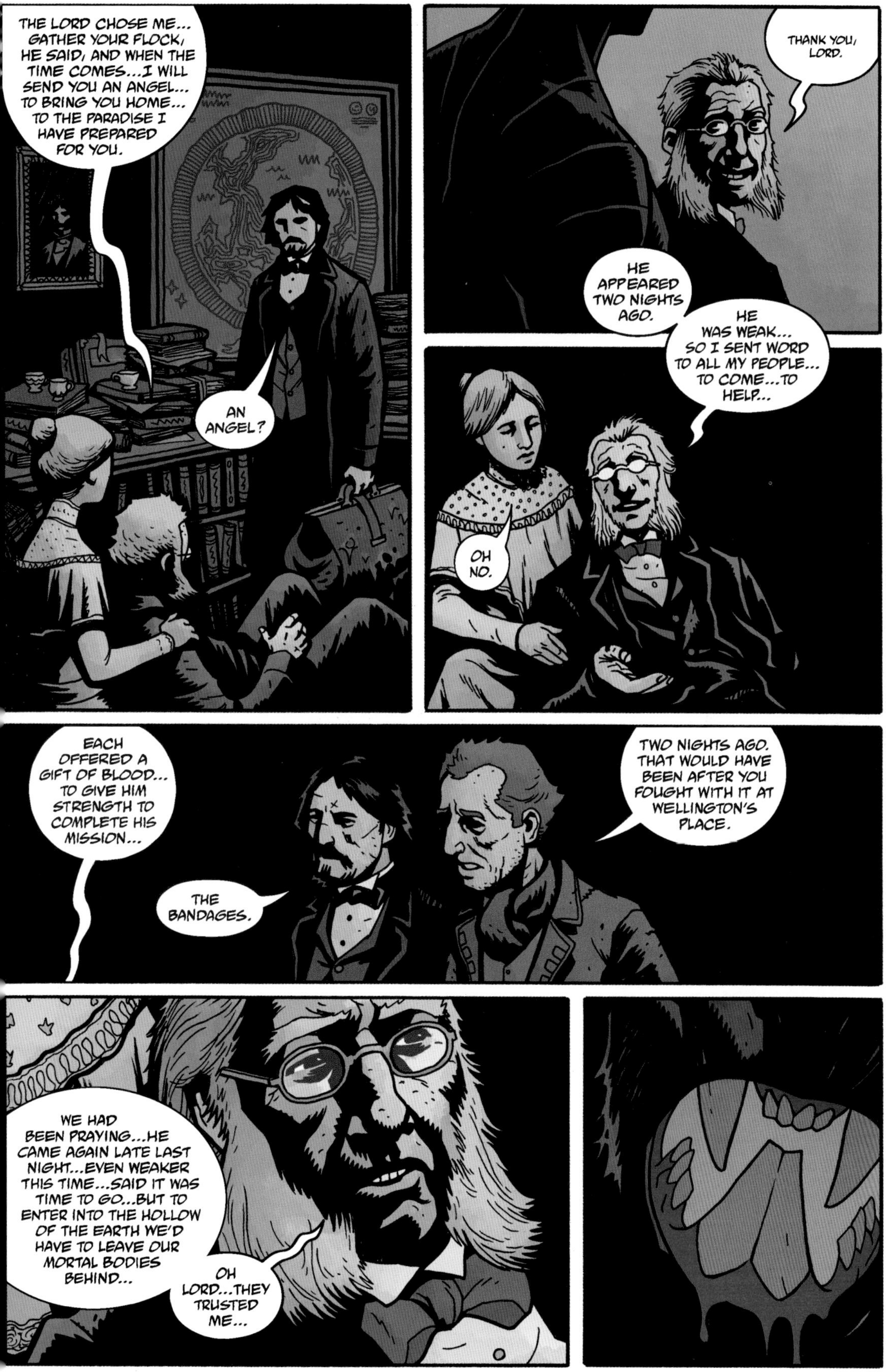
THE LORD CHOSE ME... GATHER YOUR FLOCK, HE SAID, AND WHEN THE TIME COMES...I WILL SEND YOU AN ANGEL... TO BRING YOU HOME... TO THE PARADISE I HAVE PREPARED FOR YOU.
AN ANGEL?
THANK YOU, LORD.
HE APPEARED TWO NIGHTS AGO.
HE WAS WEAK... SO I SENT WORD TO ALL MY PEOPLE... TO COME...TO HELP...
OH NO.
EACH OFFERED A GIFT OF BLOOD... TO GIVE HIM STRENGTH TO COMPLETE HIS MISSION...
THE BANDAGES.
TWO NIGHTS AGO. THAT WOULD HAVE BEEN AFTER YOU FOUGHT WITH IT AT WELLINGTON'S PLACE.
WE HAD BEEN PRAYING...HE CAME AGAIN LATE LAST NIGHT...EVEN WEAKER THIS TIME...SAID IT WAS TIME TO GO...BUT TO ENTER INTO THE HOLLOW OF THE EARTH WE'D HAVE TO LEAVE OUR MORTAL BODIES BEHIND...
OH LORD...THEY TRUSTED ME...

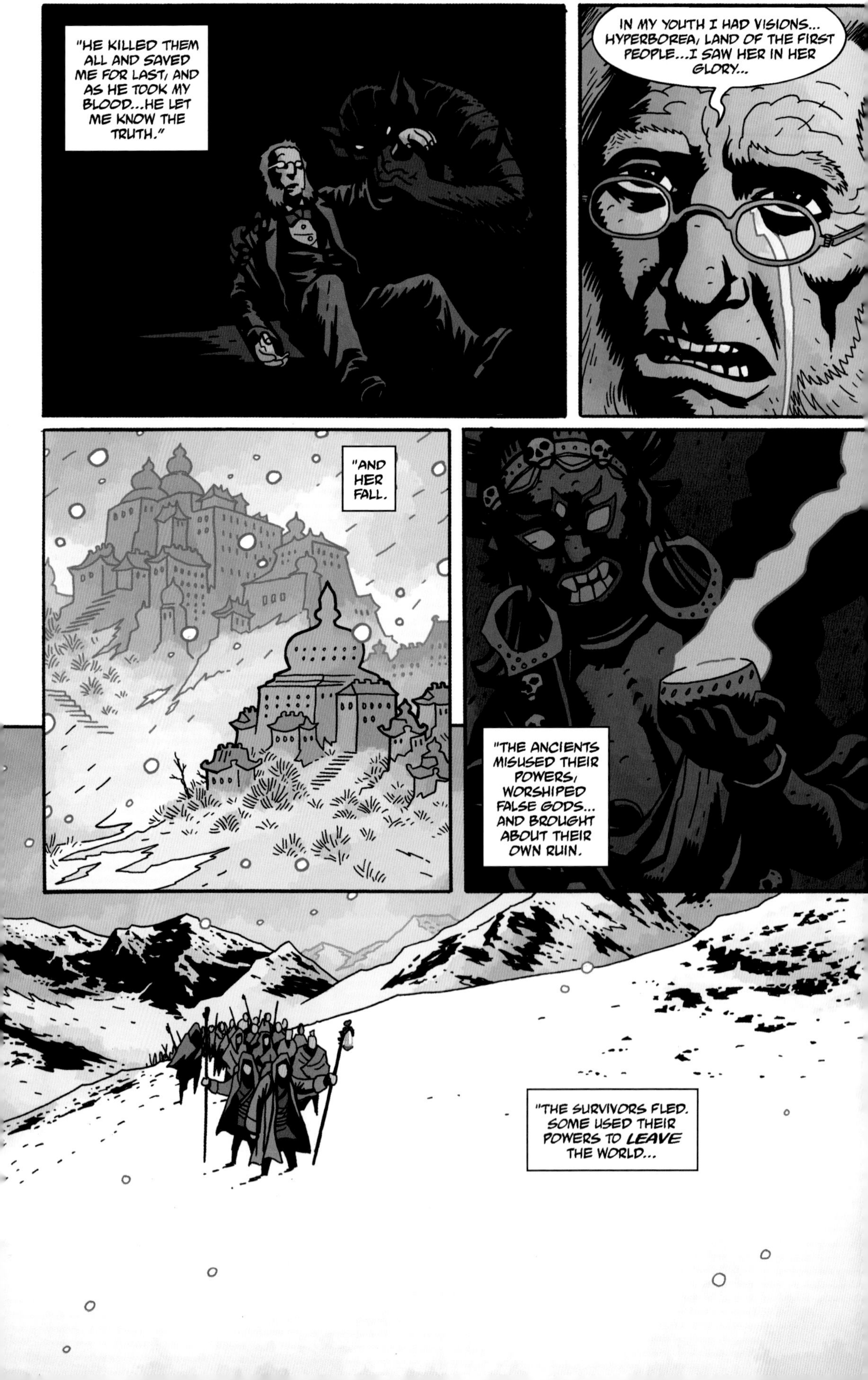
"HE KILLED THEM ALL AND SAVED ME FOR LAST, AND AS HE TOOK MY BLOOD...HE LET ME KNOW THE TRUTH."
IN MY YOUTH I HAD VISIONS... HYPERBOREA, LAND OF THE FIRST PEOPLE...I SAW HER IN HER GLORY...
"AND HER FALL.
"THE ANCIENTS MISUSED THEIR POWERS, WORSHIPED FALSE GODS... AND BROUGHT ABOUT THEIR OWN RUIN.
"THE SURVIVORS FLED. SOME USED THEIR POWERS TO LEAVE THE WORLD...

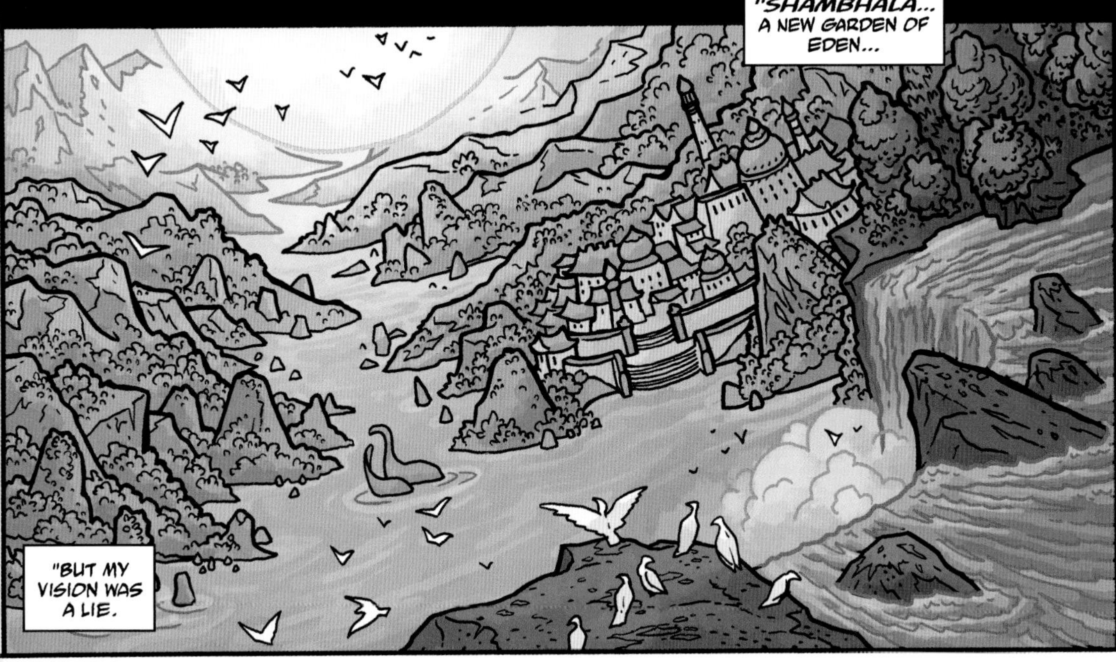
"SHAMBHALA... A NEW GARDEN OF EDEN...
"BUT MY VISION WAS A LIE.

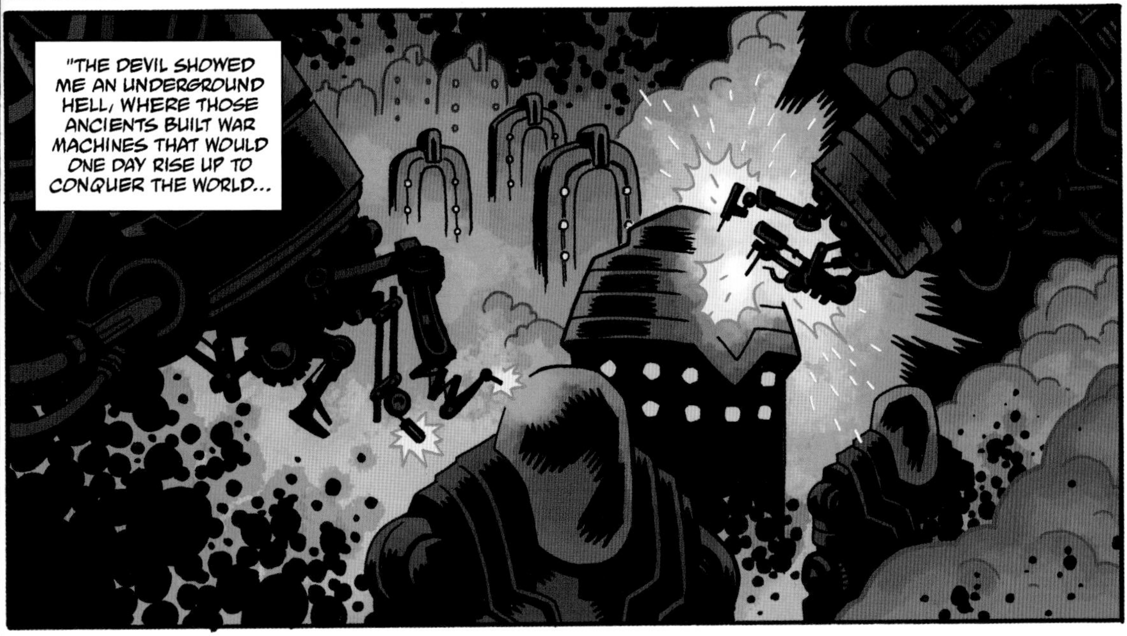
"THE DEVIL SHOWED ME AN UNDERGROUND HELL, WHERE THOSE ANCIENTS BUILT WAR MACHINES THAT WOULD ONE DAY RISE UP TO CONQUER THE WORLD...

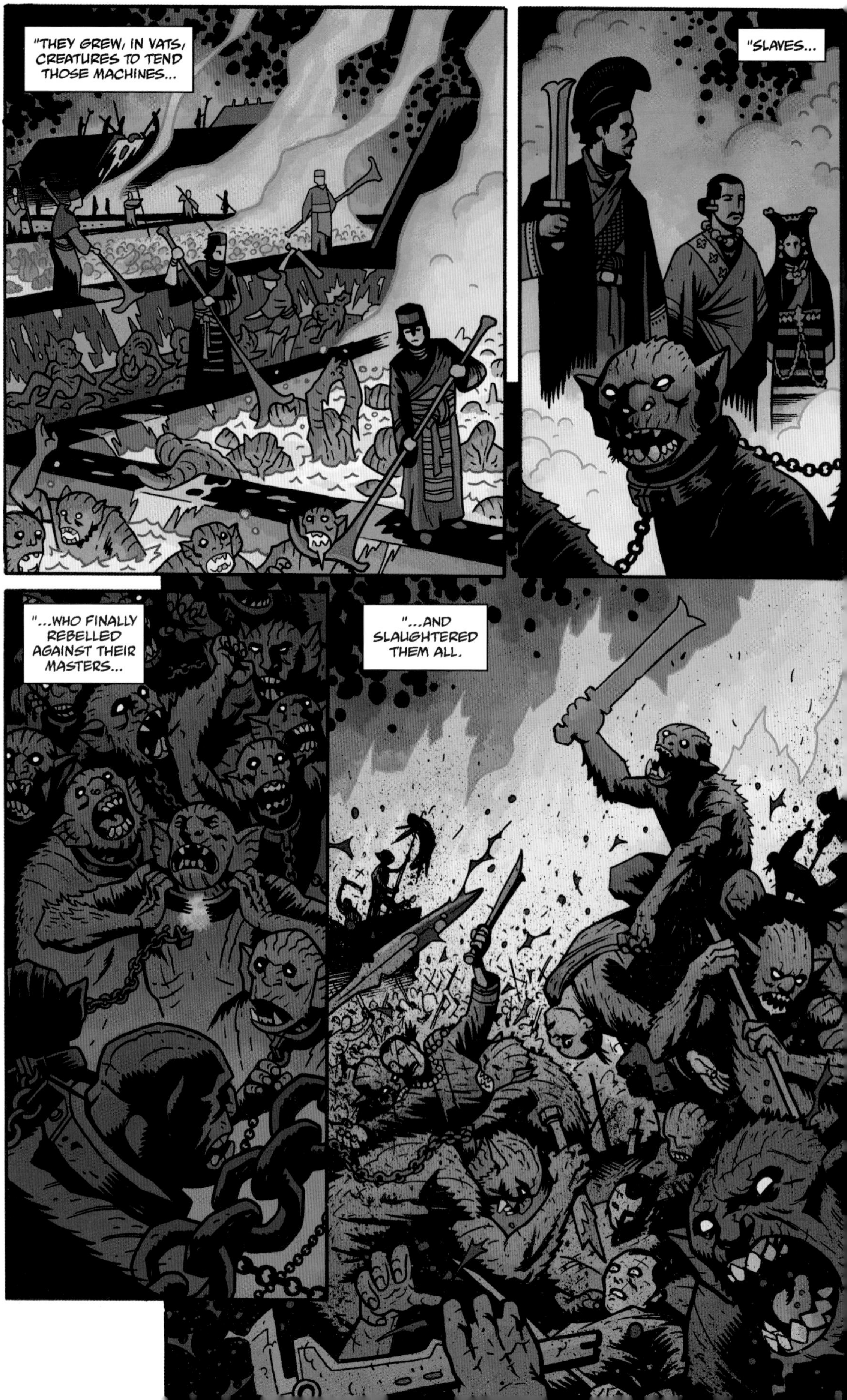
"THEY GREW, IN VATS, CREATURES TO TEND THOSE MACHINES...
"SLAVES...
"...WHO FINALLY REBELLED AGAINST THEIR MASTERS...
"...AND SLAUGHTERED THEM ALL.

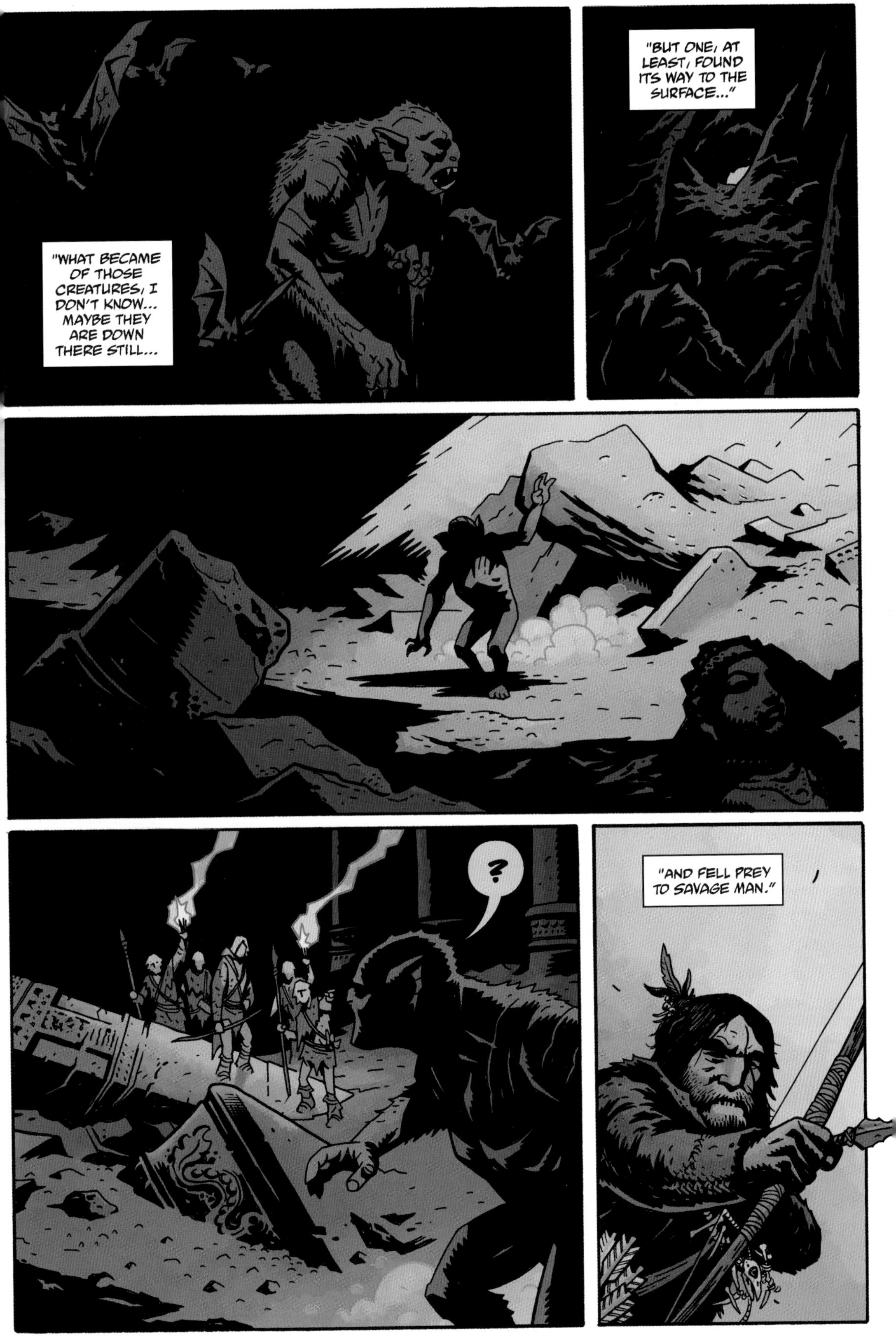
"WHAT BECAME OF THOSE CREATURES, I DON'T KNOW... MAYBE THEY ARE DOWN THERE STILL...
"BUT ONE, AT LEAST, FOUND ITS WAY TO THE SURFACE..."
?
"AND FELL PREY TO SAVAGE MAN."

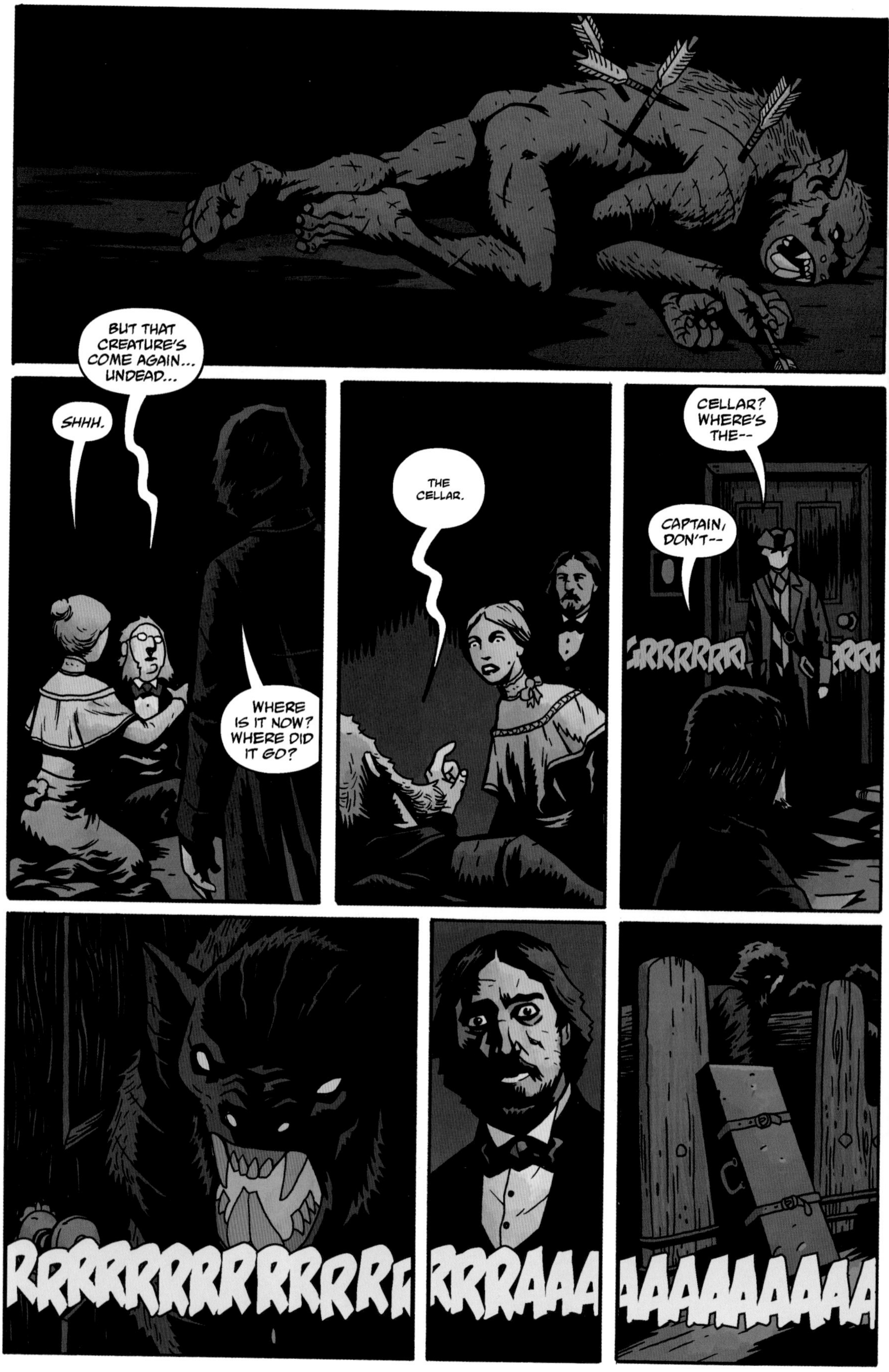

BUT THAT CREATURE'S COME AGAIN... UNDEAD...
SHHH.
WHERE IS IT NOW? WHERE DID IT GO?
THE CELLAR.
CELLAR? WHERE'S THE--
CAPTAIN, DON'T--
GRRRRRRR
RRRR
RRRRRRRRRRRRRR
RRRAAA
AAAAAAAAA

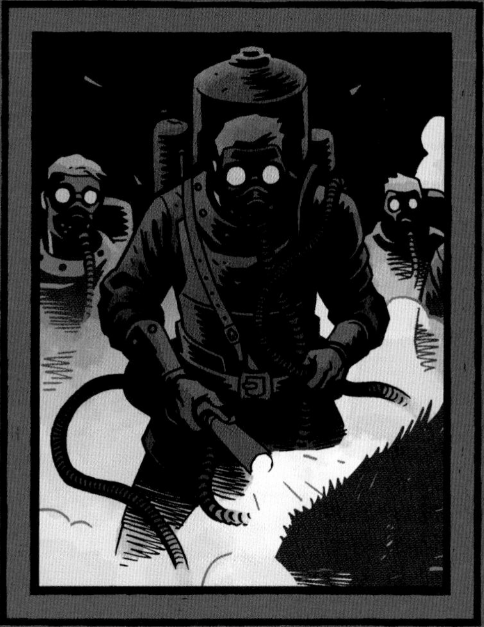

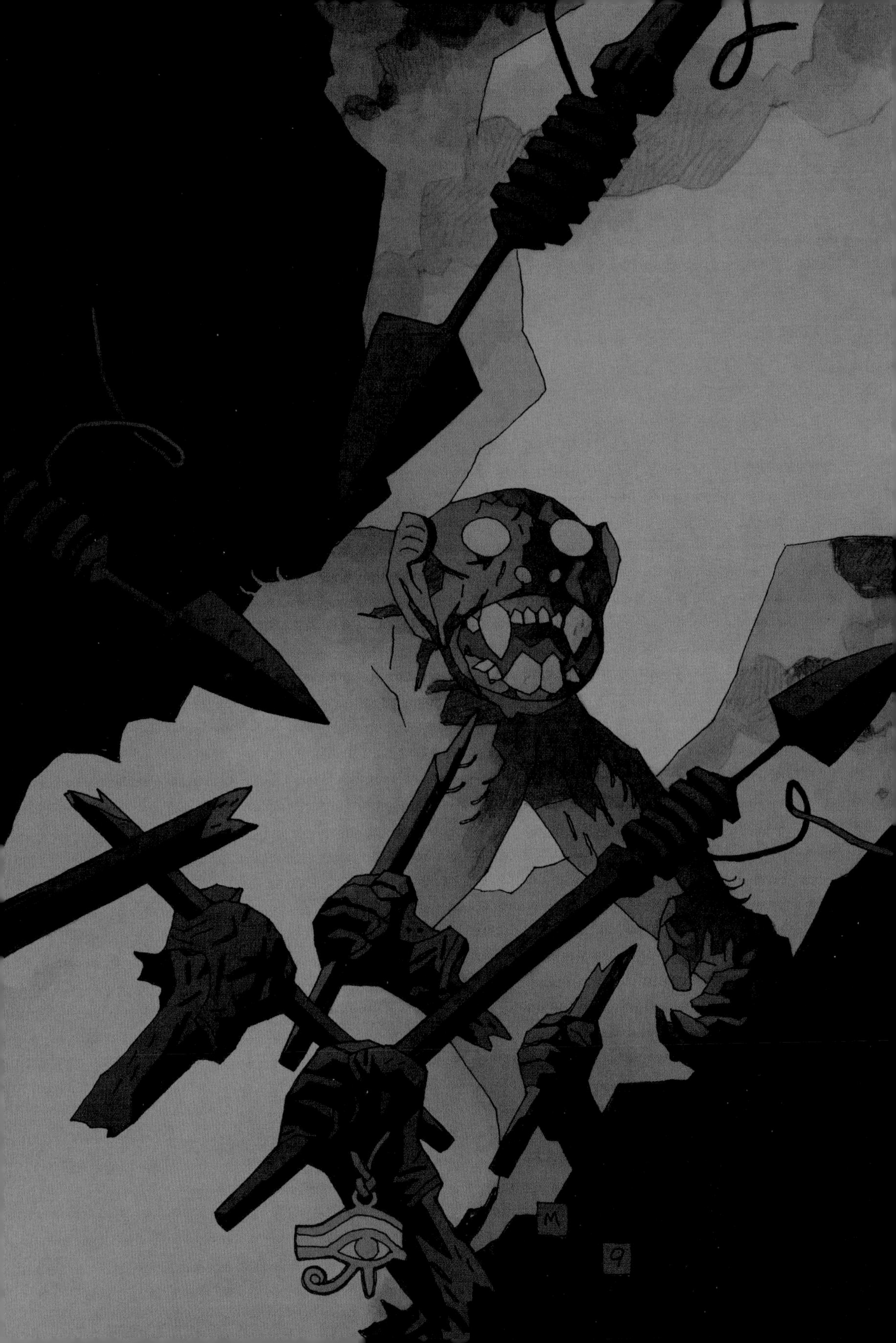

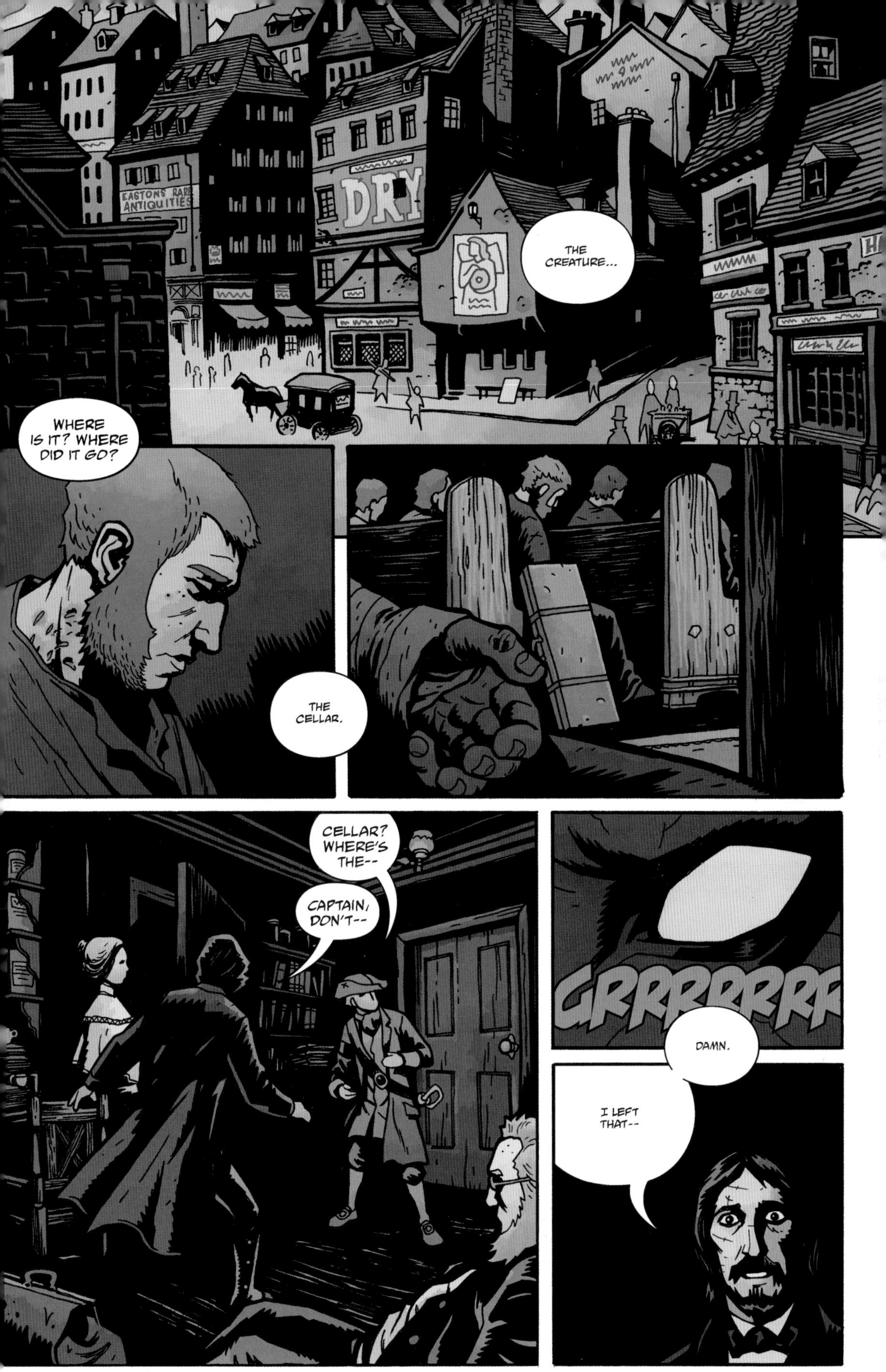
EASTONS RARE ANTIQUITIES
DRY
THE CREATURE...
WHERE IS IT? WHERE DID IT GO?
THE CELLAR.
CELLAR? WHERE'S THE--
CAPTAIN, DON'T--
GRRRRRRR
DAMN.
I LEFT THAT--

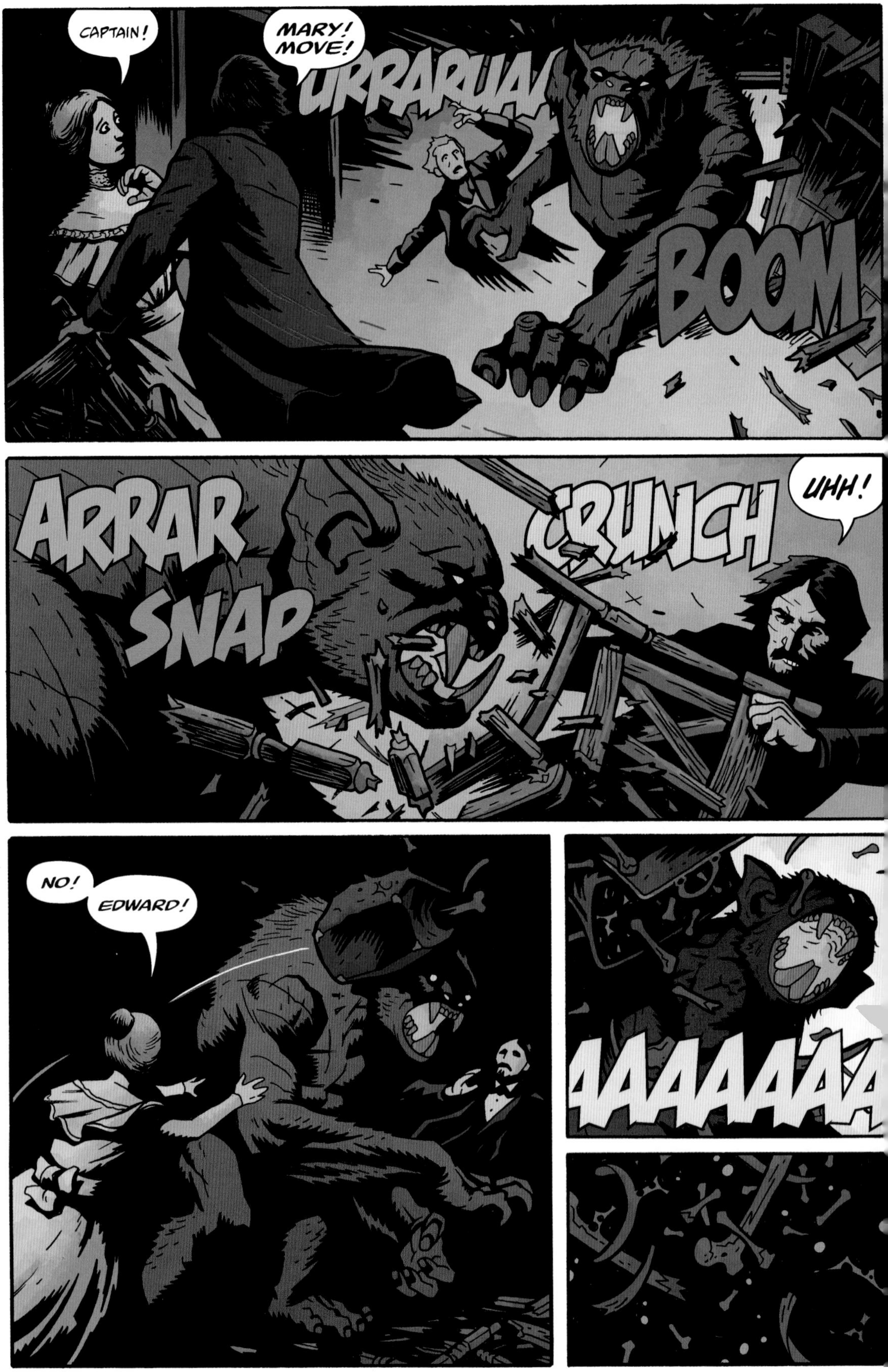
CAPTAIN!
MARY! MOVE!
URRARUA
BOOM
ARRAR
SNAP
CRUNCH
UHH!
NO!
EDWARD!
AAAAAAA

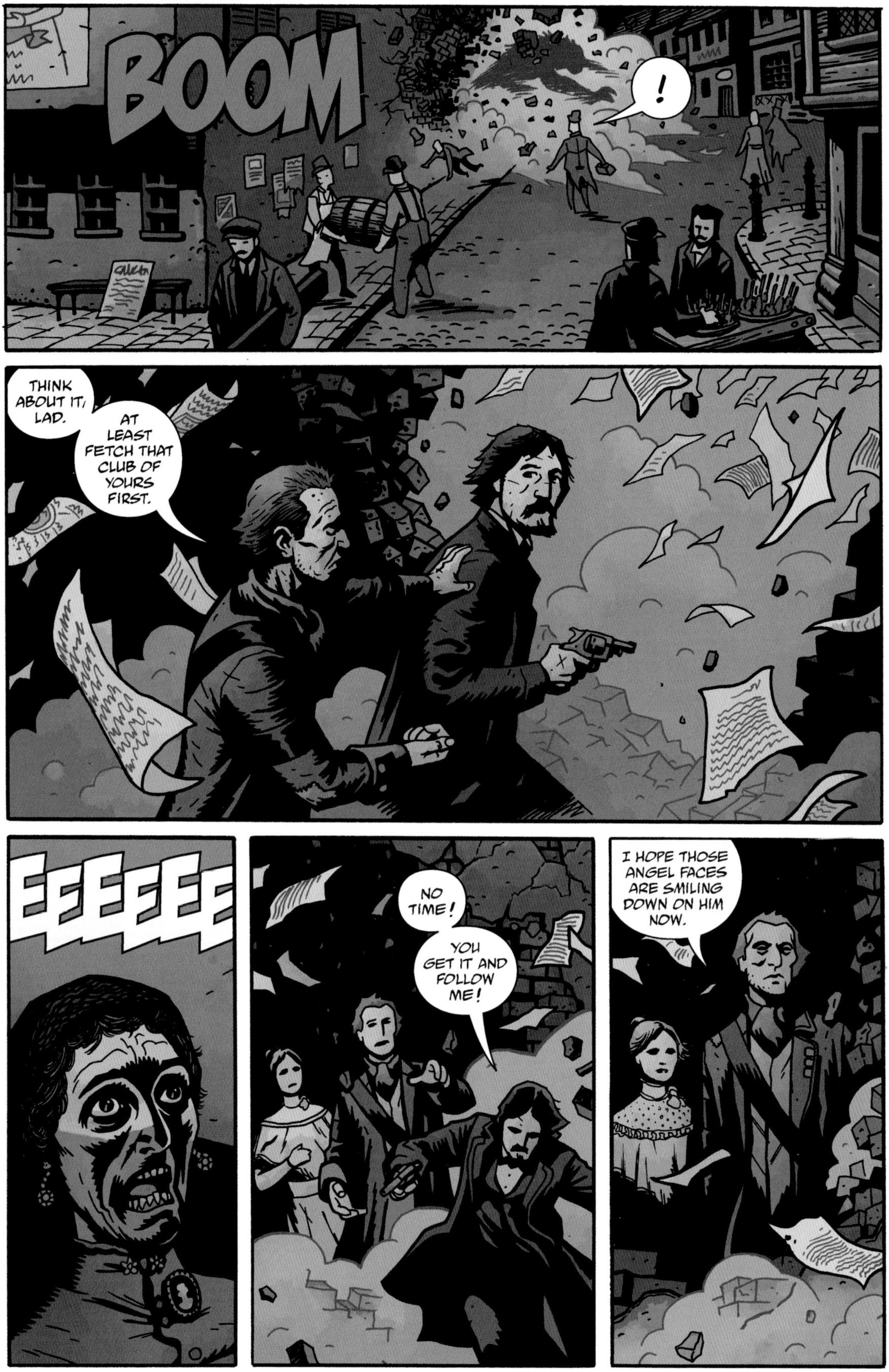
BOOM
!
THINK ABOUT IT, LAD.
AT LEAST FETCH THAT CLUB OF YOURS FIRST.
EEEEEE
NO TIME!
YOU GET IT AND FOLLOW ME!
I HOPE THOSE ANGEL FACES ARE SMILING DOWN ON HIM NOW.

CHRIST!

YOU SAW IT?

BLOODY HELL!

WHICH WAY?

THERE!

SIR!

WHAT IS IT? WHAT--

KEEP BACK. I'LL--

YOU'LL WHAT NOW?

YOU'LL DROP THAT GUN. THAT'LL DO FOR A START.

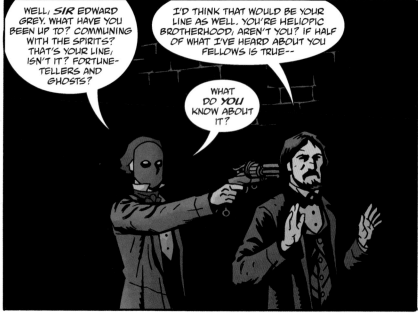

WELL, SIR EDWARD GREY. WHAT HAVE YOU BEEN UP TO? COMMUNING WITH THE SPIRITS? THAT'S YOUR LINE, ISN'T IT? FORTUNE-TELLERS AND GHOSTS?

I'D THINK THAT WOULD BE YOUR LINE AS WELL. YOU'RE HELIOPIC BROTHERHOOD, AREN'T YOU? IF HALF OF WHAT I'VE HEARD ABOUT YOU FELLOWS IS TRUE--

WHAT DO YOU KNOW ABOUT IT?

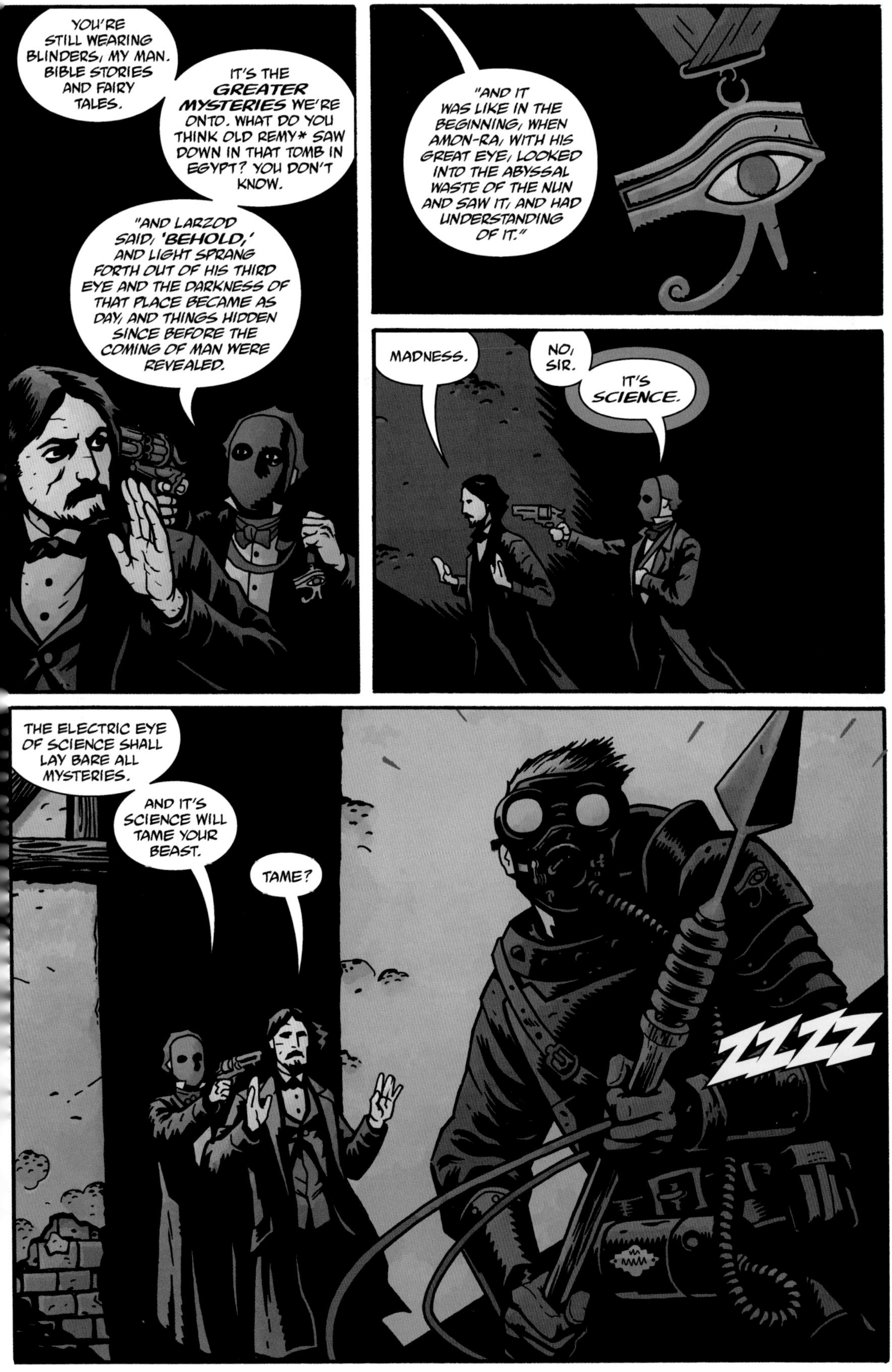
YOU'RE STILL WEARING BLINDERS, MY MAN. BIBLE STORIES AND FAIRY TALES.
IT'S THE GREATER MYSTERIES WE'RE ONTO. WHAT DO YOU THINK OLD REMY* SAW DOWN IN THAT TOMB IN EGYPT? YOU DON'T KNOW.
"AND LARZOD SAID, 'BEHOLD,' AND LIGHT SPRANG FORTH OUT OF HIS THIRD EYE AND THE DARKNESS OF THAT PLACE BECAME AS DAY, AND THINGS HIDDEN SINCE BEFORE THE COMING OF MAN WERE REVEALED.
"AND IT WAS LIKE IN THE BEGINNING, WHEN AMON-RA, WITH HIS GREAT EYE, LOOKED INTO THE ABYSSAL WASTE OF THE NUN AND SAW IT, AND HAD UNDERSTANDING OF IT."
MADNESS.
NO, SIR.
IT'S SCIENCE.
THE ELECTRIC EYE OF SCIENCE SHALL LAY BARE ALL MYSTERIES.
AND IT'S SCIENCE WILL TAME YOUR BEAST.
TAME?
ZZZZ

*EUGENE REMY, FOUNDER OF THE HELIOPIC BROTHERHOOD OF RA. 1692-1745.

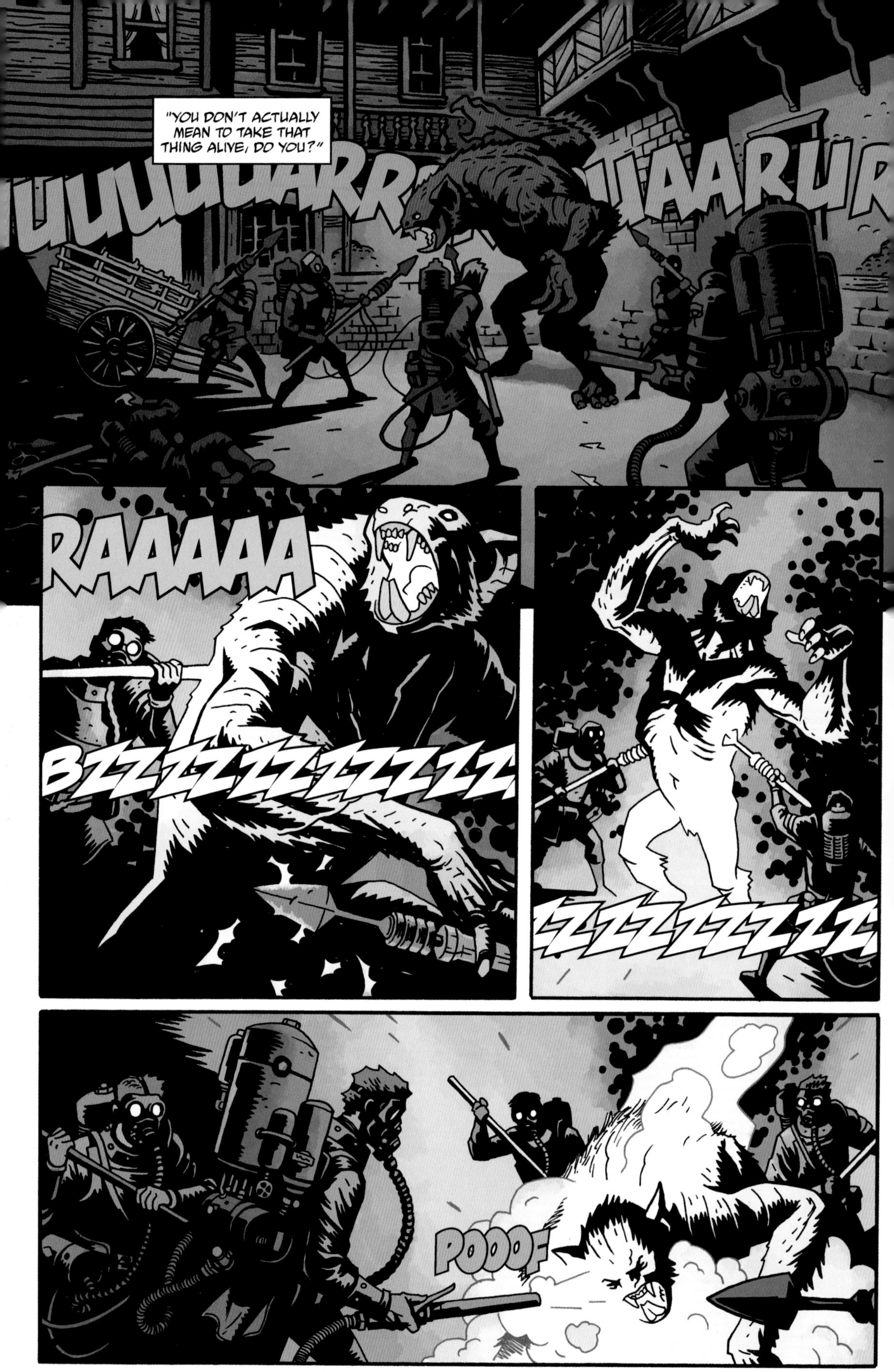
"YOU DON'T ACTUALLY MEAN TO TAKE THAT THING ALIVE, DO YOU?"
UUUUUARR
UAARUR
RAAAAA
BZZZZZZZZZZZ
ZZZZZZZZZZ
POOOF

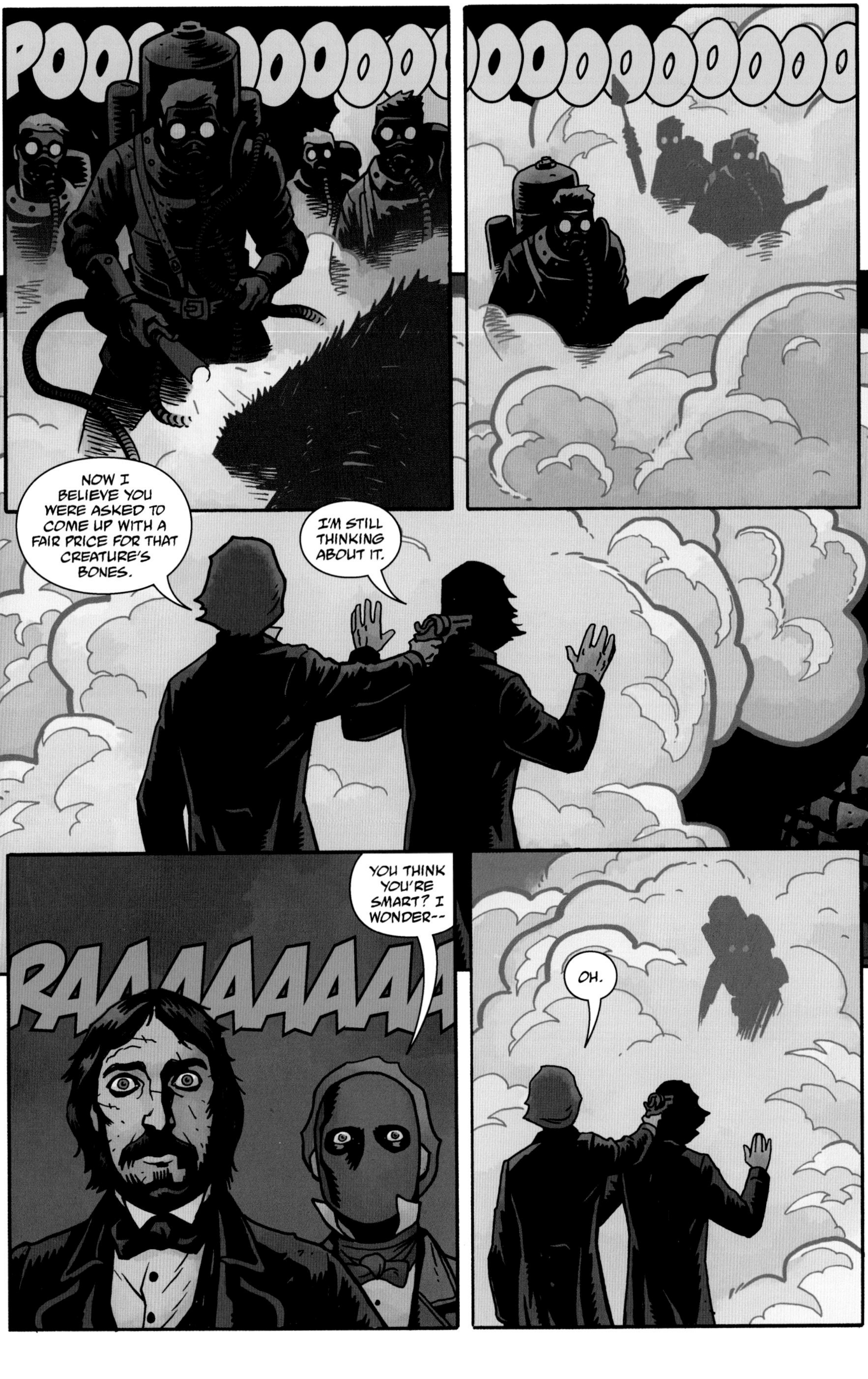
POOOOOOOOOOOOOOOOOOOOOOO
NOW I BELIEVE YOU WERE ASKED TO COME UP WITH A FAIR PRICE FOR THAT CREATURE'S BONES.
I'M STILL THINKING ABOUT IT.
RAAAAAAAA
YOU THINK YOU'RE SMART? I WONDER--
OH.

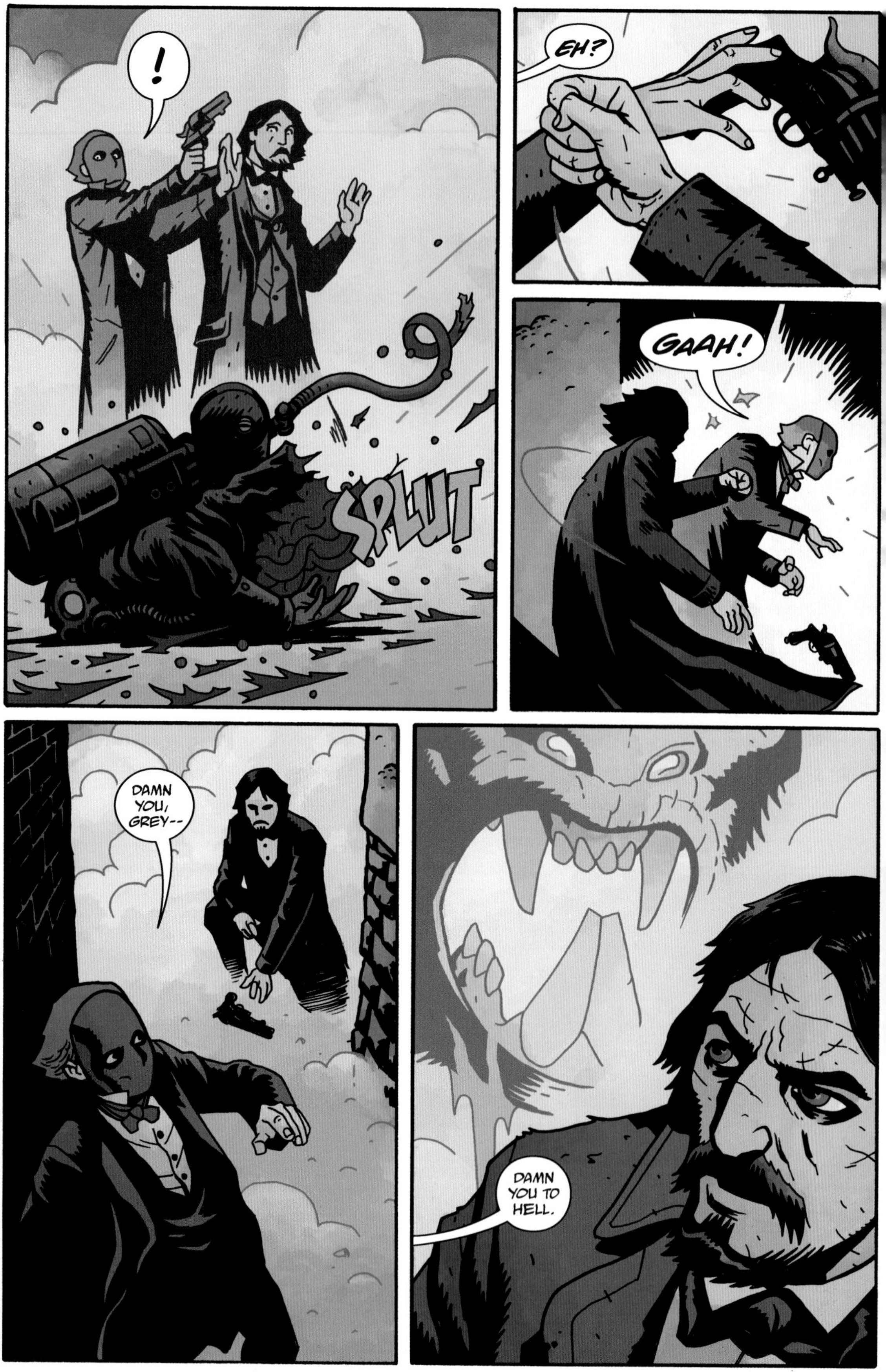
!
EH?
SPLUT
GAAH!
DAMN YOU, GREY--
DAMN YOU TO HELL.

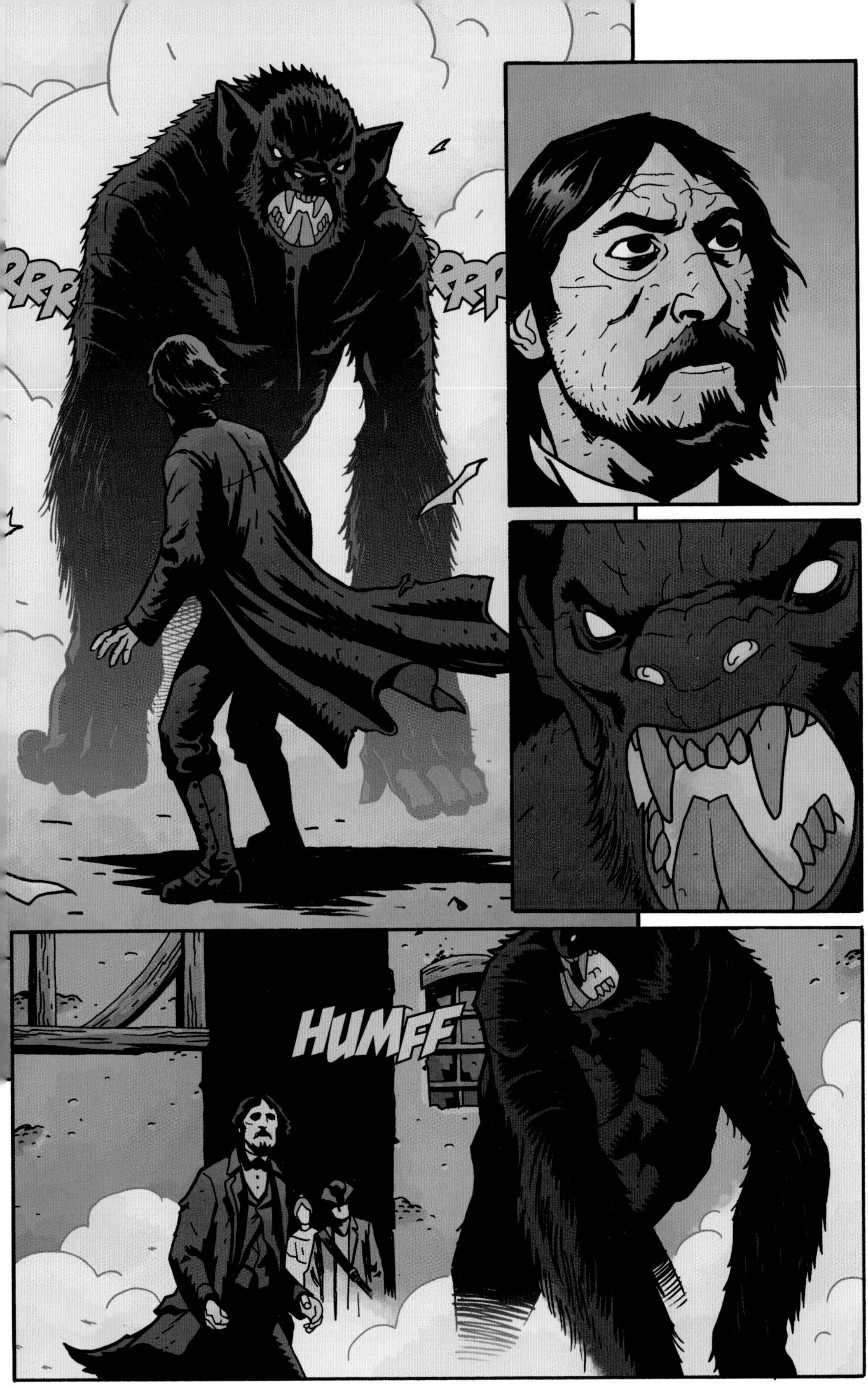
RRRR
RRRR
HUMFF

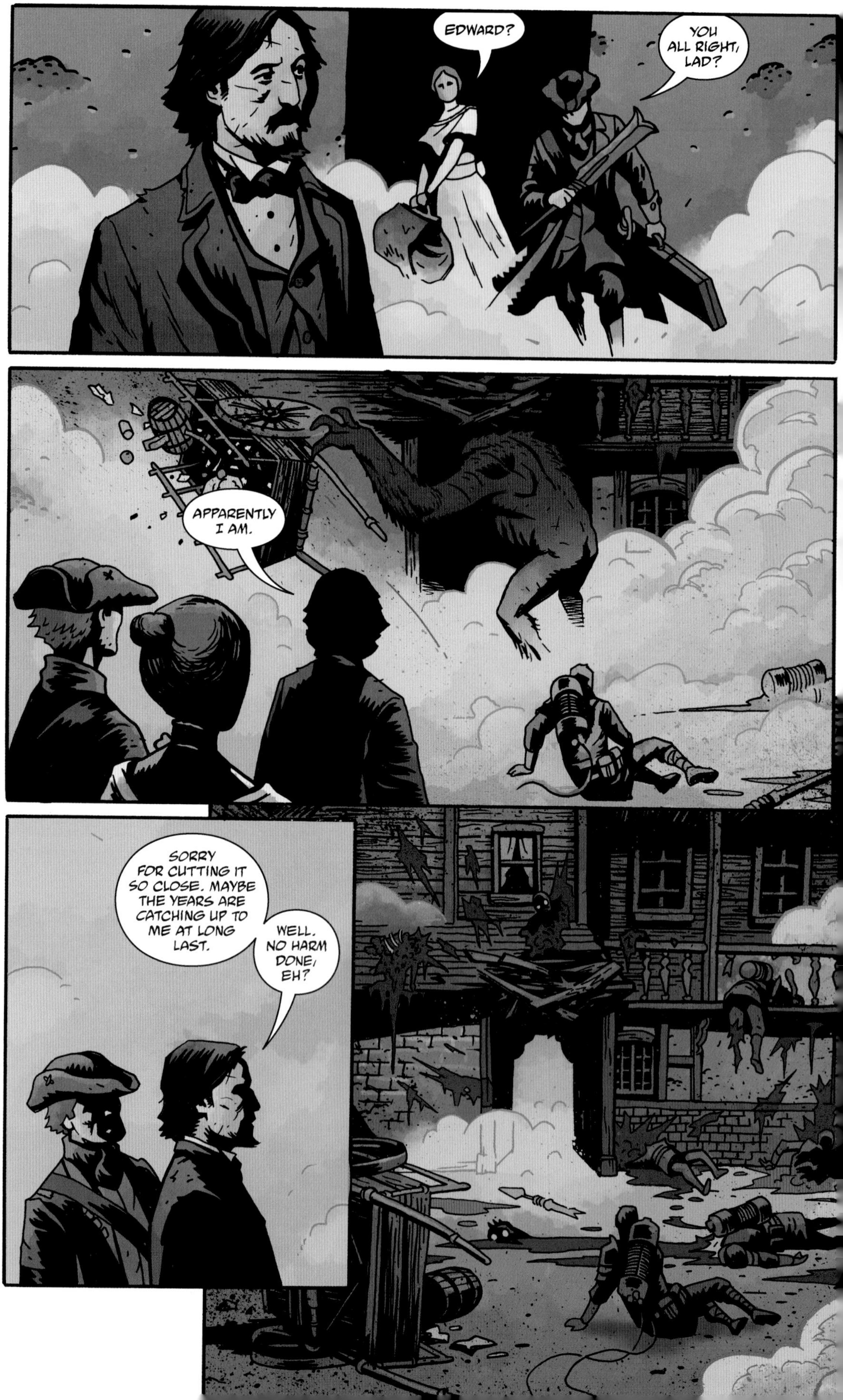
EDWARD?
YOU ALL RIGHT, LAD?
APPARENTLY I AM.
SORRY FOR CUTTING IT SO CLOSE. MAYBE THE YEARS ARE CATCHING UP TO ME AT LONG LAST.
WELL. NO HARM DONE, EH?

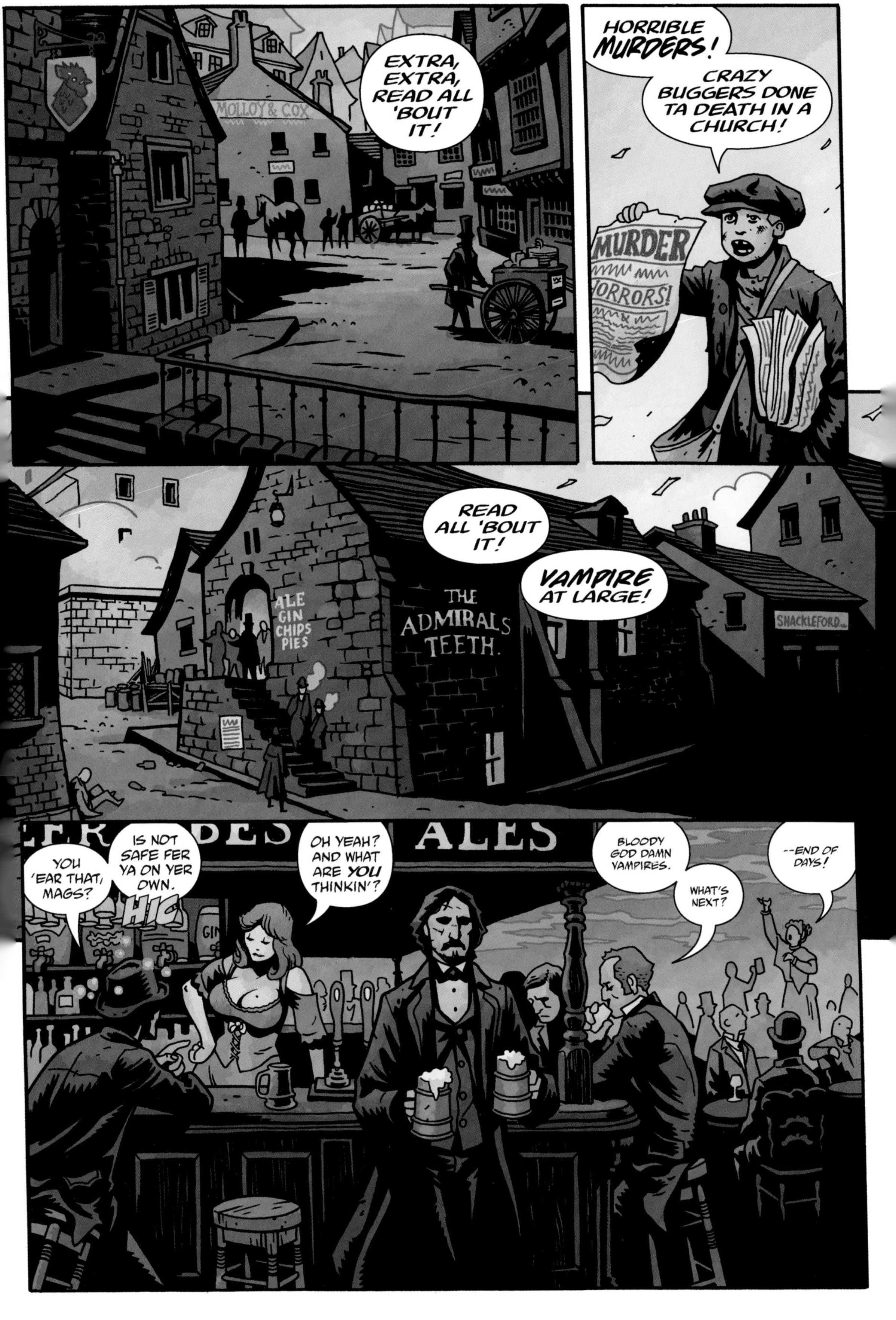
MOLLOY & COX
EXTRA, EXTRA, READ ALL 'BOUT IT!
HORRIBLE MURDERS!
CRAZY BUGGERS DONE TA DEATH IN A CHURCH!
MURDER
HORRORS!
READ ALL 'BOUT IT!
VAMPIRE AT LARGE!
ALE GIN CHIPS PIES
THE ADMIRALS TEETH.
SHACKLEFORD
ALES
YOU 'EAR THAT, MAGS?
IS NOT SAFE FER YA ON YER OWN.
HIC
OH YEAH? AND WHAT ARE YOU THINKIN'?
BLOODY GOD DAMN VAMPIRES.
WHAT'S NEXT?
--END OF DAYS!

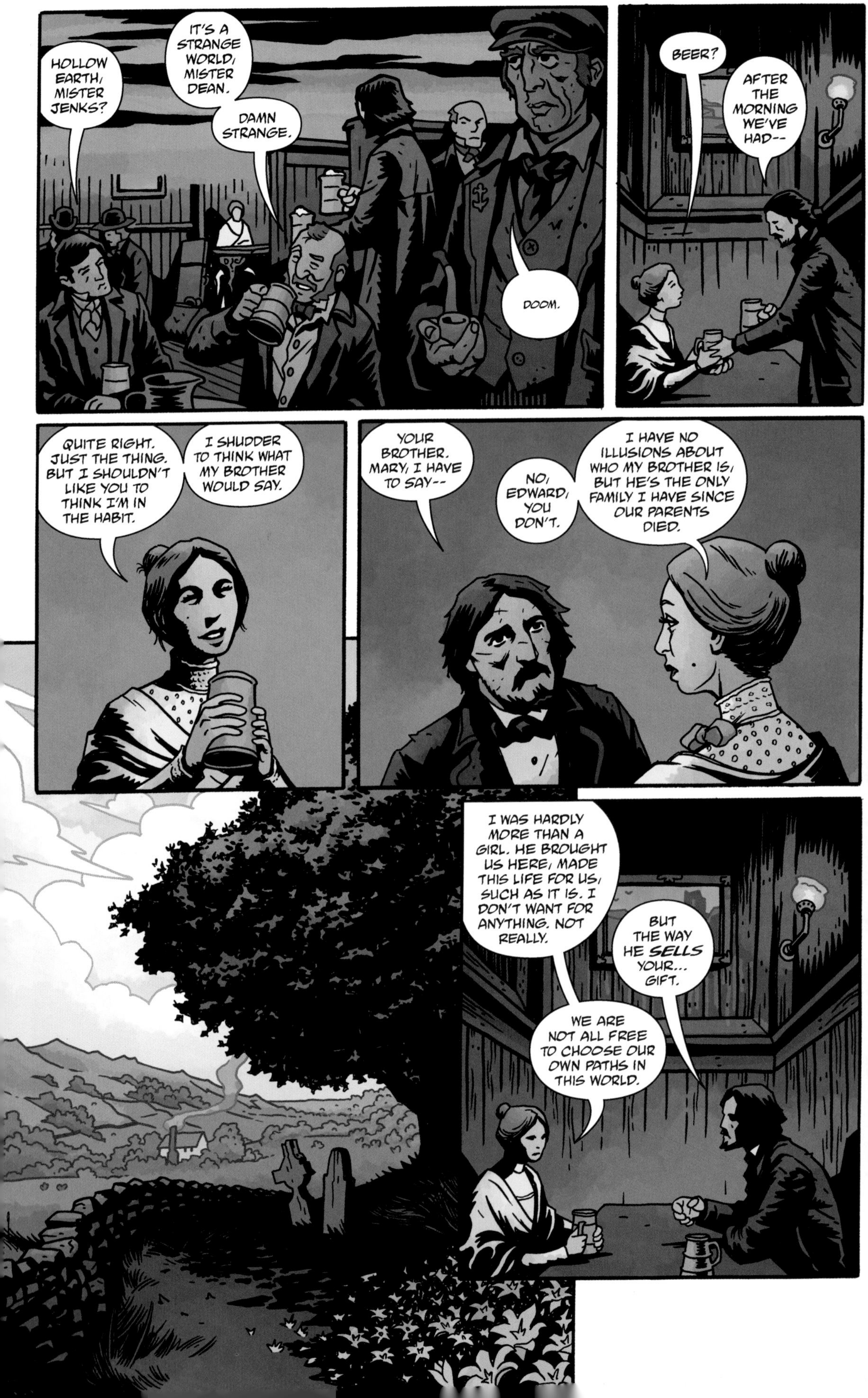
HOLLOW EARTH, MISTER JENKS?
IT'S A STRANGE WORLD, MISTER DEAN.
DAMN STRANGE.
DOOM.
BEER?
AFTER THE MORNING WE'VE HAD--
QUITE RIGHT. JUST THE THING. BUT I SHOULDN'T LIKE YOU TO THINK I'M IN THE HABIT.
I SHUDDER TO THINK WHAT MY BROTHER WOULD SAY.
YOUR BROTHER. MARY, I HAVE TO SAY--
NO, EDWARD, YOU DON'T.
I HAVE NO ILLUSIONS ABOUT WHO MY BROTHER IS, BUT HE'S THE ONLY FAMILY I HAVE SINCE OUR PARENTS DIED.
I WAS HARDLY MORE THAN A GIRL. HE BROUGHT US HERE, MADE THIS LIFE FOR US, SUCH AS IT IS. I DON'T WANT FOR ANYTHING. NOT REALLY.
BUT THE WAY HE SELLS YOUR... GIFT.
WE ARE NOT ALL FREE TO CHOOSE OUR OWN PATHS IN THIS WORLD.

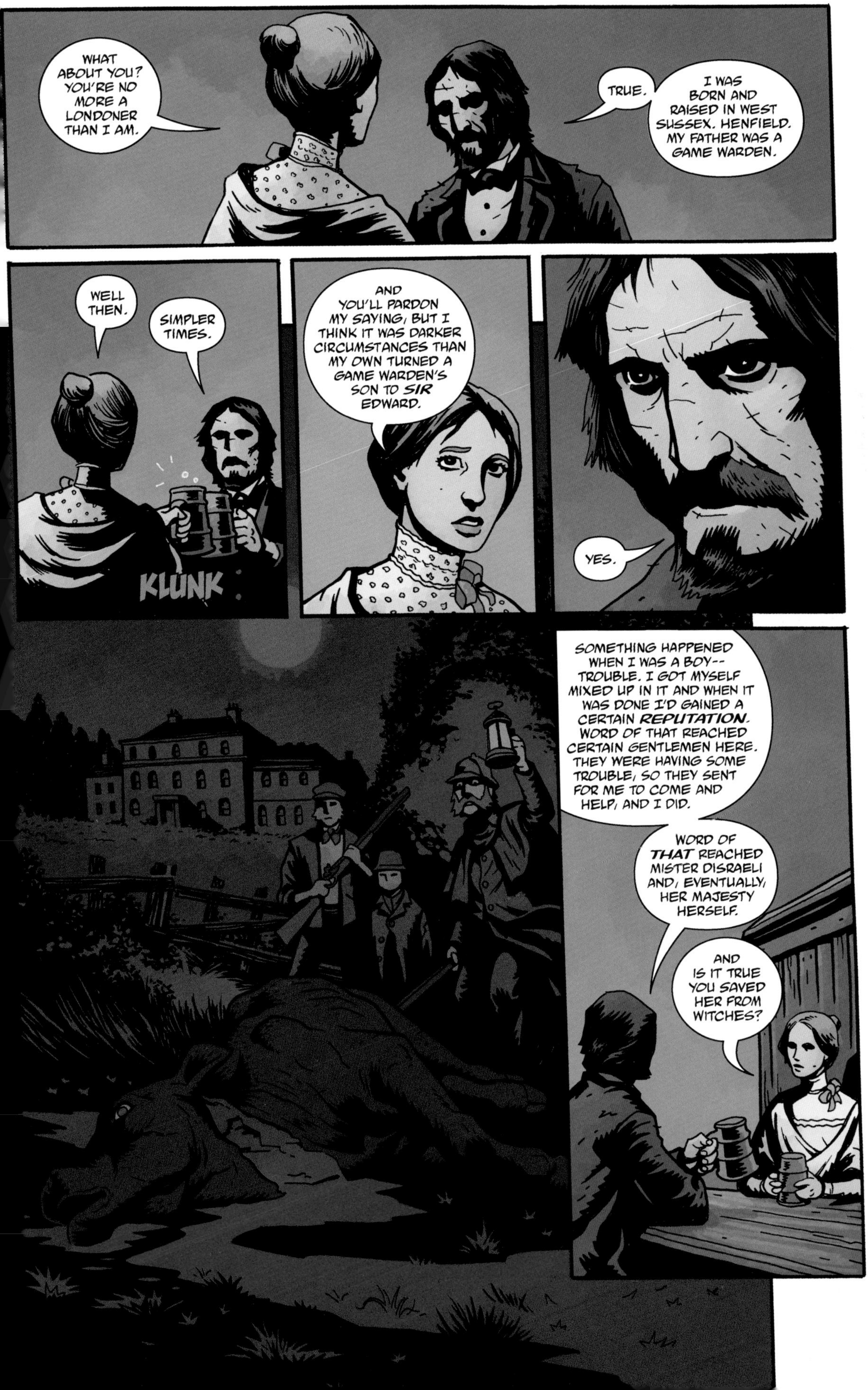
WHAT ABOUT YOU? YOU'RE NO MORE A LONDONER THAN I AM.
TRUE.
I WAS BORN AND RAISED IN WEST SUSSEX. HENFIELD. MY FATHER WAS A GAME WARDEN.
WELL THEN.
SIMPLER TIMES.
KLUNK
AND YOU'LL PARDON MY SAYING, BUT I THINK IT WAS DARKER CIRCUMSTANCES THAN MY OWN TURNED A GAME WARDEN'S SON TO SIR EDWARD.
YES.
SOMETHING HAPPENED WHEN I WAS A BOY-- TROUBLE. I GOT MYSELF MIXED UP IN IT AND WHEN IT WAS DONE I'D GAINED A CERTAIN REPUTATION. WORD OF THAT REACHED CERTAIN GENTLEMEN HERE. THEY WERE HAVING SOME TROUBLE, SO THEY SENT FOR ME TO COME AND HELP, AND I DID.
WORD OF THAT REACHED MISTER DISRAELI AND, EVENTUALLY, HER MAJESTY HERSELF.
AND IS IT TRUE YOU SAVED HER FROM WITCHES?

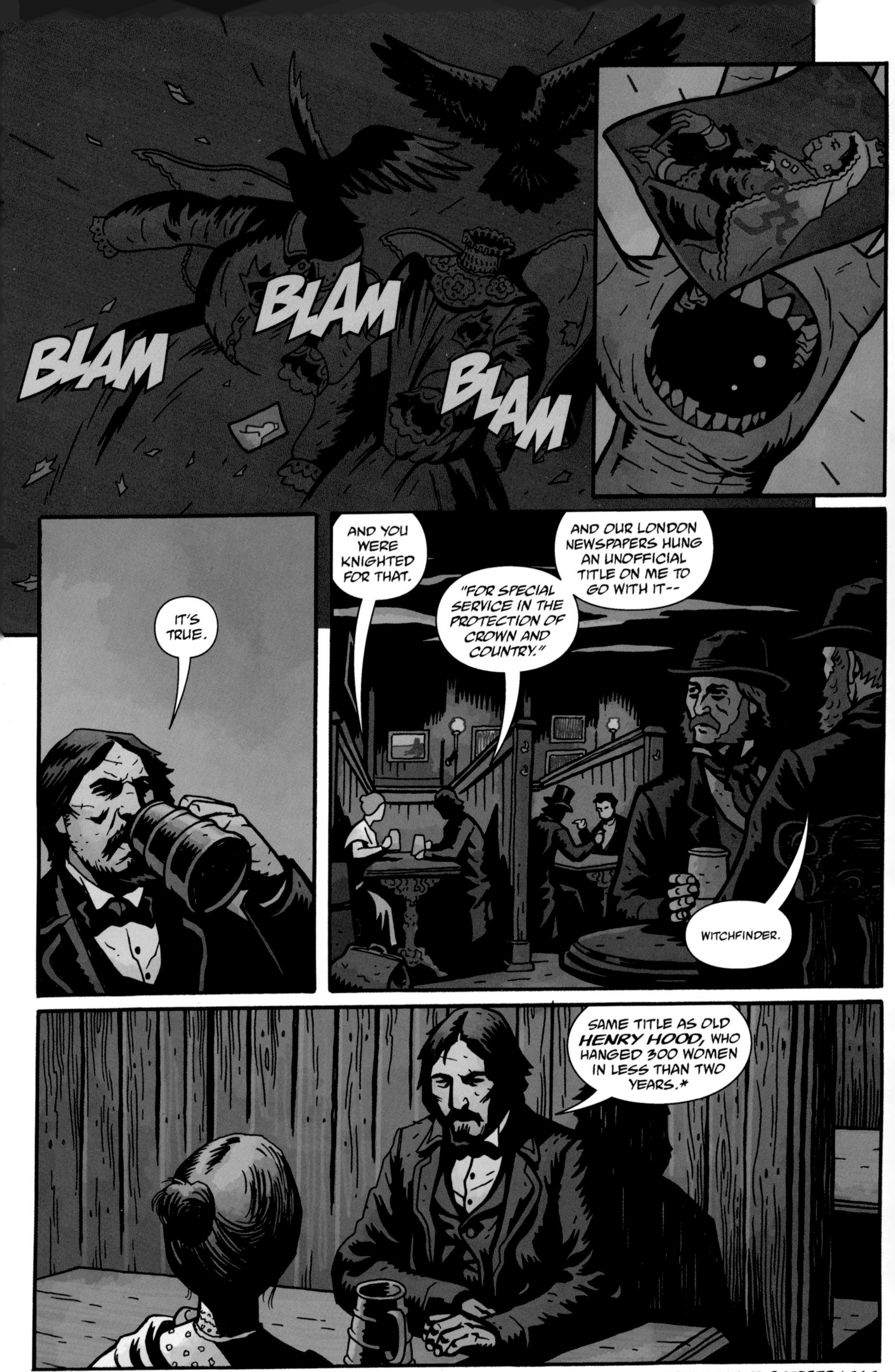
BLAM
BLAM
BLAM
IT'S TRUE.
AND YOU WERE KNIGHTED FOR THAT.
"FOR SPECIAL SERVICE IN THE PROTECTION OF CROWN AND COUNTRY."
AND OUR LONDON NEWSPAPERS HUNG AN UNOFFICIAL TITLE ON ME TO GO WITH IT--
WITCHFINDER.
SAME TITLE AS OLD HENRY HOOD, WHO HANGED 300 WOMEN IN LESS THAN TWO YEARS.*

*APRIL 1645 TO OCTOBER 1646.

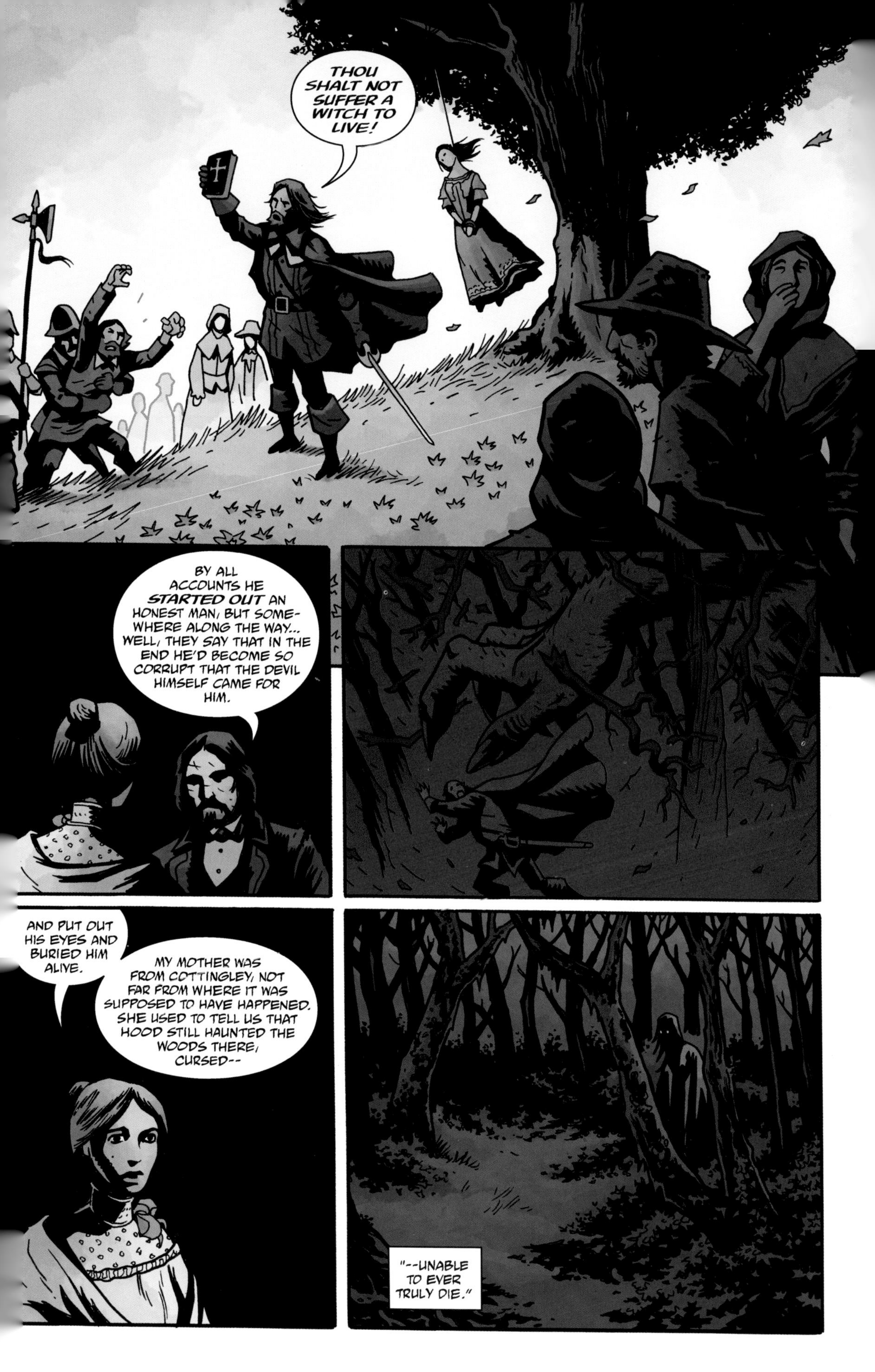
THOU SHALT NOT SUFFER A WITCH TO LIVE!
BY ALL ACCOUNTS HE STARTED OUT AN HONEST MAN, BUT SOME-WHERE ALONG THE WAY... WELL, THEY SAY THAT IN THE END HE'D BECOME SO CORRUPT THAT THE DEVIL HIMSELF CAME FOR HIM.
AND PUT OUT HIS EYES AND BURIED HIM ALIVE.
MY MOTHER WAS FROM COTTINGLEY, NOT FAR FROM WHERE IT WAS SUPPOSED TO HAVE HAPPENED. SHE USED TO TELL US THAT HOOD STILL HAUNTED THE WOODS THERE, CURSED--
"--UNABLE TO EVER TRULY DIE."

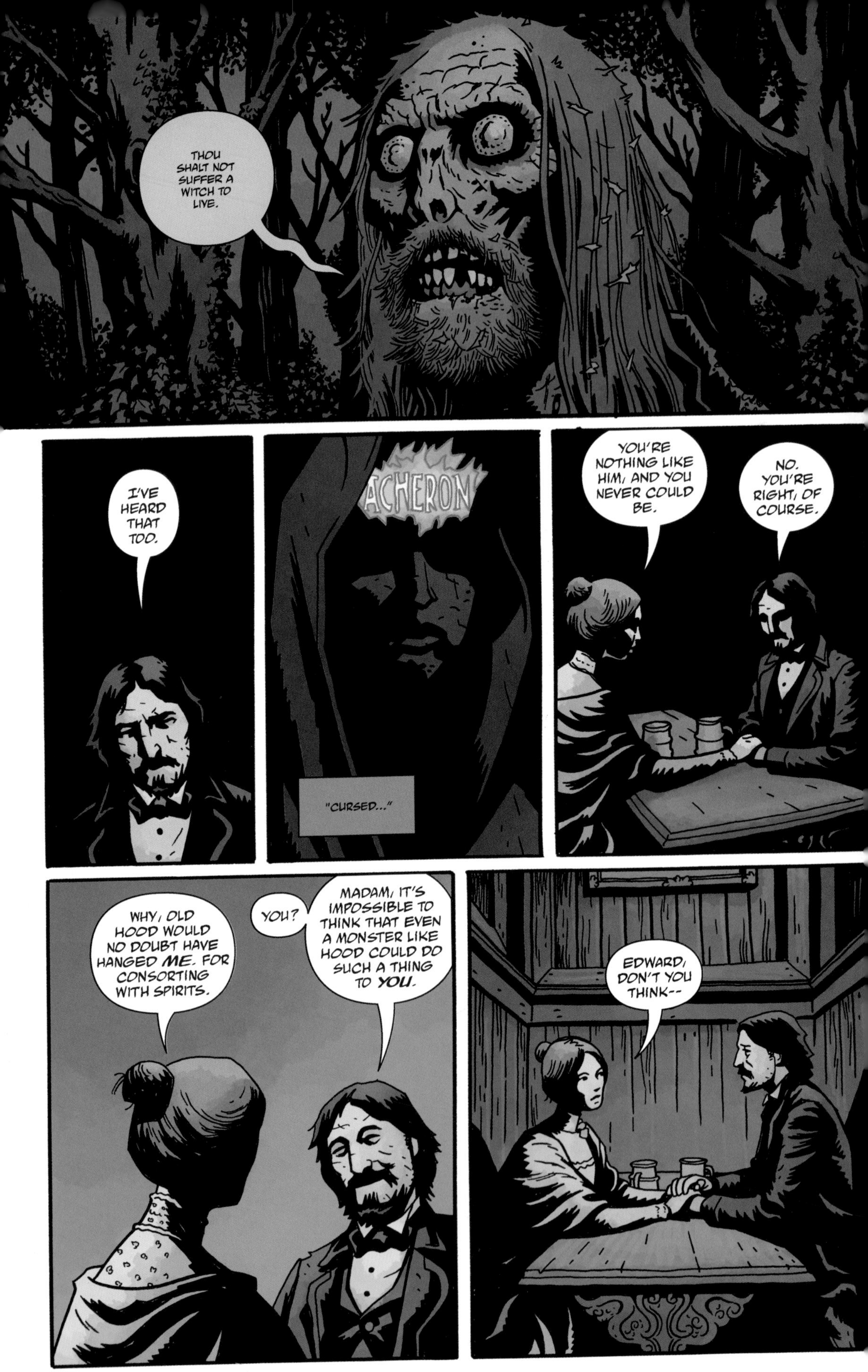
THOU SHALT NOT SUFFER A WITCH TO LIVE.
I'VE HEARD THAT TOO.
ACHERON
"CURSED..."
YOU'RE NOTHING LIKE HIM, AND YOU NEVER COULD BE.
NO. YOU'RE RIGHT, OF COURSE.
WHY, OLD HOOD WOULD NO DOUBT HAVE HANGED ME. FOR CONSORTING WITH SPIRITS.
YOU?
MADAM, IT'S IMPOSSIBLE TO THINK THAT EVEN A MONSTER LIKE HOOD COULD DO SUCH A THING TO YOU.
EDWARD, DON'T YOU THINK--

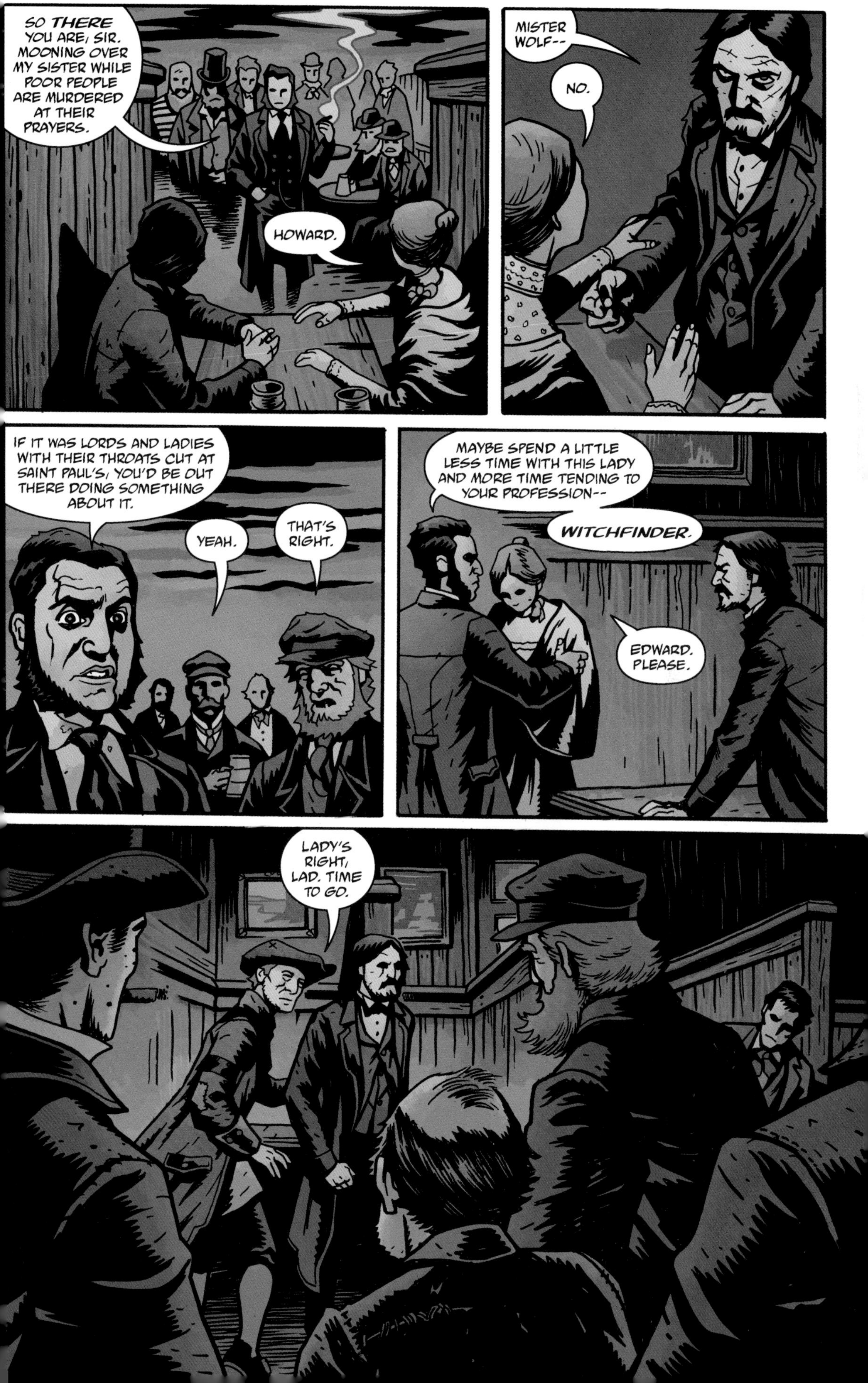
SO THERE YOU ARE, SIR. MOONING OVER MY SISTER WHILE POOR PEOPLE ARE MURDERED AT THEIR PRAYERS.
HOWARD.
MISTER WOLF--
NO.
IF IT WAS LORDS AND LADIES WITH THEIR THROATS CUT AT SAINT PAUL'S, YOU'D BE OUT THERE DOING SOMETHING ABOUT IT.
YEAH.
THAT'S RIGHT.
MAYBE SPEND A LITTLE LESS TIME WITH THIS LADY AND MORE TIME TENDING TO YOUR PROFESSION--
WITCHFINDER.
EDWARD. PLEASE.
LADY'S RIGHT, LAD. TIME TO GO.

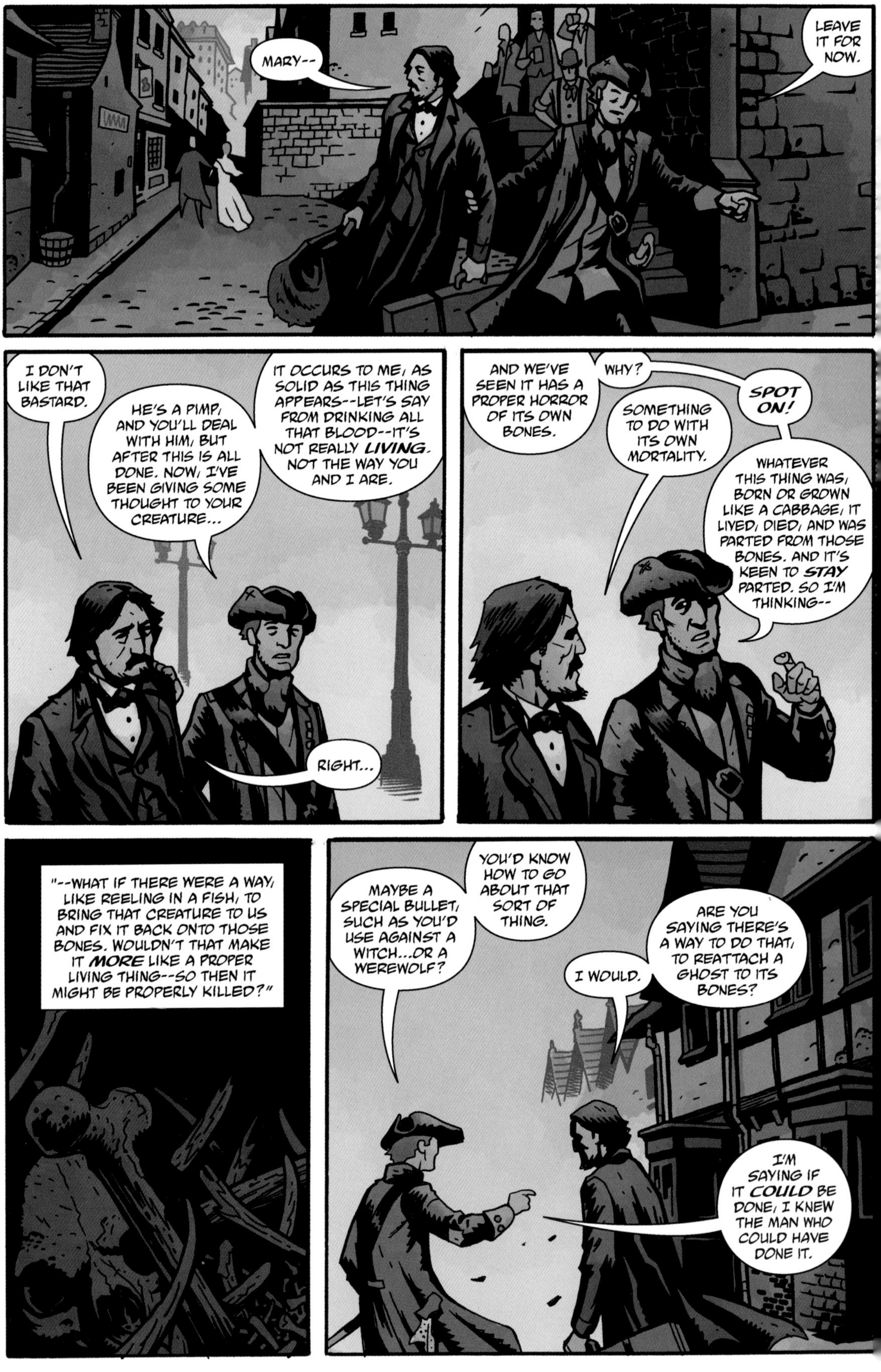
MARY--
LEAVE IT FOR NOW.
I DON'T LIKE THAT BASTARD.
HE'S A PIMP, AND YOU'LL DEAL WITH HIM, BUT AFTER THIS IS ALL DONE. NOW, I'VE BEEN GIVING SOME THOUGHT TO YOUR CREATURE...
RIGHT...
IT OCCURS TO ME, AS SOLID AS THIS THING APPEARS--LET'S SAY FROM DRINKING ALL THAT BLOOD--IT'S NOT REALLY LIVING. NOT THE WAY YOU AND I ARE.
AND WE'VE SEEN IT HAS A PROPER HORROR OF ITS OWN BONES.
WHY?
SOMETHING TO DO WITH ITS OWN MORTALITY.
SPOT ON!
WHATEVER THIS THING WAS, BORN OR GROWN LIKE A CABBAGE, IT LIVED, DIED, AND WAS PARTED FROM THOSE BONES. AND IT'S KEEN TO STAY PARTED. SO I'M THINKING--
"--WHAT IF THERE WERE A WAY, LIKE REELING IN A FISH, TO BRING THAT CREATURE TO US AND FIX IT BACK ONTO THOSE BONES. WOULDN'T THAT MAKE IT MORE LIKE A PROPER LIVING THING--SO THEN IT MIGHT BE PROPERLY KILLED?"
MAYBE A SPECIAL BULLET, SUCH AS YOU'D USE AGAINST A WITCH...OR A WEREWOLF?
YOU'D KNOW HOW TO GO ABOUT THAT SORT OF THING.
I WOULD.
ARE YOU SAYING THERE'S A WAY TO DO THAT, TO REATTACH A GHOST TO ITS BONES?
I'M SAYING IF IT COULD BE DONE, I KNEW THE MAN WHO COULD HAVE DONE IT.

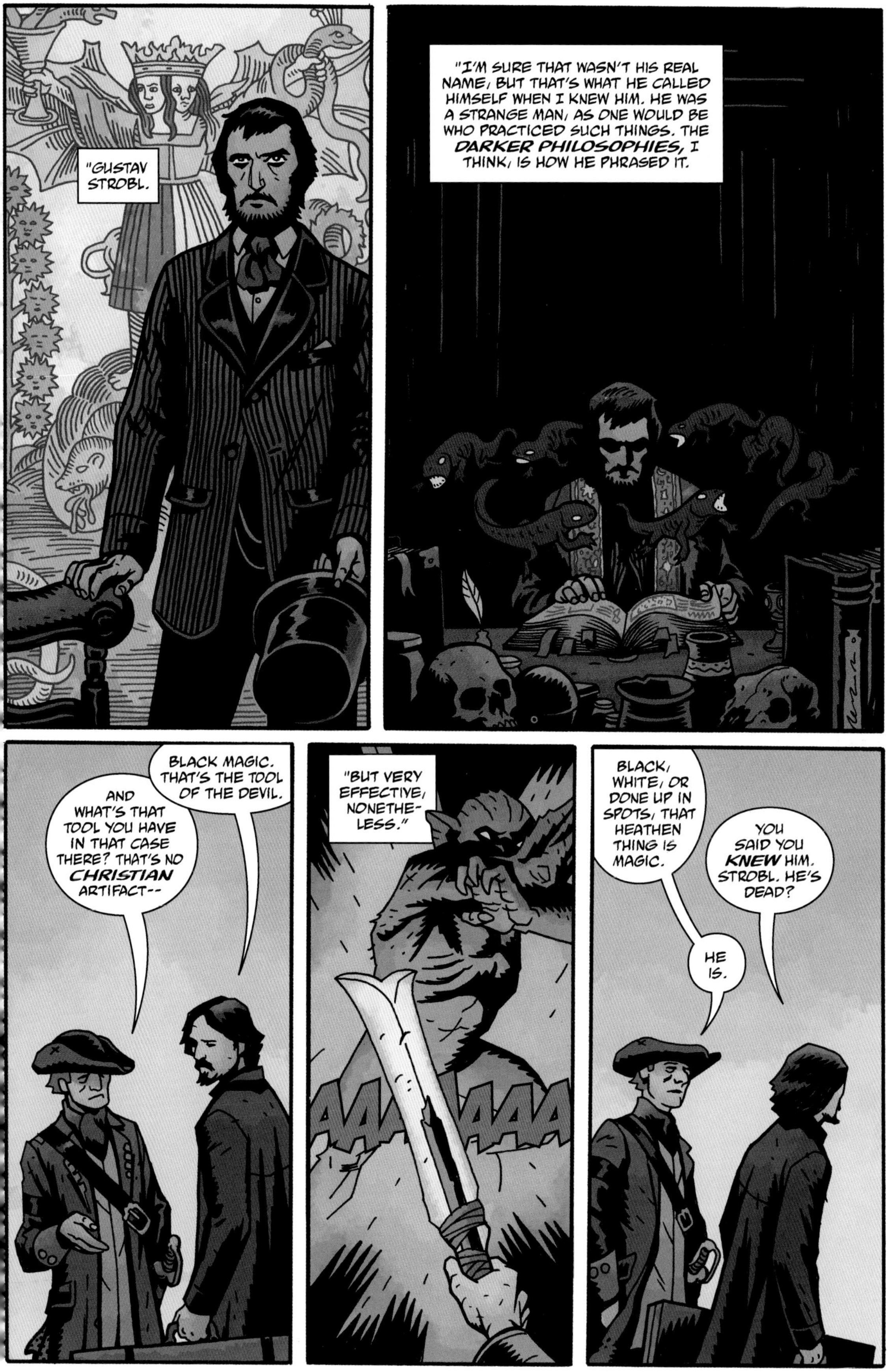
"GUSTAV STROBL.
"I'M SURE THAT WASN'T HIS REAL NAME, BUT THAT'S WHAT HE CALLED HIMSELF WHEN I KNEW HIM. HE WAS A STRANGE MAN, AS ONE WOULD BE WHO PRACTICED SUCH THINGS. THE DARKER PHILOSOPHIES, I THINK, IS HOW HE PHRASED IT.
BLACK MAGIC. THAT'S THE TOOL OF THE DEVIL.
AND WHAT'S THAT TOOL YOU HAVE IN THAT CASE THERE? THAT'S NO CHRISTIAN ARTIFACT--
"BUT VERY EFFECTIVE, NONETHELESS."
AAAAAAAA
BLACK, WHITE, OR DONE UP IN SPOTS, THAT HEATHEN THING IS MAGIC.
YOU SAID YOU KNEW HIM. STROBL. HE'S DEAD?
HE IS.

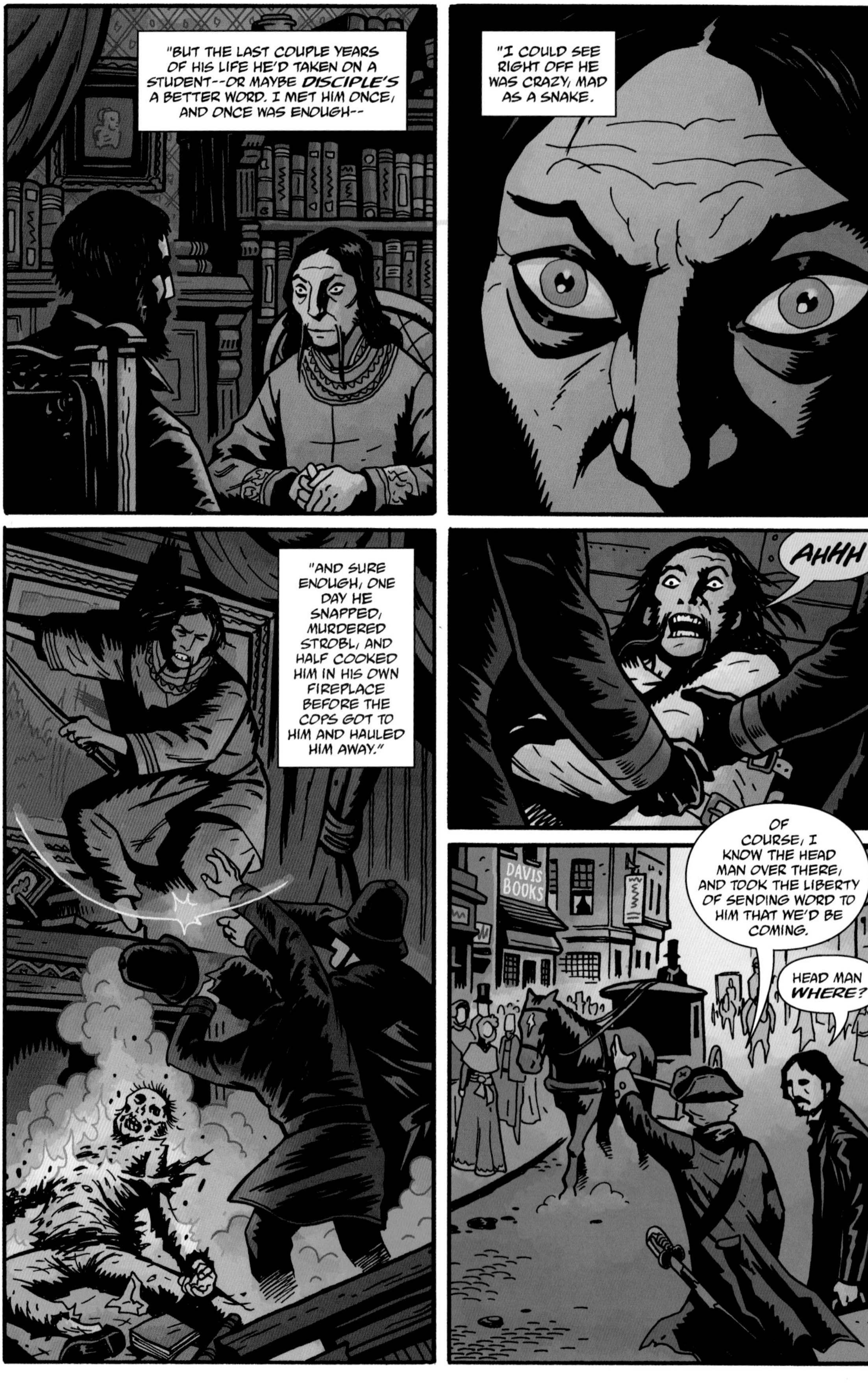
"BUT THE LAST COUPLE YEARS OF HIS LIFE HE'D TAKEN ON A STUDENT--OR MAYBE DISCIPLE'S A BETTER WORD. I MET HIM ONCE, AND ONCE WAS ENOUGH--
"I COULD SEE RIGHT OFF HE WAS CRAZY, MAD AS A SNAKE.
"AND SURE ENOUGH, ONE DAY HE SNAPPED, MURDERED STROBL, AND HALF COOKED HIM IN HIS OWN FIREPLACE BEFORE THE COPS GOT TO HIM AND HAULED HIM AWAY."
AHHH
DAVIS BOOKS
OF COURSE, I KNOW THE HEAD MAN OVER THERE, AND TOOK THE LIBERTY OF SENDING WORD TO HIM THAT WE'D BE COMING.
HEAD MAN WHERE?

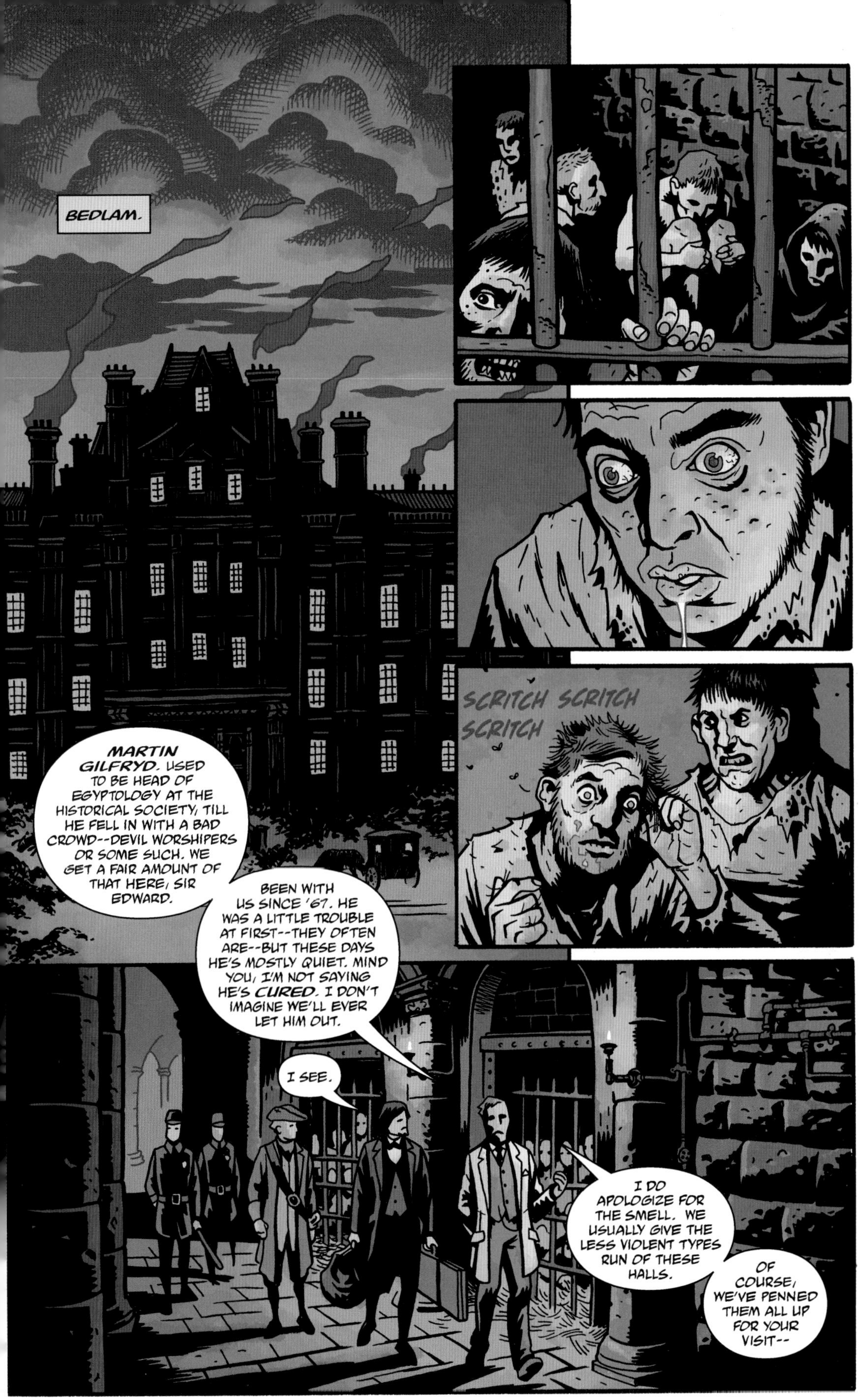
BEDLAM.
SCRITCH SCRITCH SCRITCH
MARTIN GILFRYD. USED TO BE HEAD OF EGYPTOLOGY AT THE HISTORICAL SOCIETY, TILL HE FELL IN WITH A BAD CROWD--DEVIL WORSHIPERS OR SOME SUCH. WE GET A FAIR AMOUNT OF THAT HERE, SIR EDWARD.
BEEN WITH US SINCE '67. HE WAS A LITTLE TROUBLE AT FIRST--THEY OFTEN ARE--BUT THESE DAYS HE'S MOSTLY QUIET. MIND YOU, I'M NOT SAYING HE'S CURED. I DON'T IMAGINE WE'LL EVER LET HIM OUT.
I SEE.
I DO APOLOGIZE FOR THE SMELL. WE USUALLY GIVE THE LESS VIOLENT TYPES RUN OF THESE HALLS.
OF COURSE, WE'VE PENNED THEM ALL UP FOR YOUR VISIT--

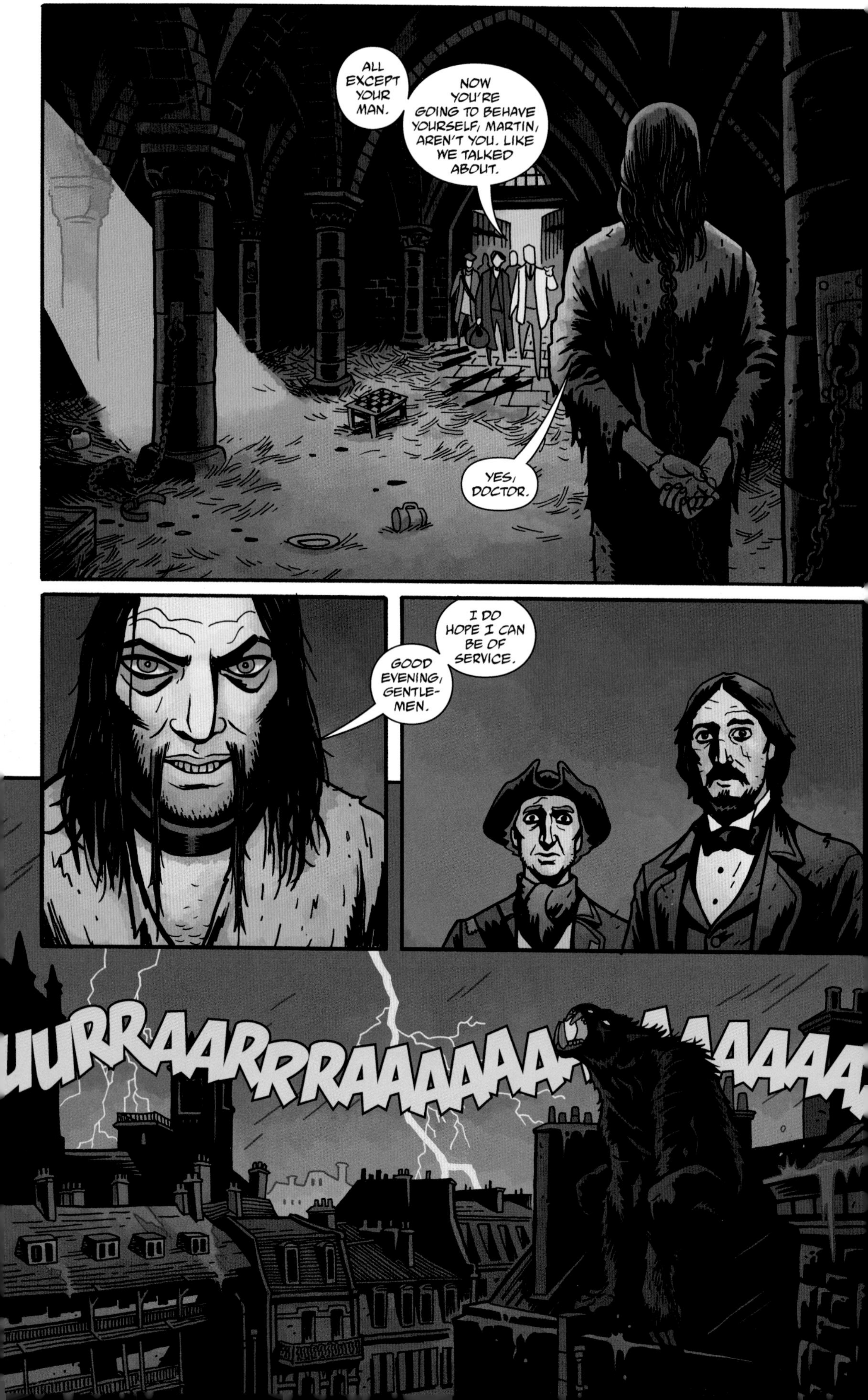
ALL EXCEPT YOUR MAN.
NOW YOU'RE GOING TO BEHAVE YOURSELF, MARTIN, AREN'T YOU. LIKE WE TALKED ABOUT.
YES, DOCTOR.
GOOD EVENING, GENTLE-MEN.
I DO HOPE I CAN BE OF SERVICE.
UURRAARRRAAAAAAAAAAAAA

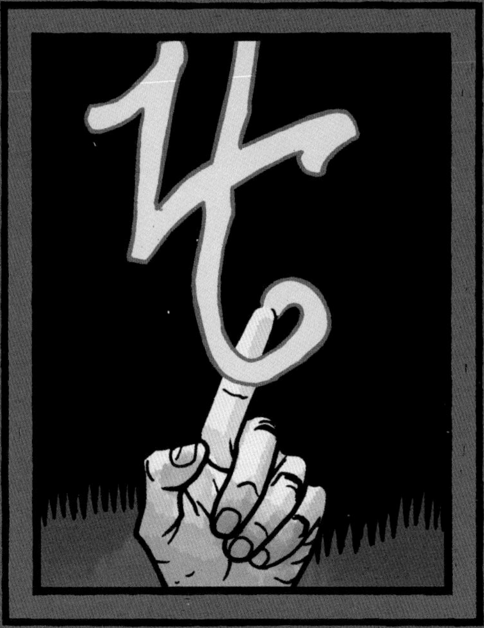

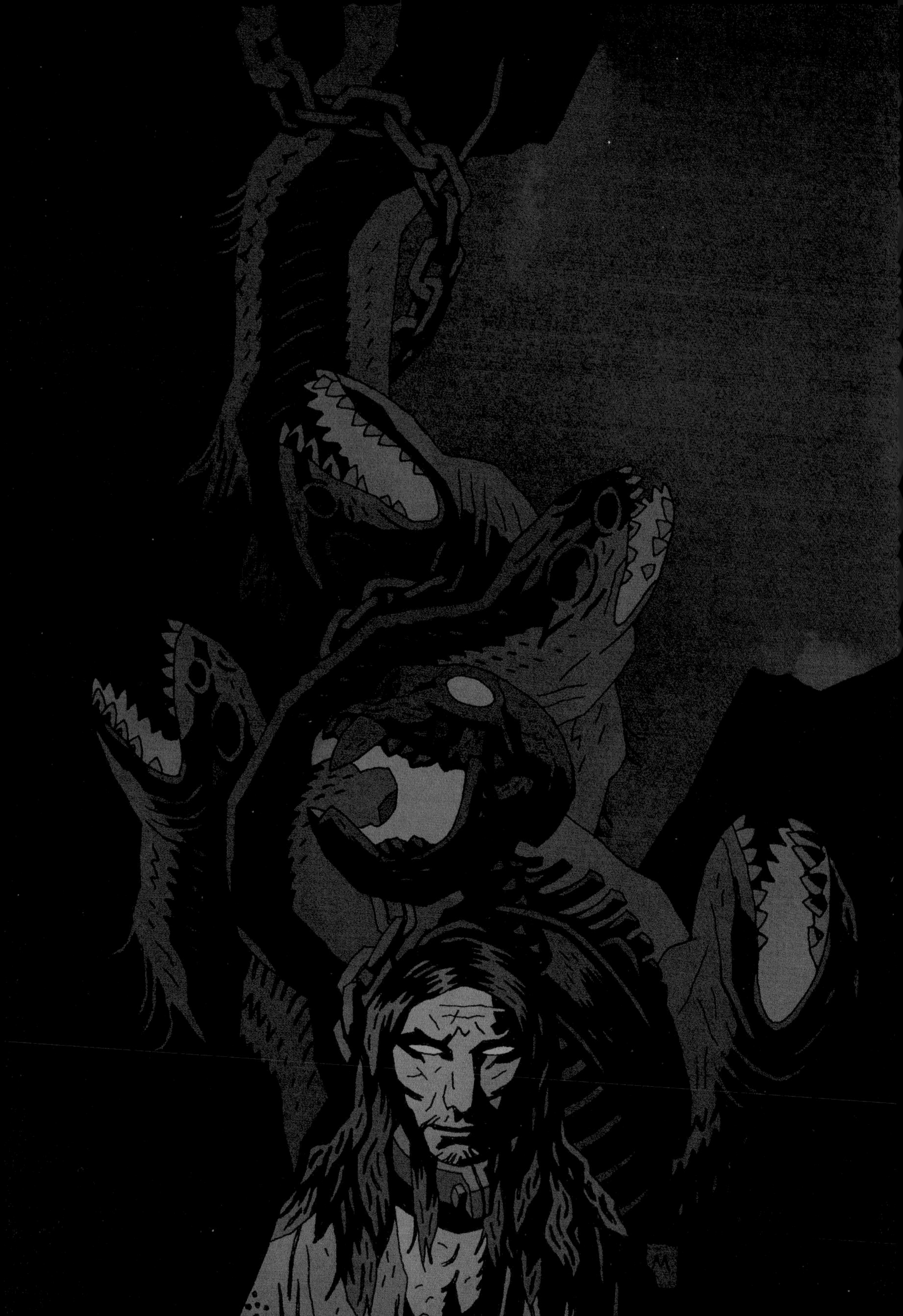

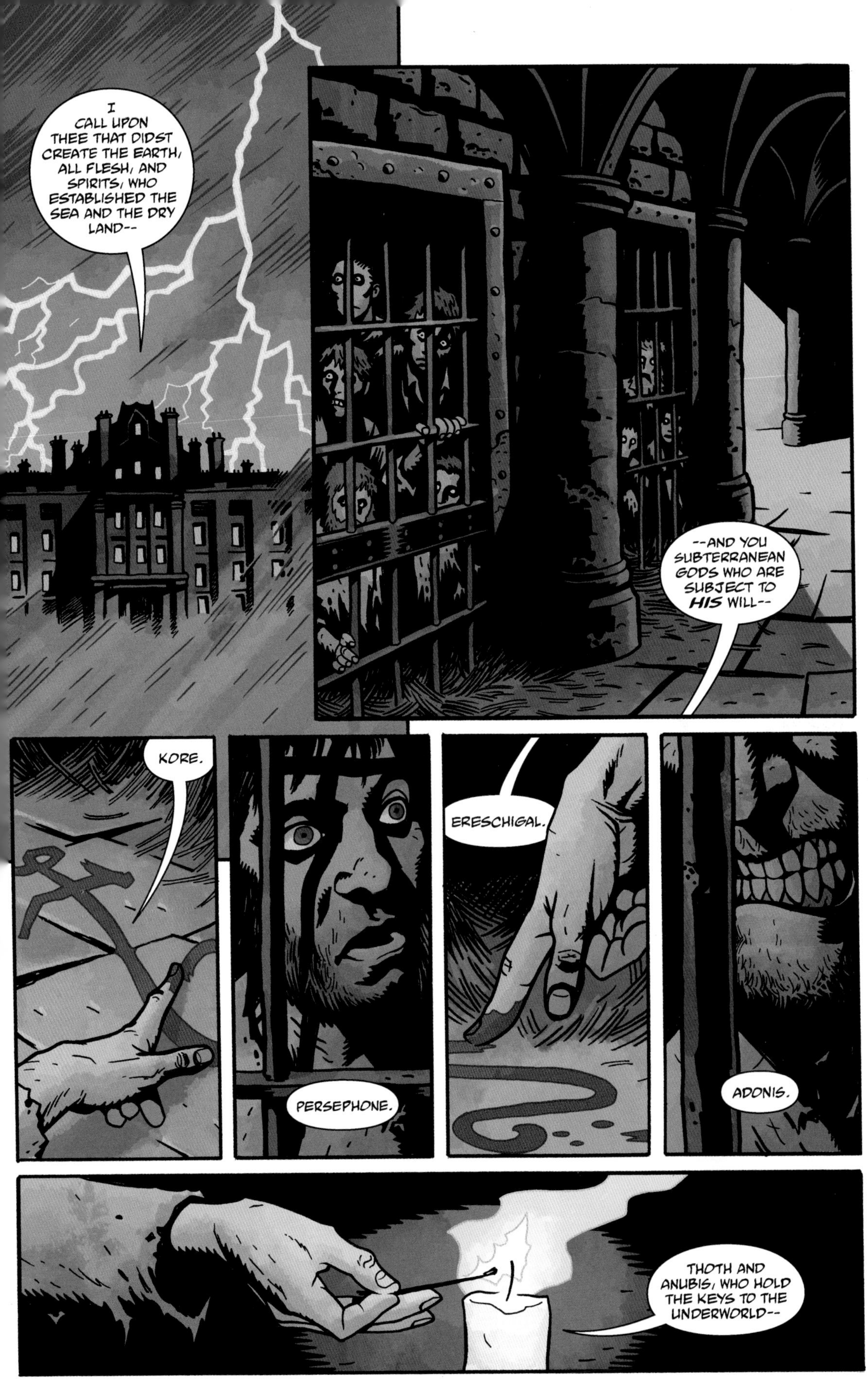

I CALL UPON THEE THAT DIDST CREATE THE EARTH, ALL FLESH, AND SPIRITS, WHO ESTABLISHED THE SEA AND THE DRY LAND--
--AND YOU SUBTERRANEAN GODS WHO ARE SUBJECT TO **HIS** WILL--
KORE.
PERSEPHONE.
ERESCHIGAL.
ADONIS.
THOTH AND ANUBIS, WHO HOLD THE KEYS TO THE UNDERWORLD--

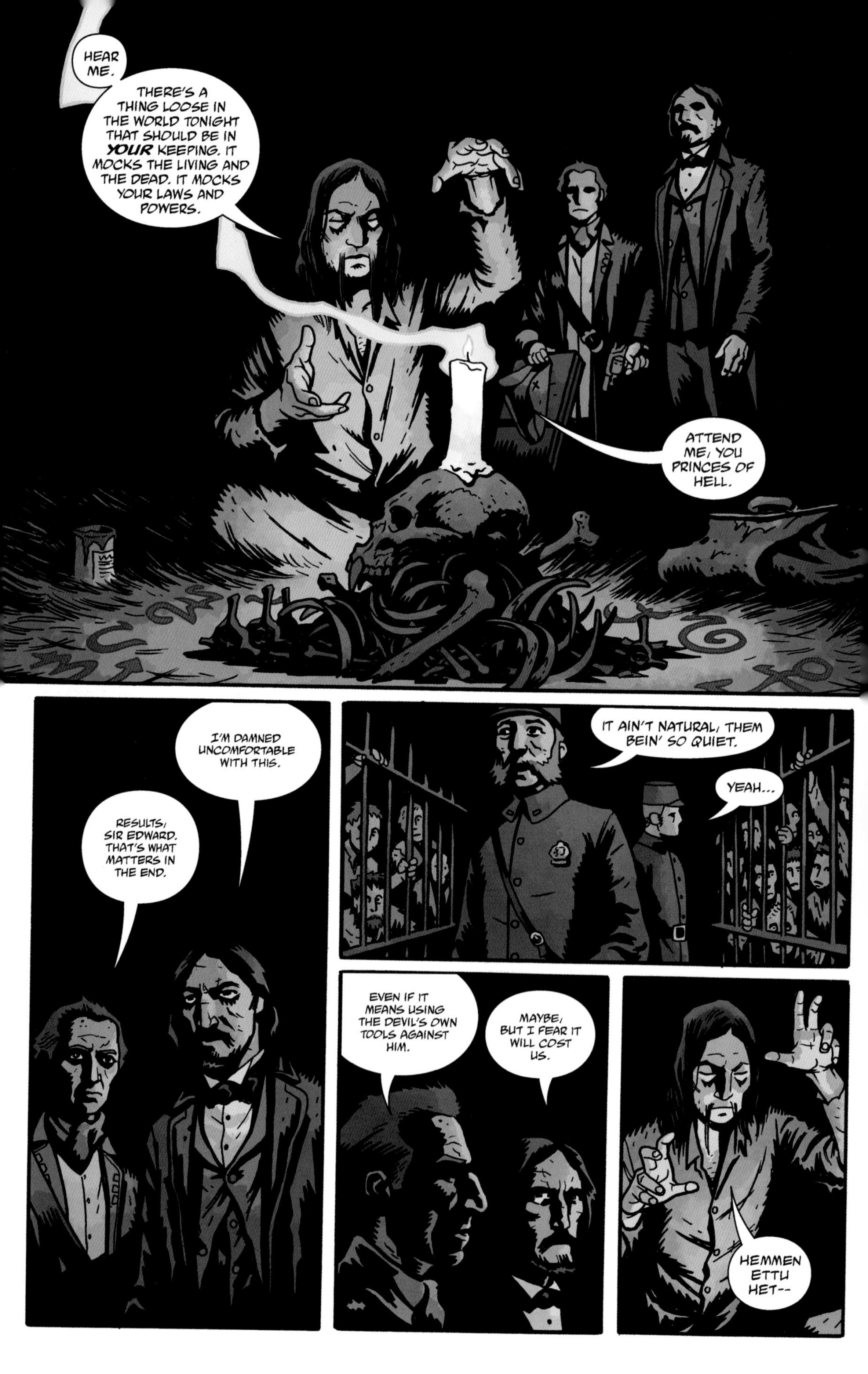
HEAR ME.
THERE'S A THING LOOSE IN THE WORLD TONIGHT THAT SHOULD BE IN YOUR KEEPING. IT MOCKS THE LIVING AND THE DEAD. IT MOCKS YOUR LAWS AND POWERS.
ATTEND ME, YOU PRINCES OF HELL.
I'M DAMNED UNCOMFORTABLE WITH THIS.
RESULTS, SIR EDWARD. THAT'S WHAT MATTERS IN THE END.
IT AIN'T NATURAL, THEM BEIN' SO QUIET.
YEAH...
EVEN IF IT MEANS USING THE DEVIL'S OWN TOOLS AGAINST HIM.
MAYBE, BUT I FEAR IT WILL COST US.
HEMMEN ETTU HET--

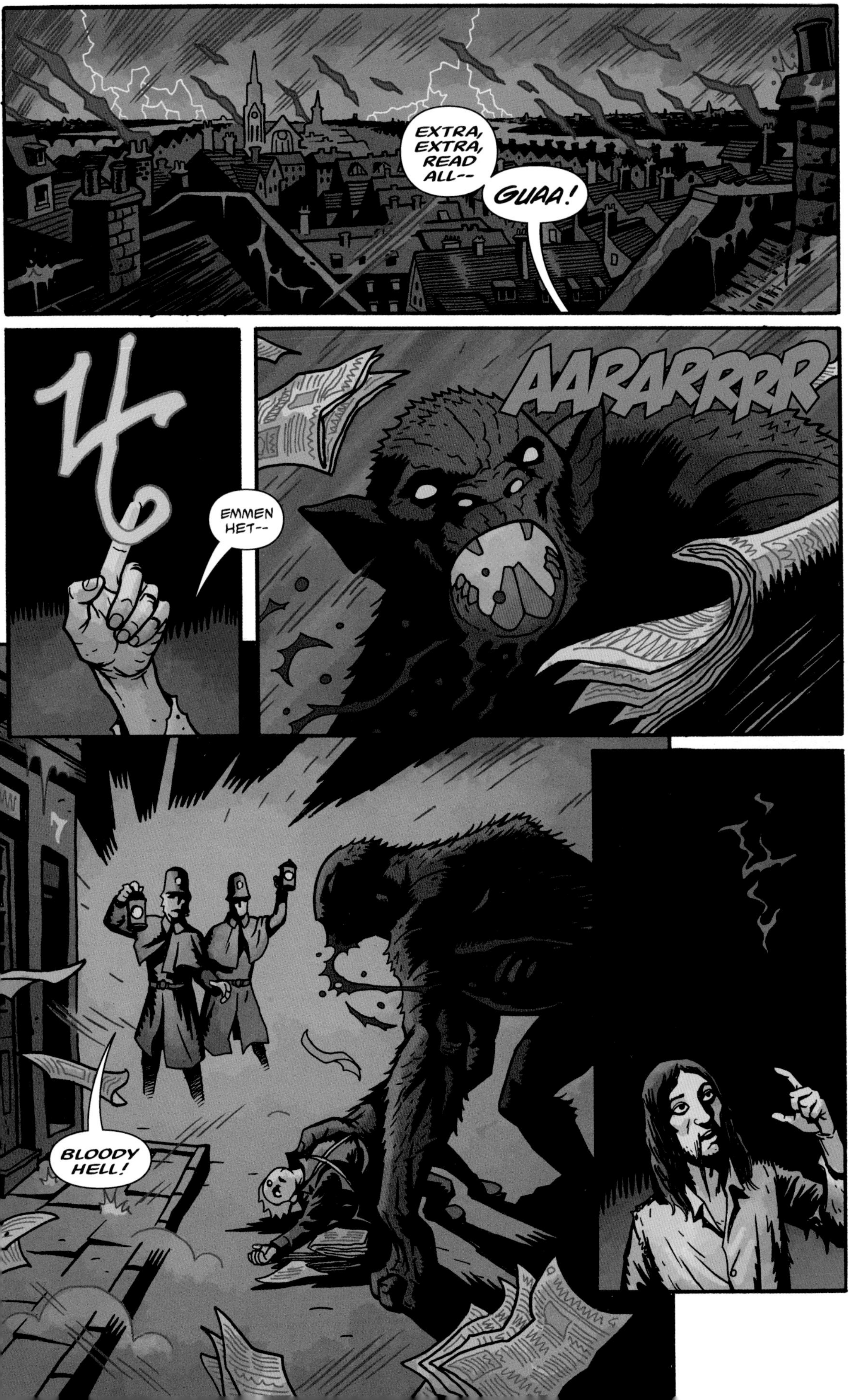
EXTRA, EXTRA, READ ALL--
GUAA!
EMMEN HET--
AARARRRR
BLOODY HELL!

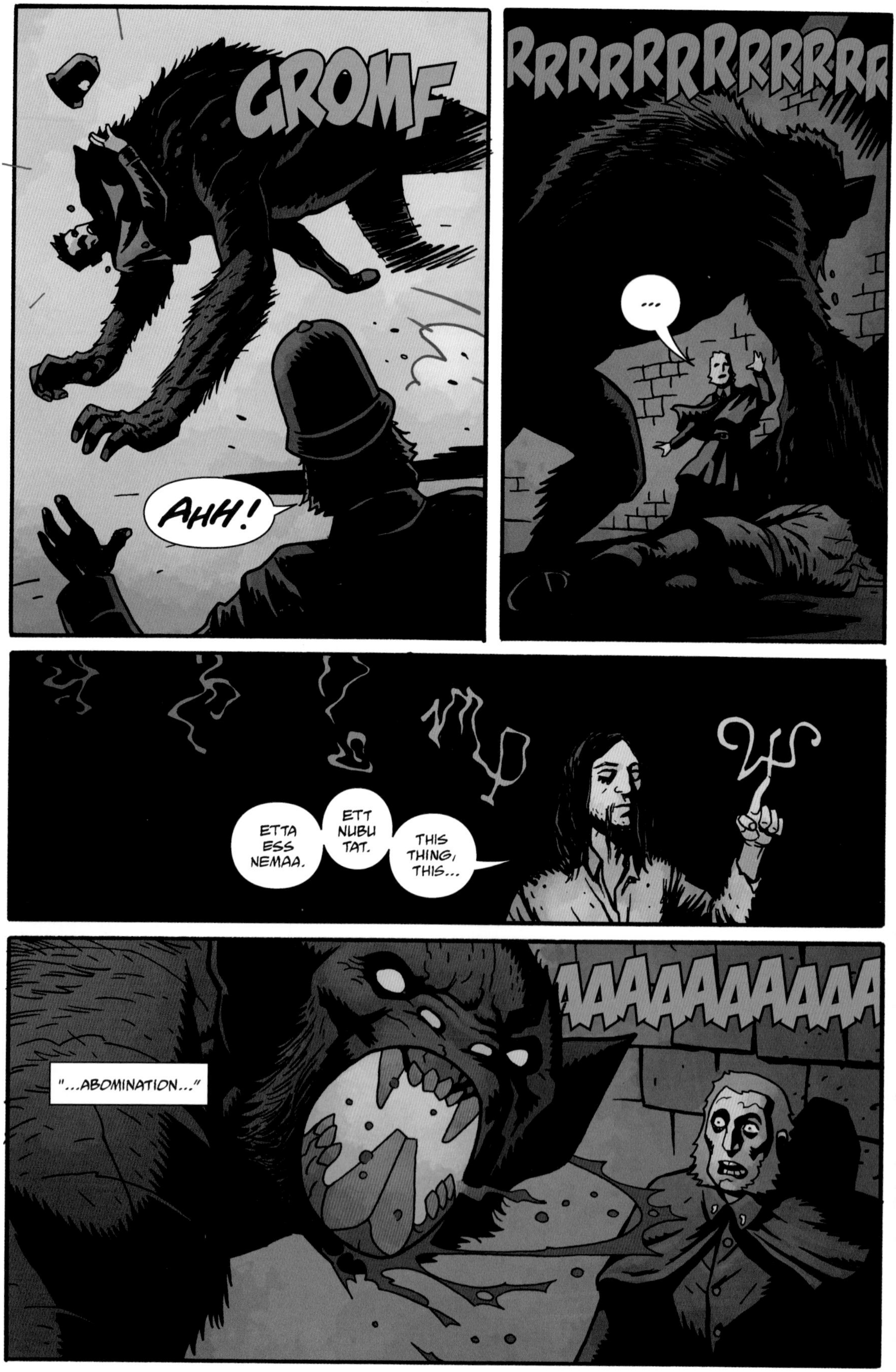
GROMF
AHH!
RRRRRRRRRRRRR
...
ETTA ESS NEMAA.
ETT NUBU TAT.
THIS THING, THIS...
AAAAAAAAAAA
"...ABOMINATION..."

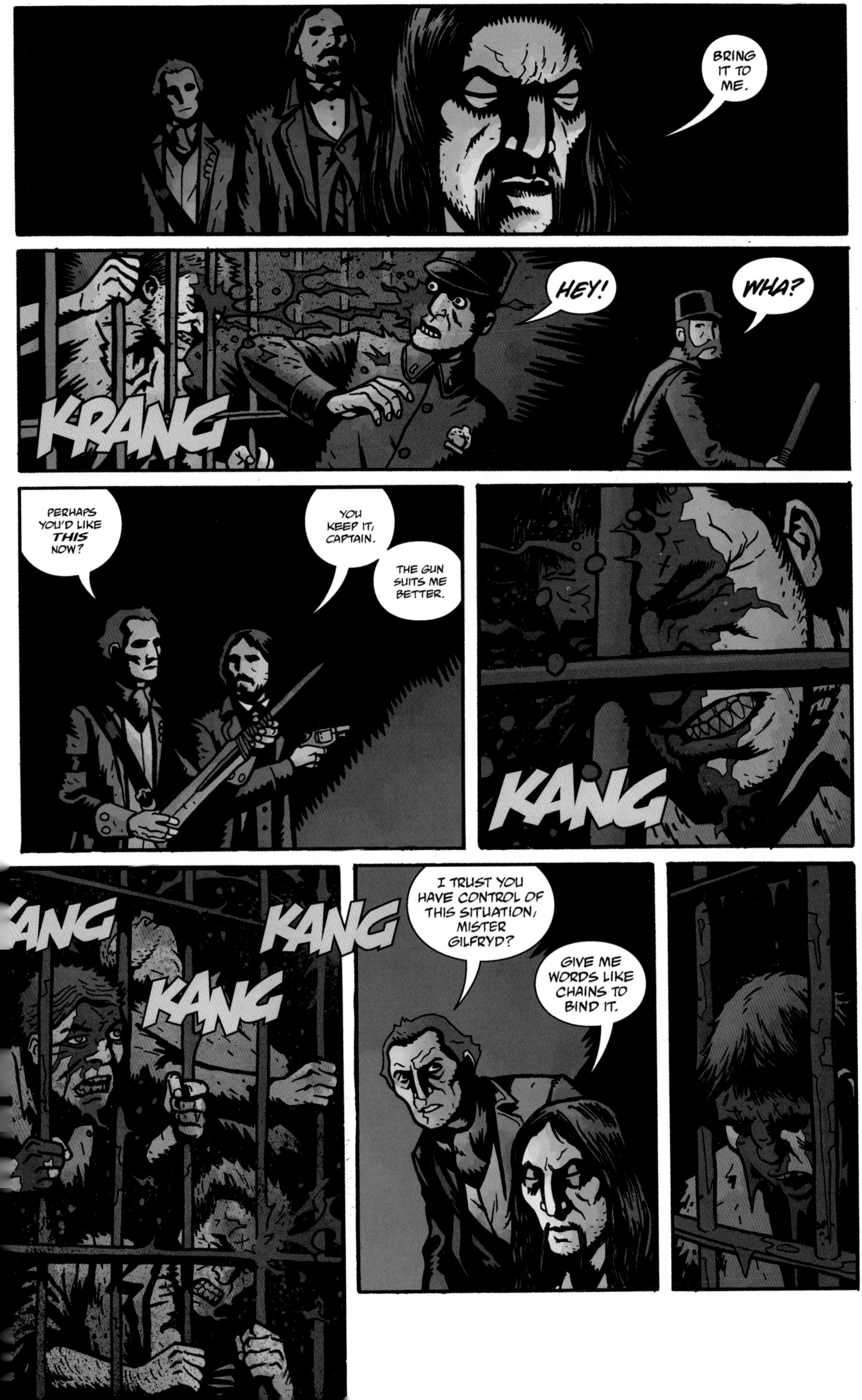
BRING IT TO ME.
HEY!
WHA?
KRANG
PERHAPS YOU'D LIKE THIS NOW?
YOU KEEP IT, CAPTAIN.
THE GUN SUITS ME BETTER.
KANG
KANG
KANG
I TRUST YOU HAVE CONTROL OF THIS SITUATION, MISTER GILFRYD?
GIVE ME WORDS LIKE CHAINS TO BIND IT.

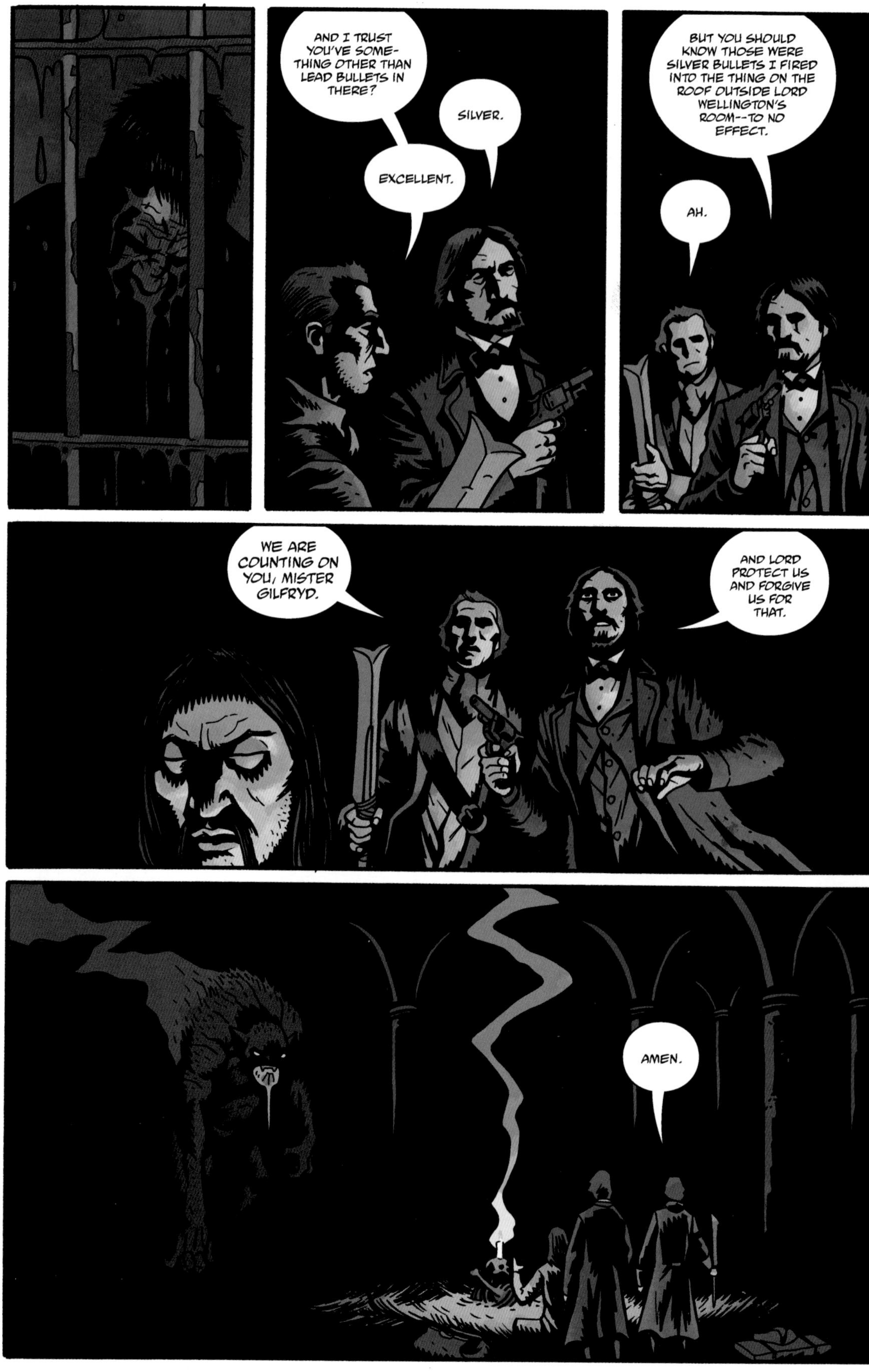
AND I TRUST YOU'VE SOME-THING OTHER THAN LEAD BULLETS IN THERE?
SILVER.
EXCELLENT.
BUT YOU SHOULD KNOW THOSE WERE SILVER BULLETS I FIRED INTO THE THING ON THE ROOF OUTSIDE LORD WELLINGTON'S ROOM--TO NO EFFECT.
AH.
WE ARE COUNTING ON YOU, MISTER GILFRYD.
AND LORD PROTECT US AND FORGIVE US FOR THAT.
AMEN.

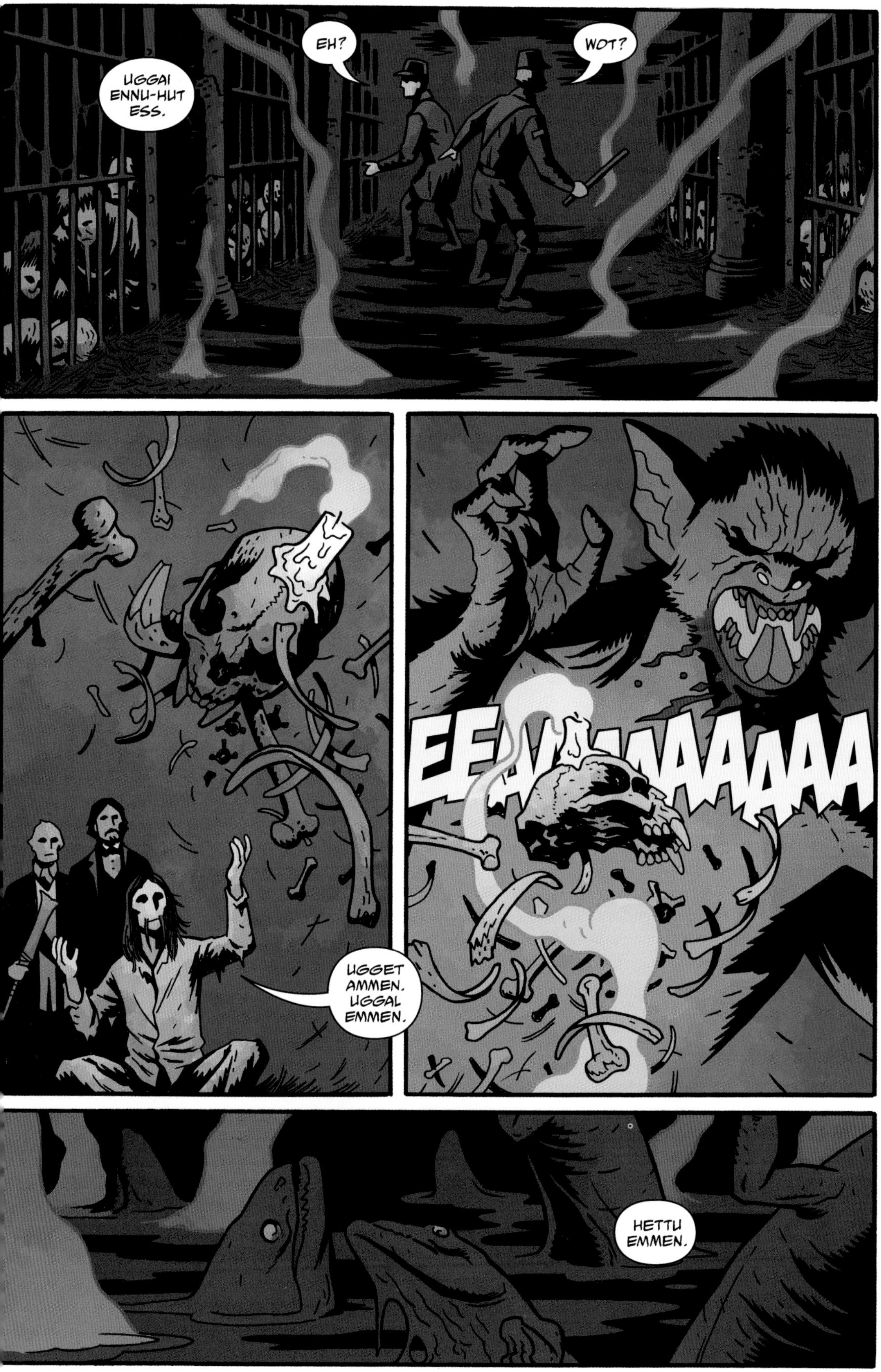

UGGAI ENNU-HUT ESS.
EH?
WOT?
UGGET AMMEN. UGGAL EMMEN.
EEAAAAAAAAA
HETTU EMMEN.

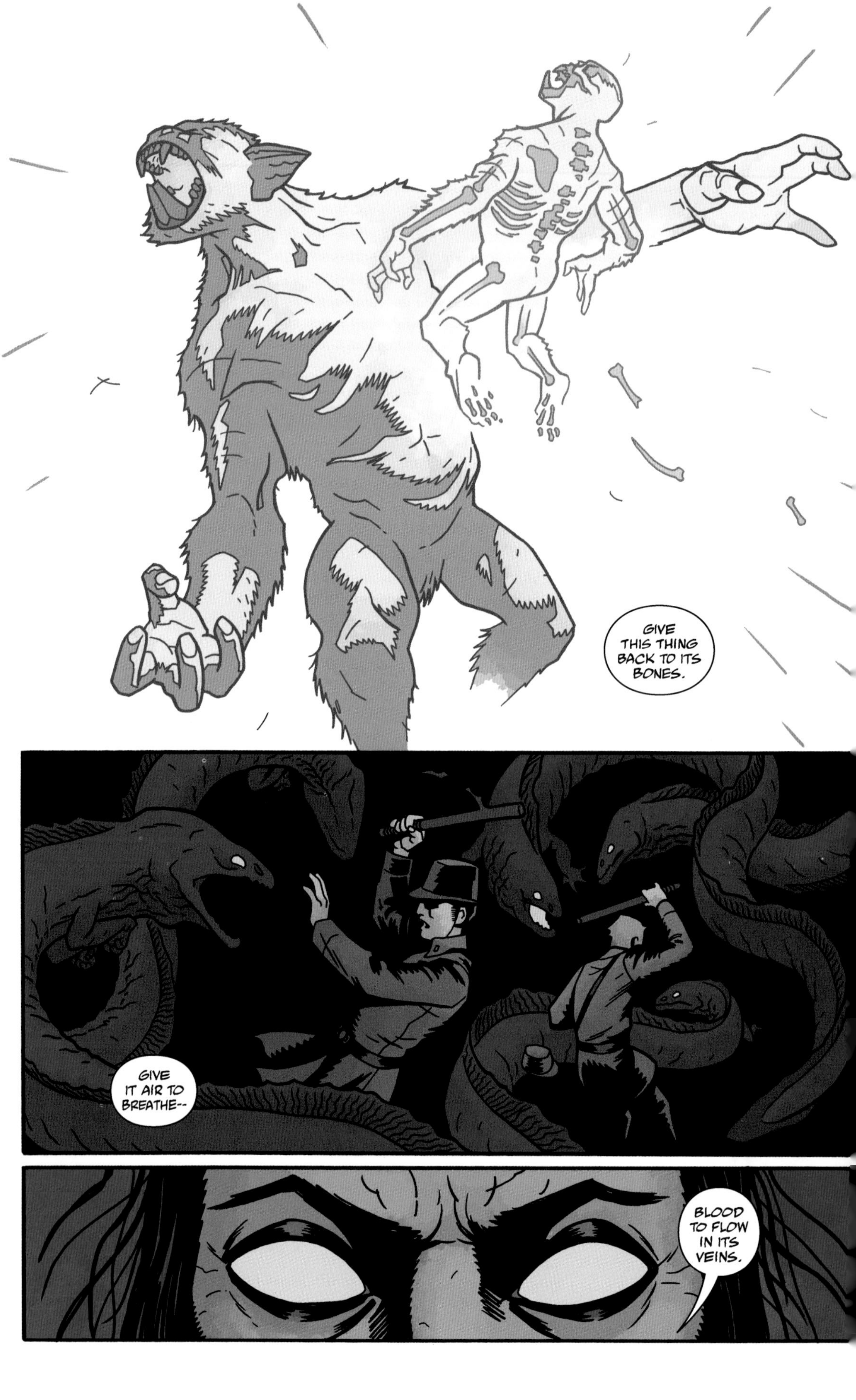
GIVE THIS THING BACK TO ITS BONES.
GIVE IT AIR TO BREATHE--
BLOOD TO FLOW IN ITS VEINS.

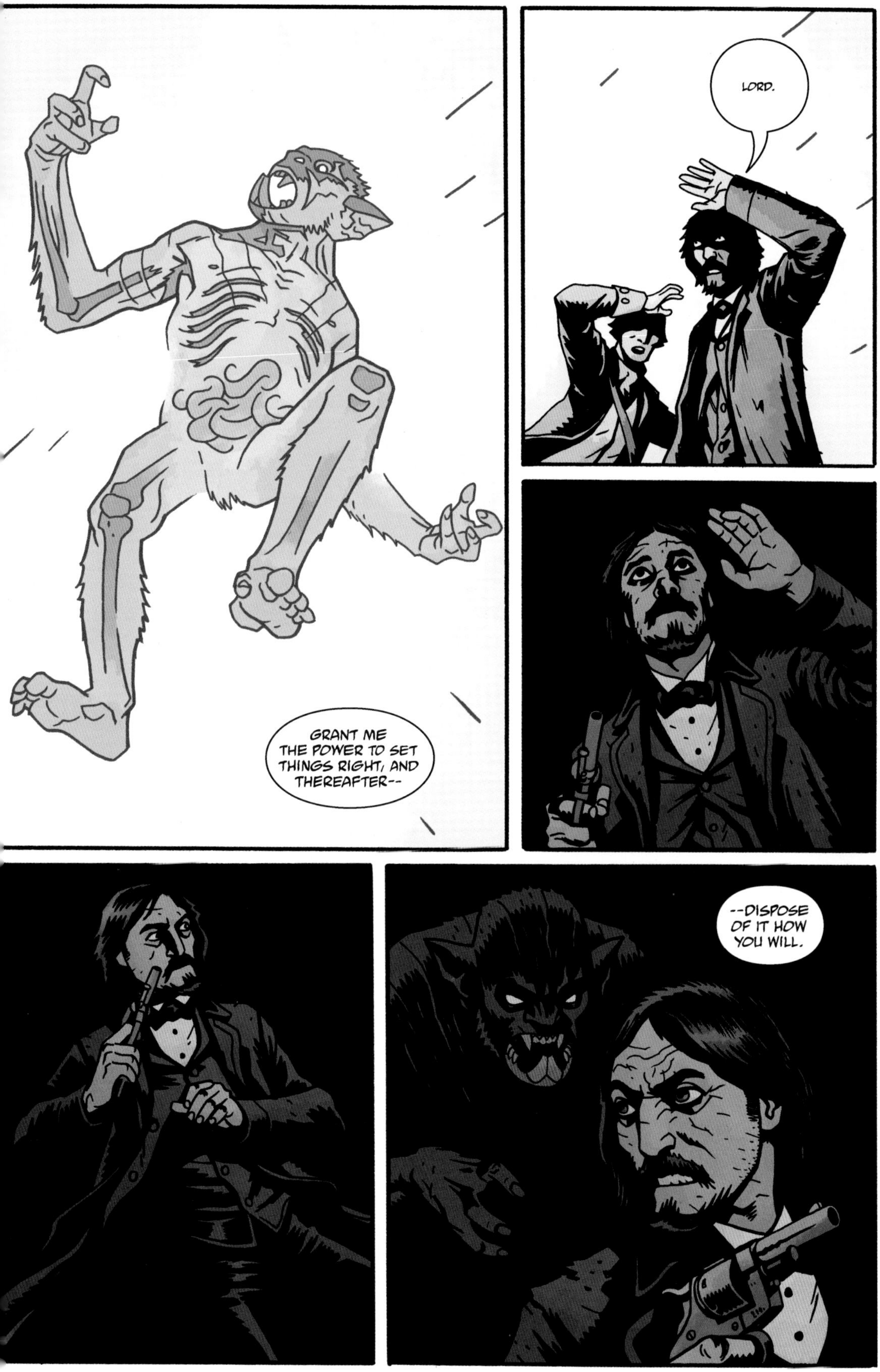
LORD.
GRANT ME THE POWER TO SET THINGS RIGHT, AND THEREAFTER--
--DISPOSE OF IT HOW YOU WILL.

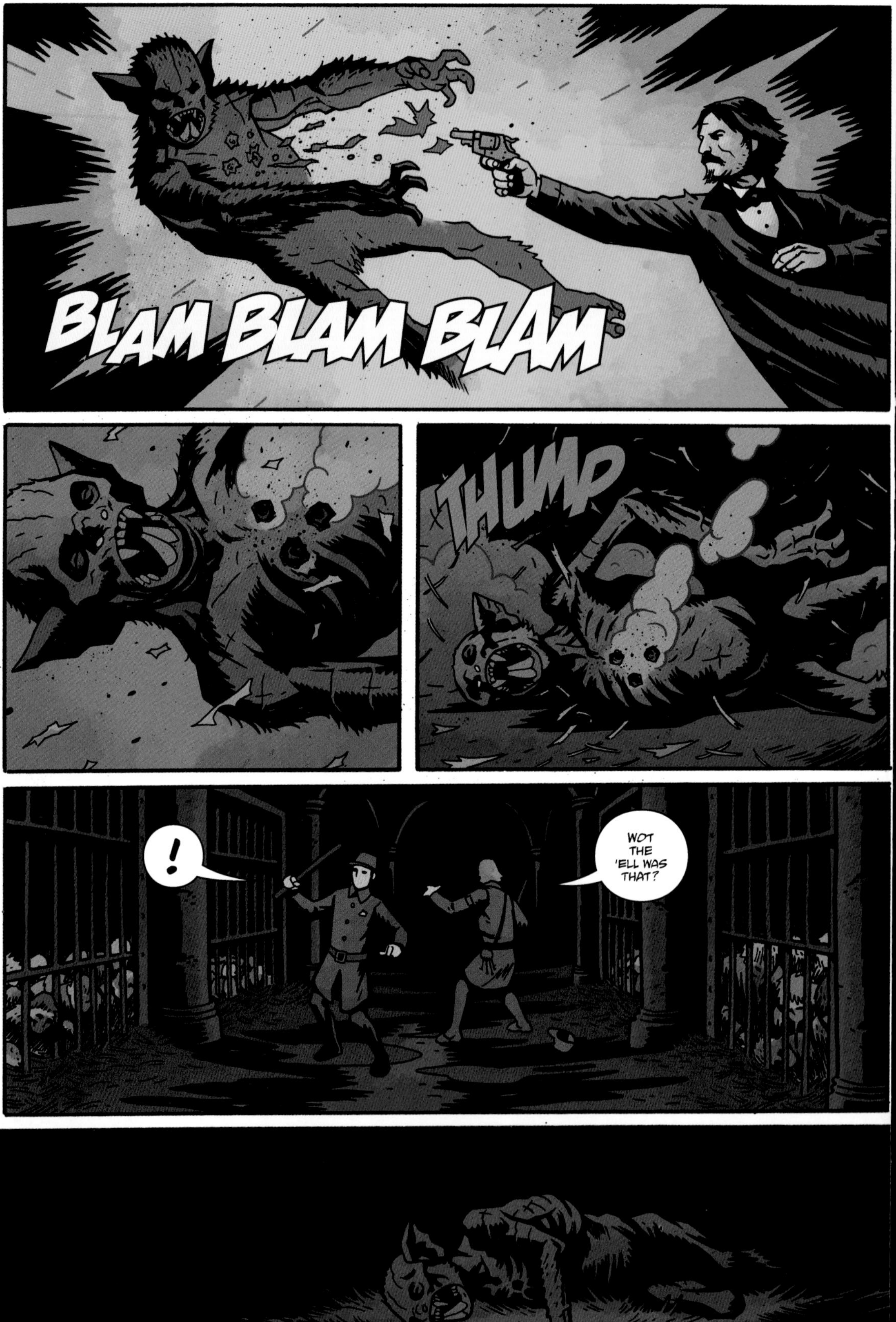
BLAM BLAM BLAM
THUMP
!
WOT THE 'ELL WAS THAT?

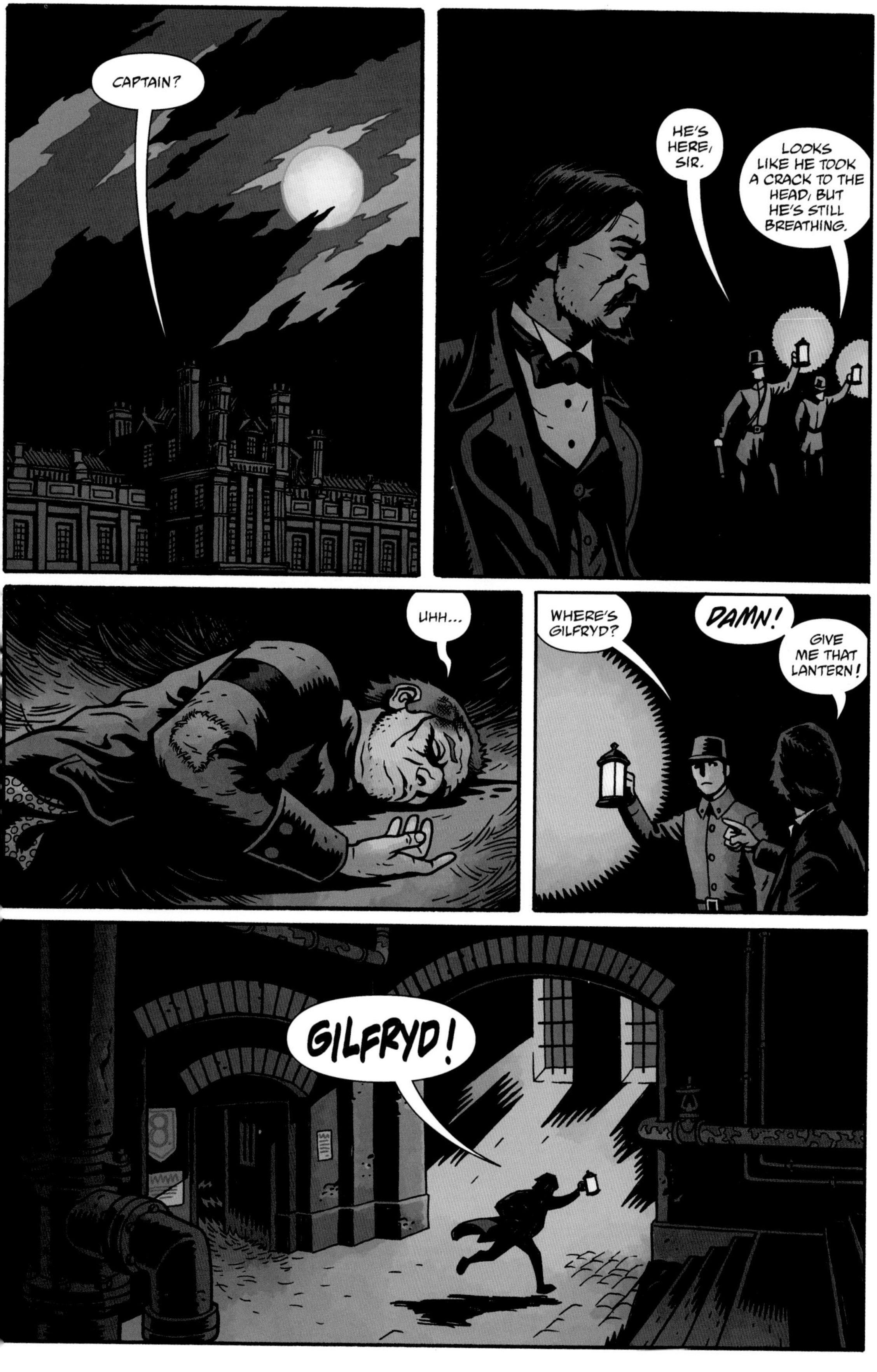
CAPTAIN?
HE'S HERE, SIR.
LOOKS LIKE HE TOOK A CRACK TO THE HEAD, BUT HE'S STILL BREATHING.
UHH...
WHERE'S GILFRYD?
DAMN!
GIVE ME THAT LANTERN!
GILFRYD!

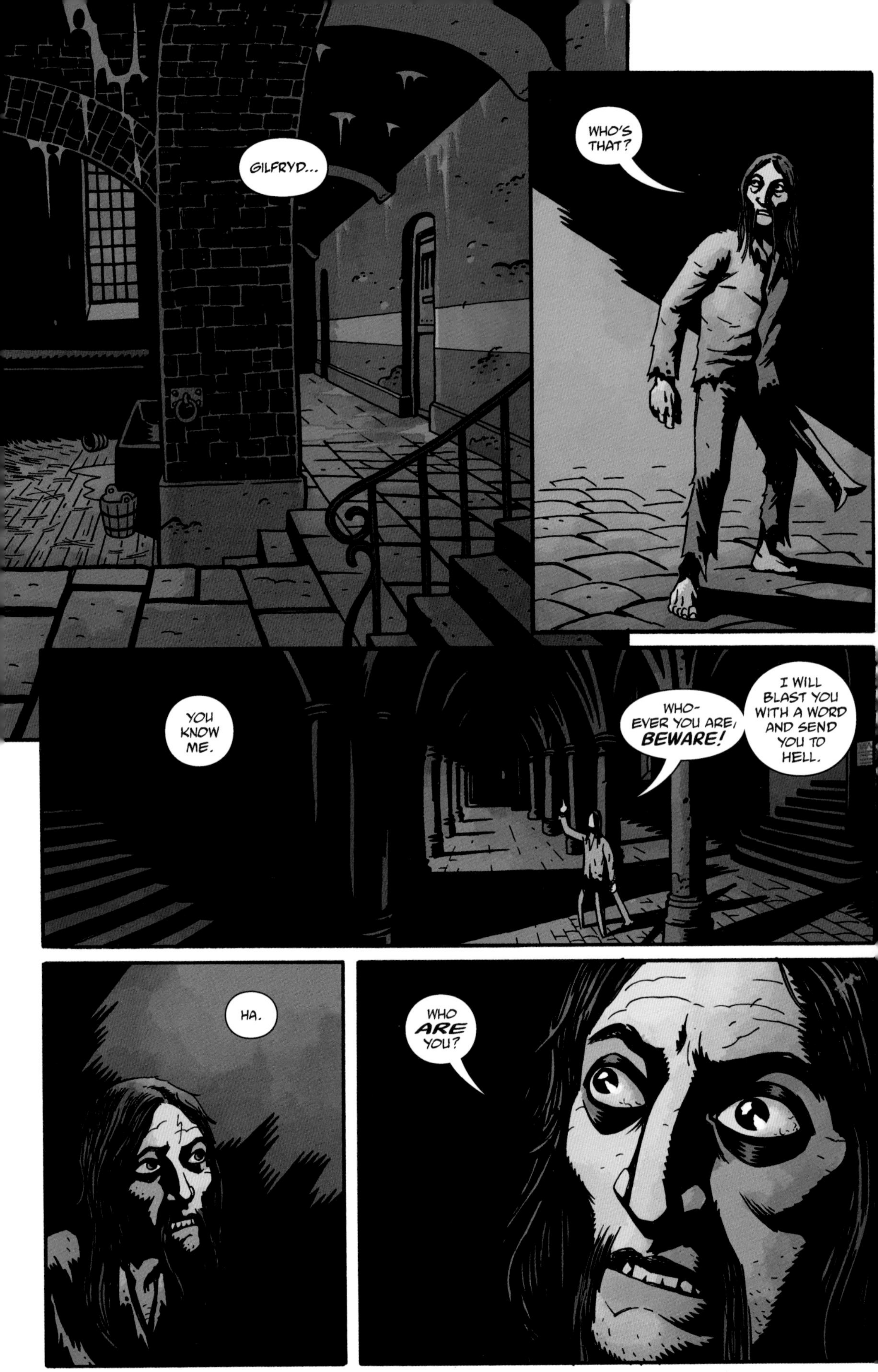
GILFRYD...
WHO'S THAT?
YOU KNOW ME.
WHO-EVER YOU ARE, **BEWARE!**
I WILL BLAST YOU WITH A WORD AND SEND YOU TO HELL.
HA.
WHO **ARE** YOU?

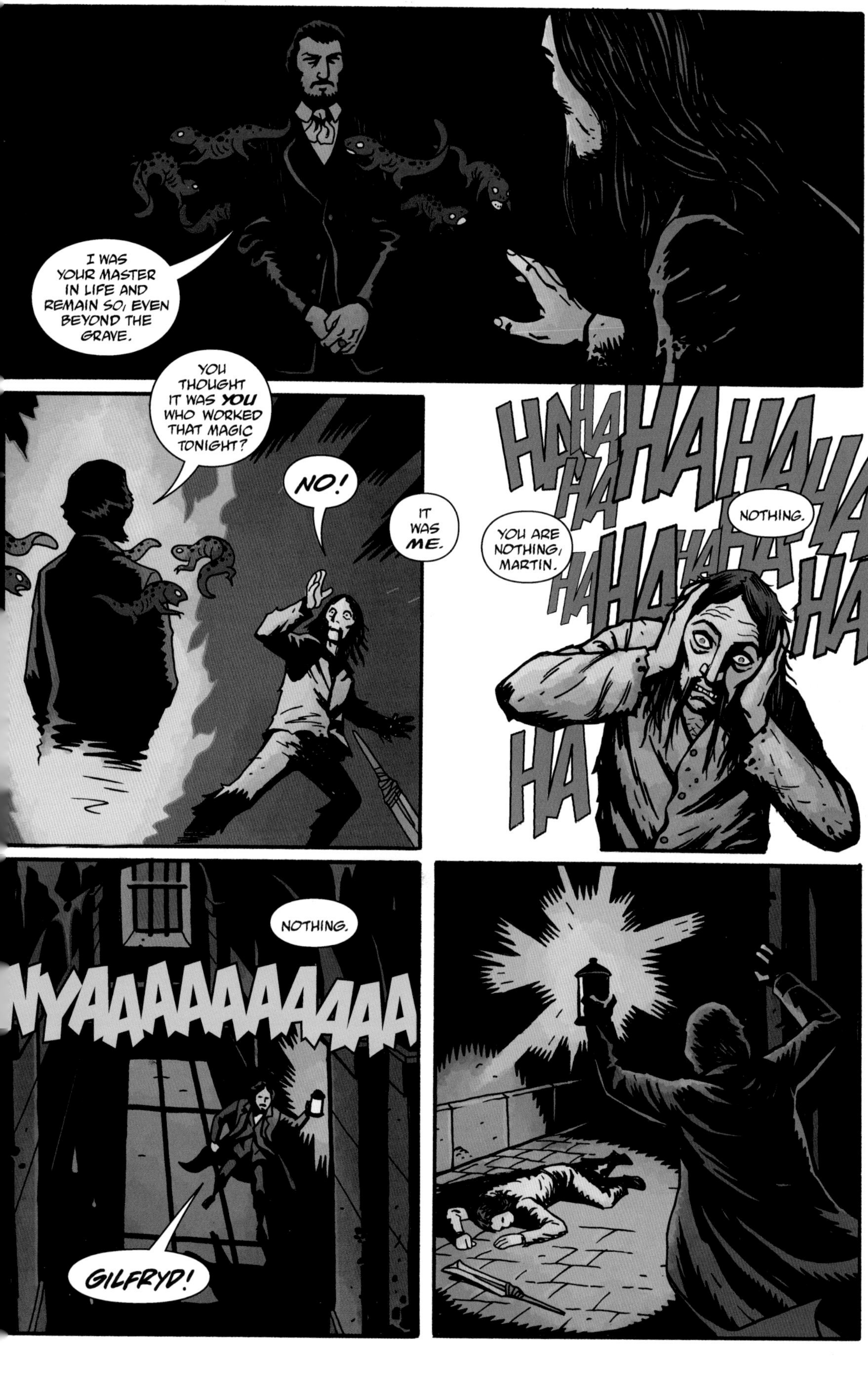
I WAS YOUR MASTER IN LIFE AND REMAIN SO, EVEN BEYOND THE GRAVE.
YOU THOUGHT IT WAS YOU WHO WORKED THAT MAGIC TONIGHT?
NO!
IT WAS ME.
HAHAHAHAHA HAHAHAHAHAHAHA HA HA
YOU ARE NOTHING, MARTIN.
NOTHING.
NOTHING.
NYAAAAAAAAAA
GILFRYD!

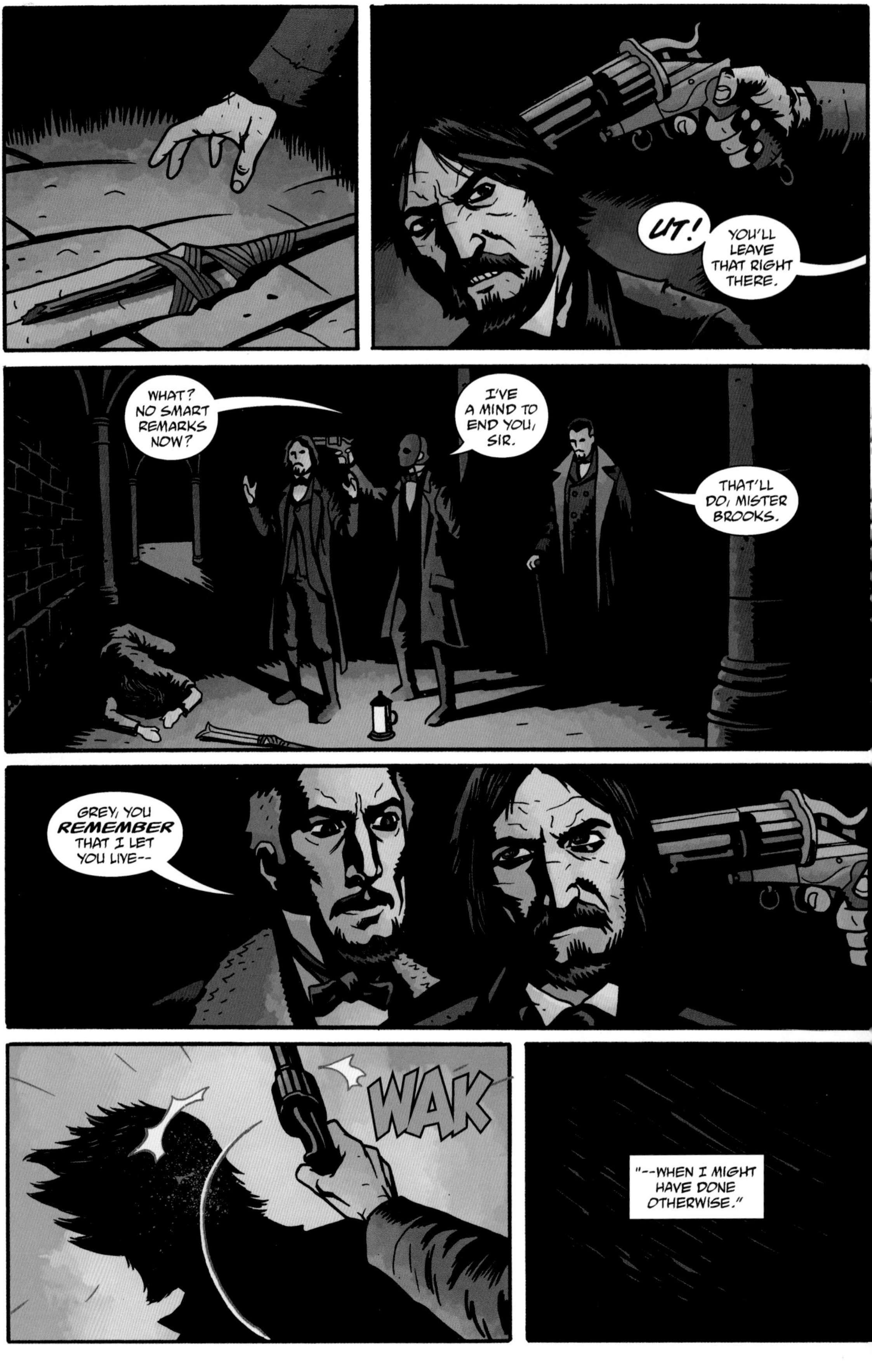
UT!
YOU'LL LEAVE THAT RIGHT THERE.
WHAT? NO SMART REMARKS NOW?
I'VE A MIND TO END YOU, SIR.
THAT'LL DO, MISTER BROOKS.
GREY, YOU REMEMBER THAT I LET YOU LIVE--
WAK
"--WHEN I MIGHT HAVE DONE OTHERWISE."

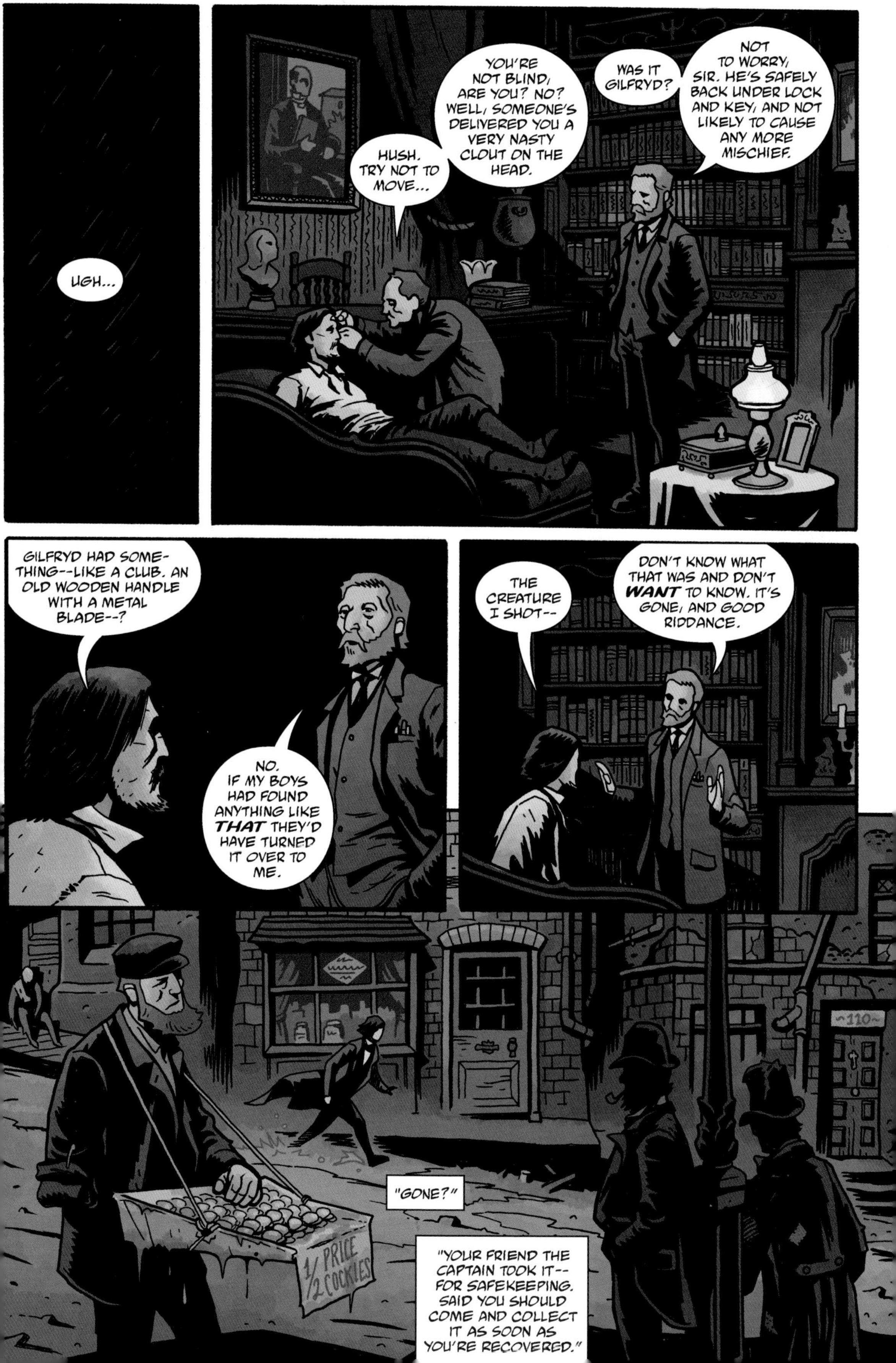
UGH...
HUSH. TRY NOT TO MOVE...
YOU'RE NOT BLIND, ARE YOU? NO? WELL, SOMEONE'S DELIVERED YOU A VERY NASTY CLOUT ON THE HEAD.
WAS IT GILFRYD?
NOT TO WORRY, SIR. HE'S SAFELY BACK UNDER LOCK AND KEY, AND NOT LIKELY TO CAUSE ANY MORE MISCHIEF.
GILFRYD HAD SOMETHING--LIKE A CLUB. AN OLD WOODEN HANDLE WITH A METAL BLADE--?
NO. IF MY BOYS HAD FOUND ANYTHING LIKE THAT THEY'D HAVE TURNED IT OVER TO ME.
THE CREATURE I SHOT--
DON'T KNOW WHAT THAT WAS AND DON'T WANT TO KNOW. IT'S GONE, AND GOOD RIDDANCE.
~110~
"GONE?"
1/2 PRICE COCKLES
"YOUR FRIEND THE CAPTAIN TOOK IT--FOR SAFEKEEPING. SAID YOU SHOULD COME AND COLLECT IT AS SOON AS YOU'RE RECOVERED."

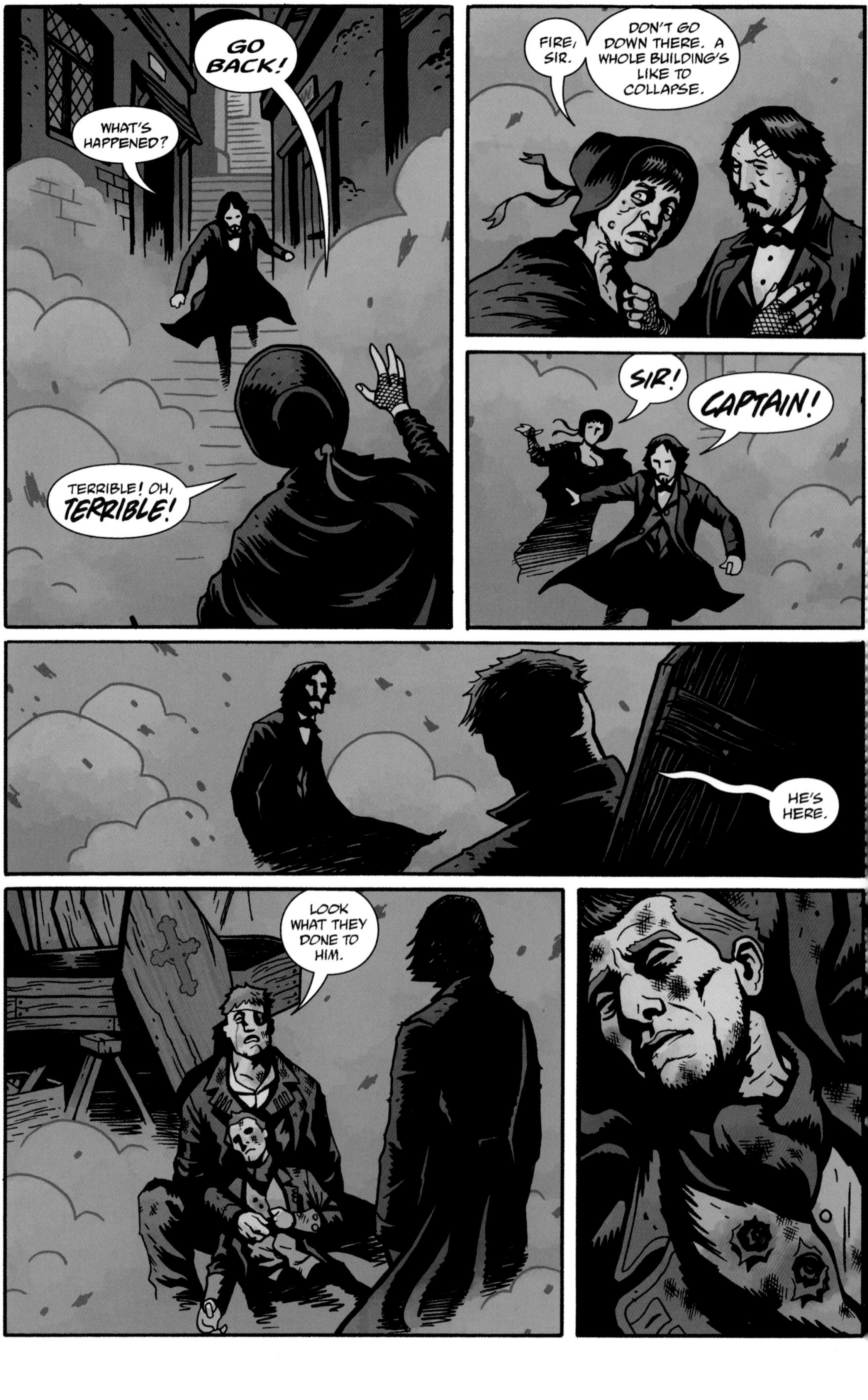
WHAT'S HAPPENED?
GO BACK!
TERRIBLE! OH, TERRIBLE!
FIRE, SIR.
DON'T GO DOWN THERE. A WHOLE BUILDING'S LIKE TO COLLAPSE.
SIR!
CAPTAIN!
HE'S HERE.
LOOK WHAT THEY DONE TO HIM.

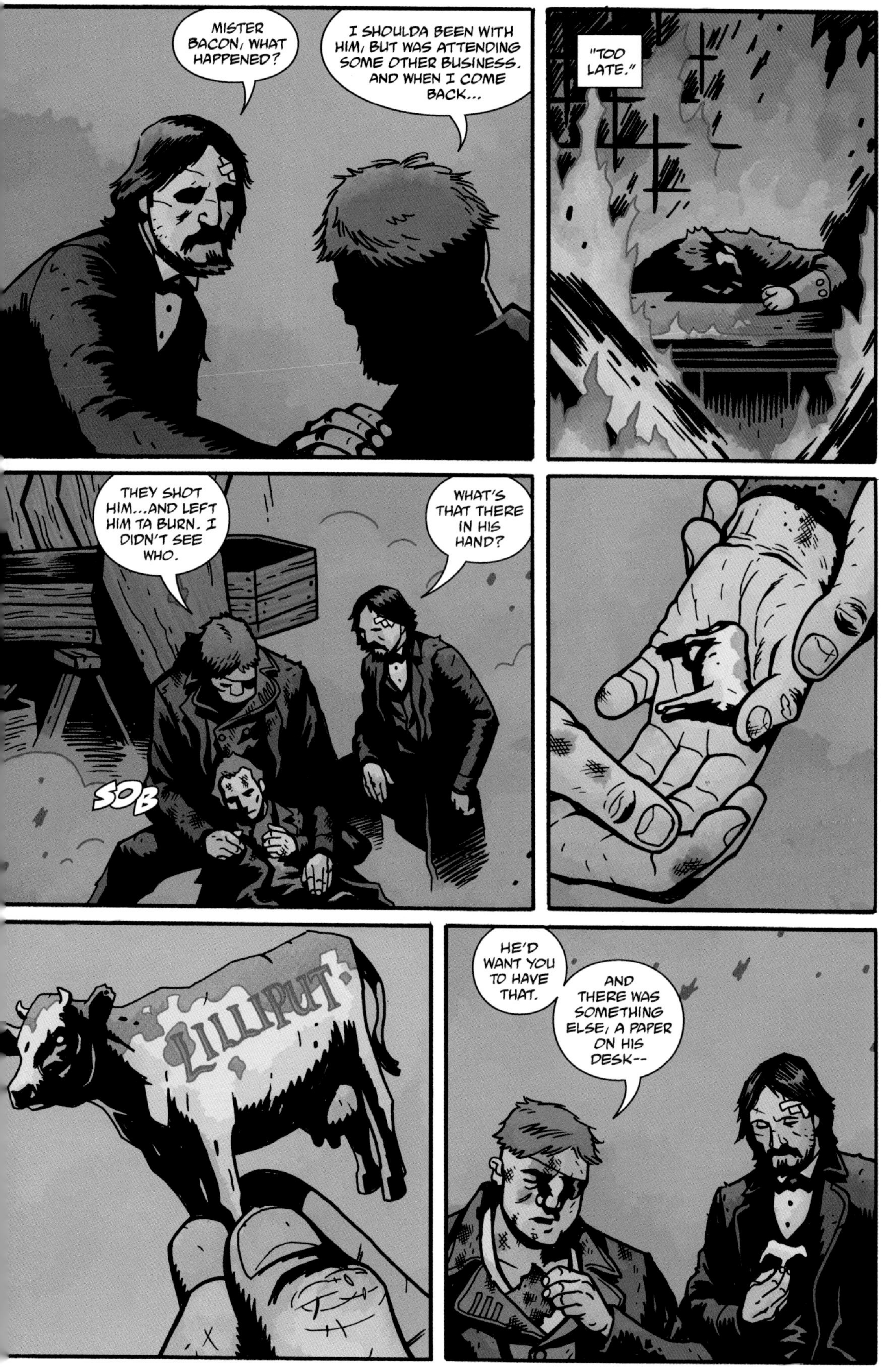
MISTER BACON, WHAT HAPPENED?
I SHOULDA BEEN WITH HIM, BUT WAS ATTENDING SOME OTHER BUSINESS. AND WHEN I COME BACK...
"TOO LATE."
THEY SHOT HIM...AND LEFT HIM TA BURN. I DIDN'T SEE WHO.
SOB
WHAT'S THAT THERE IN HIS HAND?
LILLIPUT
HE'D WANT YOU TO HAVE THAT.
AND THERE WAS SOMETHING ELSE, A PAPER ON HIS DESK--

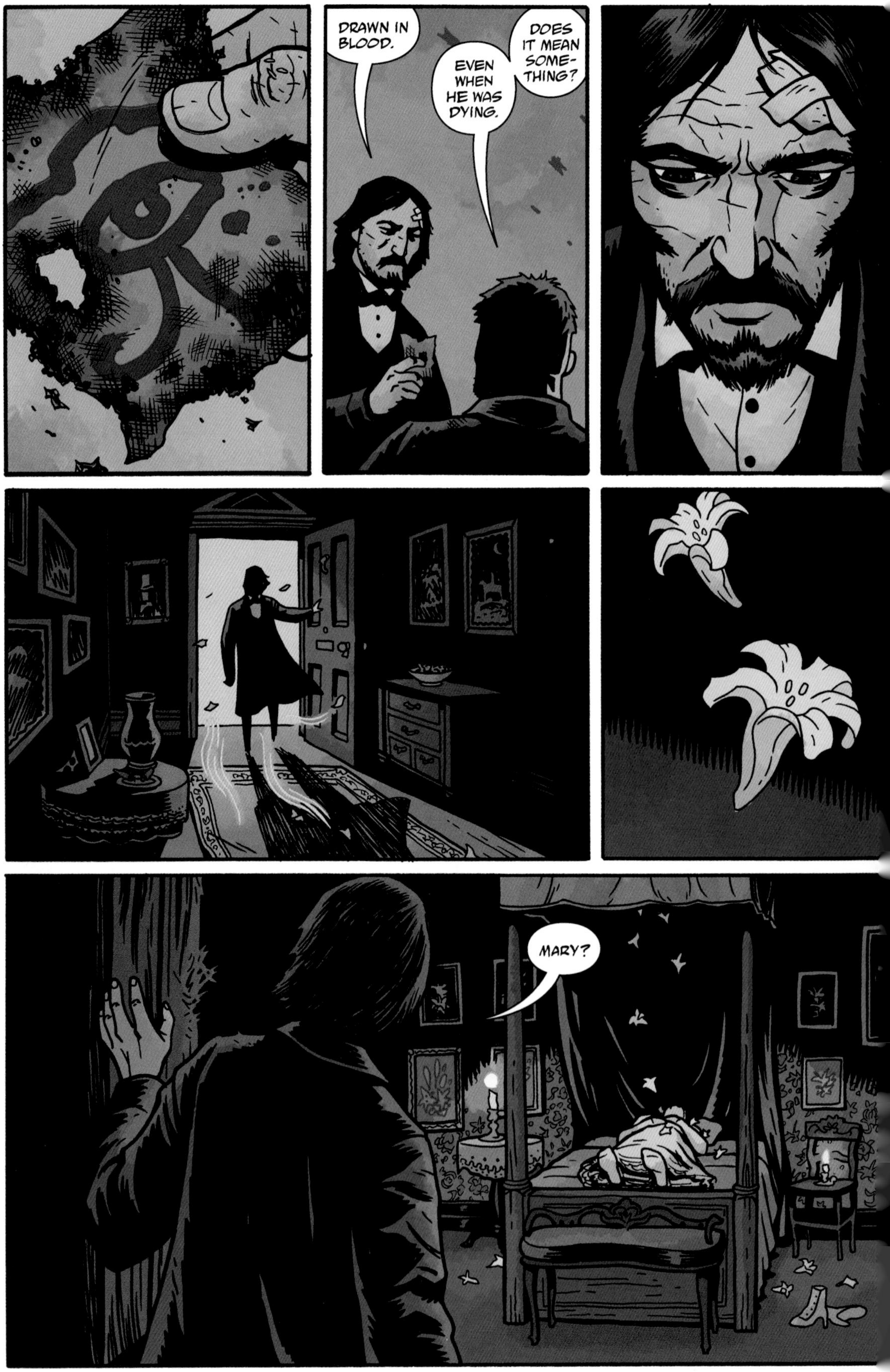
DRAWN IN BLOOD.
EVEN WHEN HE WAS DYING.
DOES IT MEAN SOME-THING?
MARY?

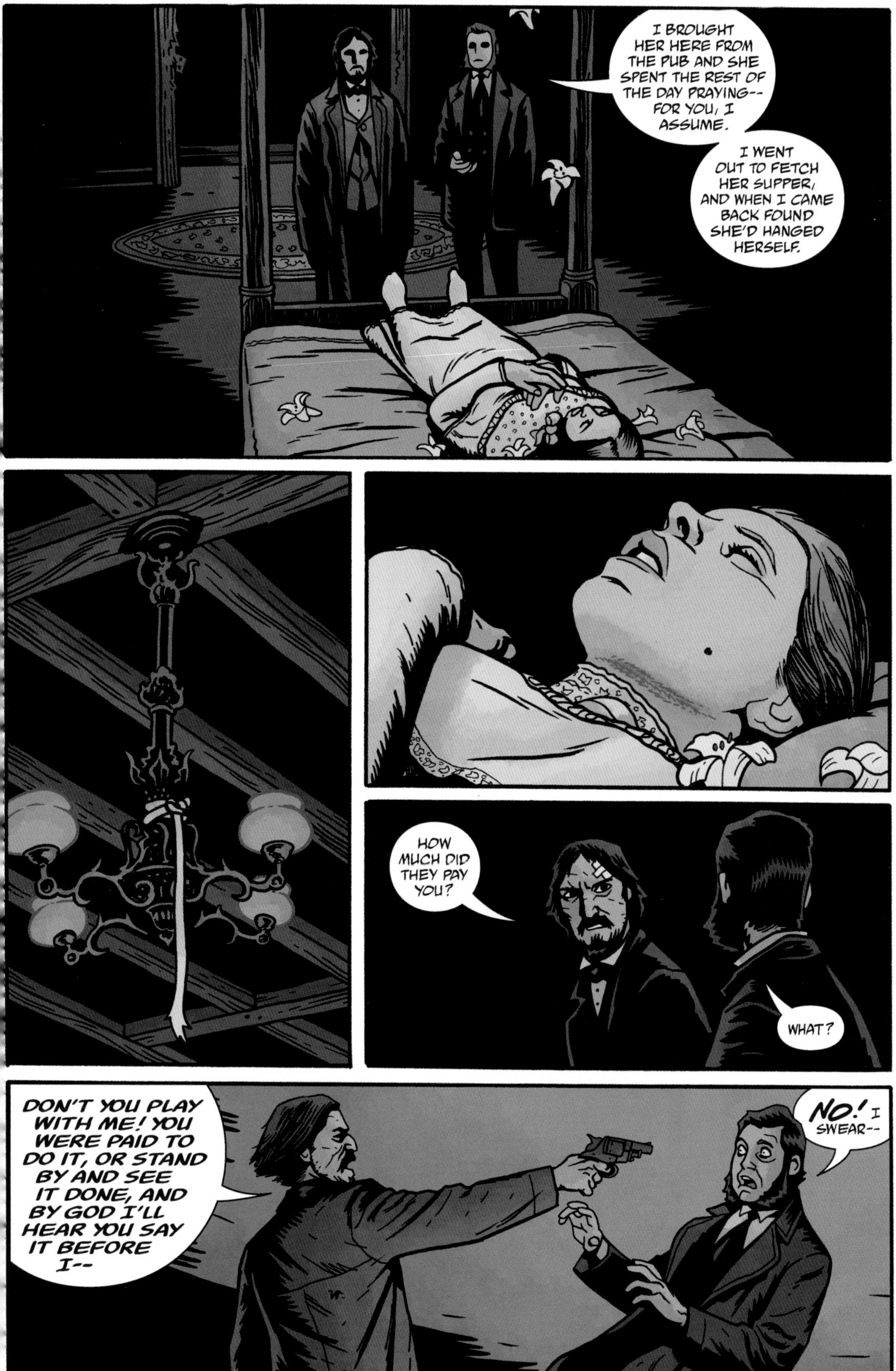
I BROUGHT HER HERE FROM THE PUB AND SHE SPENT THE REST OF THE DAY PRAYING-- FOR YOU, I ASSUME.
I WENT OUT TO FETCH HER SUPPER, AND WHEN I CAME BACK FOUND SHE'D HANGED HERSELF.
HOW MUCH DID THEY PAY YOU?
WHAT?
DON'T YOU PLAY WITH ME! YOU WERE PAID TO DO IT, OR STAND BY AND SEE IT DONE, AND BY GOD I'LL HEAR YOU SAY IT BEFORE I--
NO! I SWEAR--

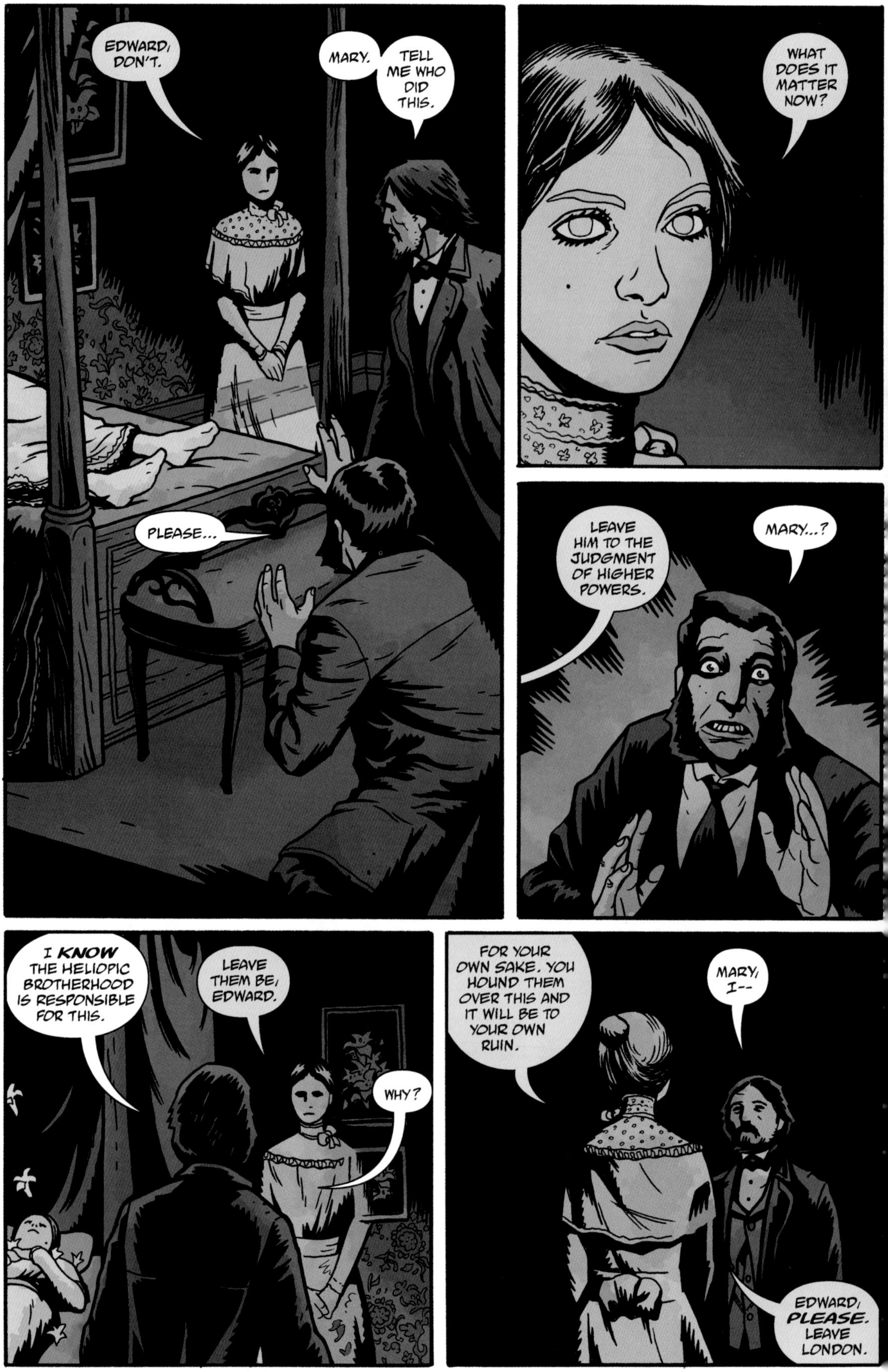
EDWARD, DON'T.
MARY.
TELL ME WHO DID THIS.
PLEASE...
WHAT DOES IT MATTER NOW?
LEAVE HIM TO THE JUDGMENT OF HIGHER POWERS.
MARY...?
I **KNOW** THE HELIOPIC BROTHERHOOD IS RESPONSIBLE FOR THIS.
LEAVE THEM BE, EDWARD.
WHY?
FOR YOUR OWN SAKE. YOU HOUND THEM OVER THIS AND IT WILL BE TO YOUR OWN RUIN.
MARY, I--
EDWARD, **PLEASE.** LEAVE LONDON.

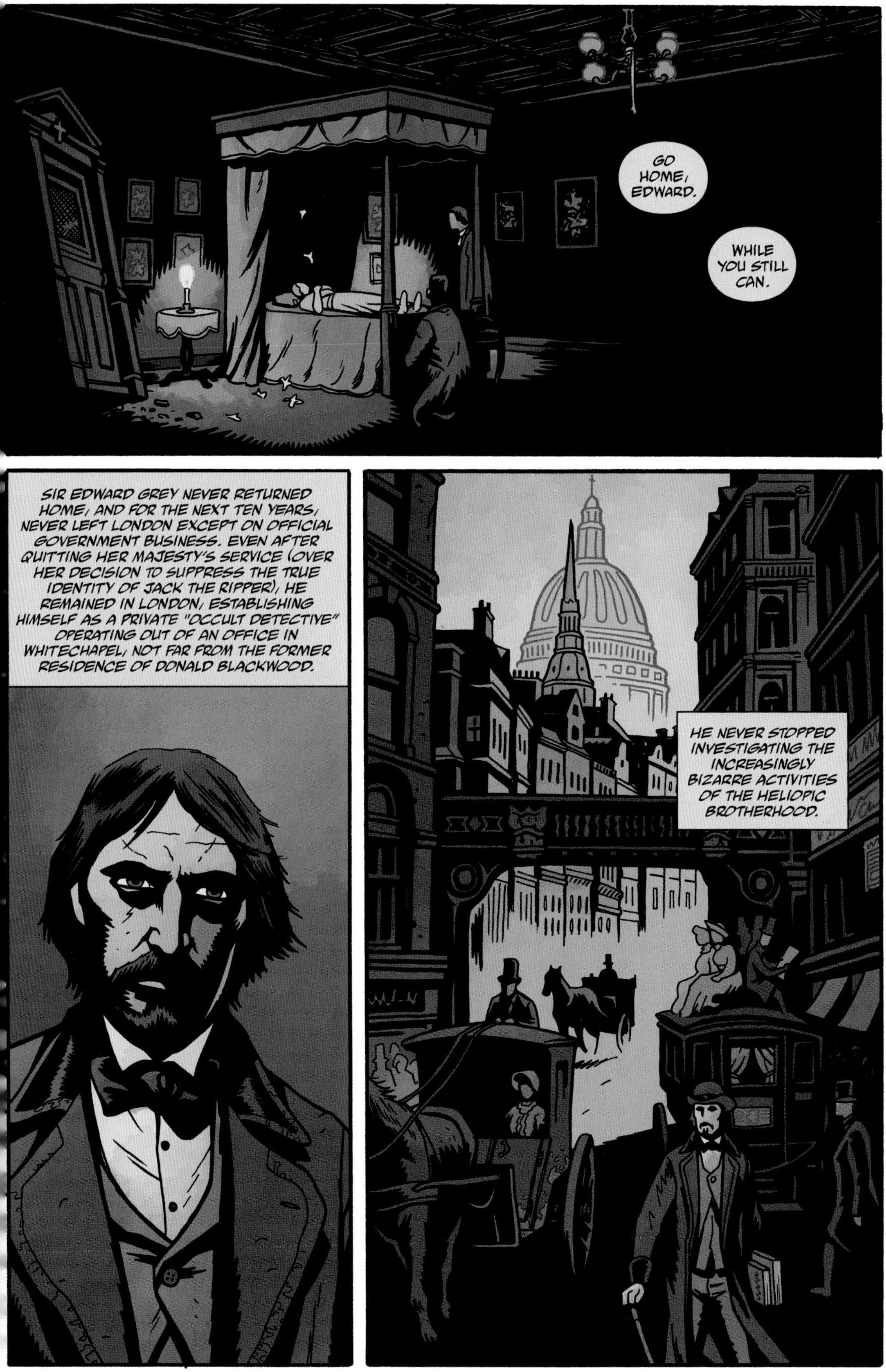
GO HOME, EDWARD.
WHILE YOU STILL CAN.
SIR EDWARD GREY NEVER RETURNED HOME, AND FOR THE NEXT TEN YEARS, NEVER LEFT LONDON EXCEPT ON OFFICIAL GOVERNMENT BUSINESS. EVEN AFTER QUITTING HER MAJESTY'S SERVICE (OVER HER DECISION TO SUPPRESS THE TRUE IDENTITY OF JACK THE RIPPER), HE REMAINED IN LONDON, ESTABLISHING HIMSELF AS A PRIVATE "OCCULT DETECTIVE" OPERATING OUT OF AN OFFICE IN WHITECHAPEL, NOT FAR FROM THE FORMER RESIDENCE OF DONALD BLACKWOOD.
HE NEVER STOPPED INVESTIGATING THE INCREASINGLY BIZARRE ACTIVITIES OF THE HELIOPIC BROTHERHOOD.

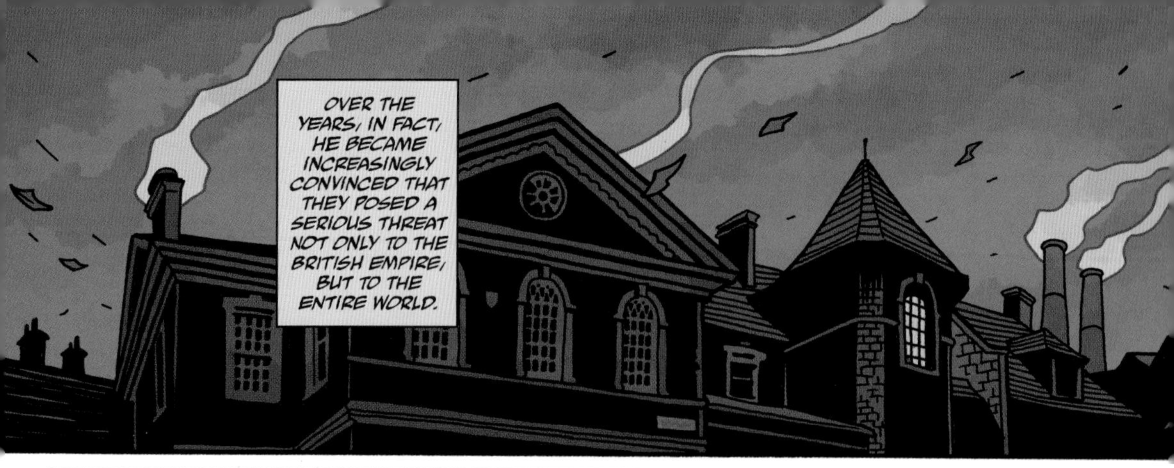
OVER THE YEARS, IN FACT, HE BECAME INCREASINGLY CONVINCED THAT THEY POSED A SERIOUS THREAT NOT ONLY TO THE BRITISH EMPIRE, BUT TO THE ENTIRE WORLD.

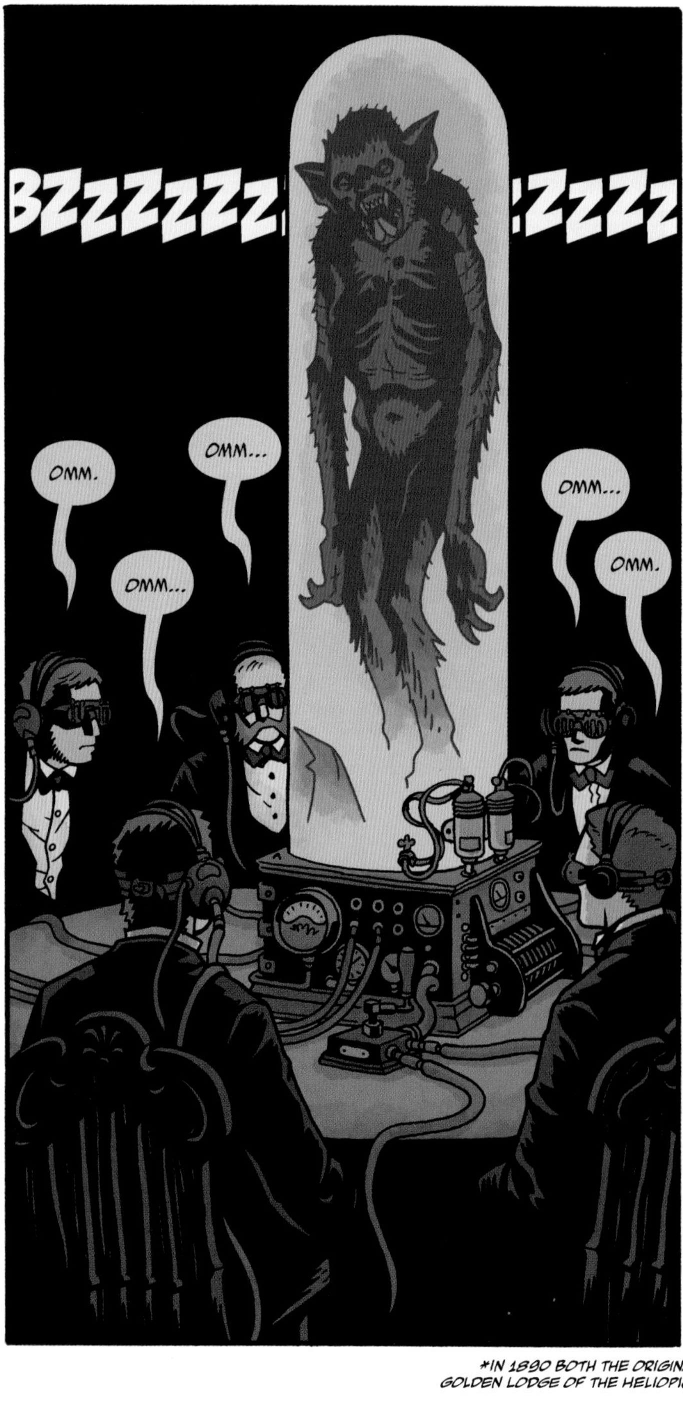
BZZZZZZ
ZZZZZ
OMM.
OMM...
OMM...
OMM...
OMM.

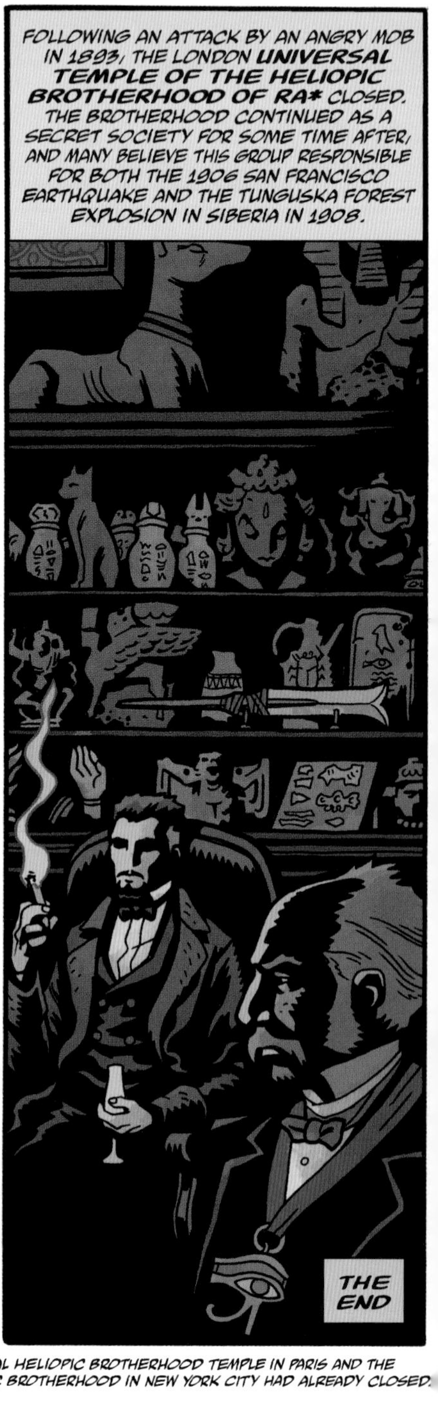
FOLLOWING AN ATTACK BY AN ANGRY MOB IN 1893, THE LONDON **UNIVERSAL TEMPLE OF THE HELIOPIC BROTHERHOOD OF RA*** CLOSED. THE BROTHERHOOD CONTINUED AS A SECRET SOCIETY FOR SOME TIME AFTER, AND MANY BELIEVE THIS GROUP RESPONSIBLE FOR BOTH THE 1906 SAN FRANCISCO EARTHQUAKE AND THE TUNGUSKA FOREST EXPLOSION IN SIBERIA IN 1908.
THE END

*IN 1890 BOTH THE ORIGINAL HELIOPIC BROTHERHOOD TEMPLE IN PARIS AND THE GOLDEN LODGE OF THE HELIOPIC BROTHERHOOD IN NEW YORK CITY HAD ALREADY CLOSED.

AFTERWORD

WHERE DID THIS THING COME FROM?

I've said it a bunch of times, and it's really true—the novel *Dracula*, which I read at the tender age of thirteen, changed my life. I probably already knew I wanted to draw monsters (I don't remember a time when I didn't), but from then on I knew what I wanted to *read*—I wanted guys in Victorian outfits creeping around foggy graveyards looking for monsters. Ask my therapist why—I don't know. I just know that from then on I loved that world. I read the well-known (and not-so-well-known-anymore) Victorian ghost-story writers—M. R. James (the master) and J. S. Le Fanu (the other master), E. F. Benson, Maupassant, Bangs, Dickens, Bierce, Riddell, Jacobs, Kipling—and somewhere in there I discovered the Occult Detectives. Now, Van Helsing (in *Dracula*) was sort of an occult detective, but we only saw him solve that one case, and he took a long time to do it. Algernon Blackwood wrote a whole series of stories about his guy (John Silence). So did William Hope Hodgson (Carnacki). And around the time these stories were being written there were real guys like Harry Price running around investigating Borley Rectory and Gef the talking mongoose. Add to that all the crazy Spiritualist stuff going on back then—Madame Blavatsky and the Theosophists, Hollow Earth theories . . . Yeah. That is my kind of stuff.

So when I started seriously thinking about creating my own comic, I *knew* I would do an occult detective.

I was planning on making my detective a regular human being, inspired by the guys (real and fictional) mentioned above. But set it in the Victorian era? Back then I had just finished the comic-book adaptation of Francis Ford Coppola's *Dracula* film. It turned out okay, but it was a lot of work. I didn't even want to *think* about drawing another coach wheel for a long time. And, I thought, if I was hoping this comic of mine would turn into a series, wouldn't it be *smarter* to set it in the modern world—so I wouldn't be constantly searching for period reference? Lazy? Maybe. I prefer to think I was just being practical. Then, of course, there was the matter of the detective himself. By then I'd been drawing comics for about ten years, and I knew a few things about myself—and as sure as I knew drawing horses and hansom cabs was going to drive me crazy, I *knew* I'd eventually get bored drawing a regular guy. Sorry. It's true. So I went with Hellboy instead, and he was supposed to be a regular guy but turned into something else— blah blah blah. I've written about that whole thing elsewhere. But everything that I like I have to have my own version of in the Hellboy world. So just like I created Lobster Johnson to stand in for all those great pulp characters of the '30s, I created Sir Edward Grey to represent the classic English occult detective.

I first mentioned Edward Grey, briefly, in the second *Hellboy* miniseries, *Wake the Devil*. He appeared (sort of) in one panel. If you blinked, you missed it. But, little by little, his Victorian world wormed its way into the Hellboy world. I created the Heliopic Brotherhood of Ra (a stand-in for any number of Victorian secret societies) for a Hellboy story called "Dr. Carp's Experiment," and a short time later Abe Sapien's Victorian roots started to show. Before you knew it, we had a Victorian submarine (you *need* one of those), Victorian cyborgs, and a living mummy (unwrapped, of course, by Victorians). We were picking up steam now. One of our major villains in the *B.P.R.D.* books turned out to have been a former curator of the British Historical Society who had done time in Victorian Bedlam. It seemed about time for Ed Grey to show up again. He appeared in the first ten pages of *Abe Sapien: The Drowning*, and after that he just didn't want to go away. I find that happens with these characters sometimes. It's hard to get them to go back to being supporting characters again. Okay, but where was I going to find an artist crazy enough to draw a whole series set in Victorian London?

Enter Ben Stenbeck. And I don't really know if he's crazy (though he *is* willing to work with me), but he is very, very good—great with characters and mood, and a nut for research. He really delivered the goods. Sometimes a character just needs to be patient and wait for the right artist to come along.

On the following pages you'll find two short stories. The first of these, "Murderous Intent," appeared online and was sort of a warm-up for Ben and me working together. It was intended as an Ed Grey "teaser," to explain why the series would be called *Witchfinder*. And speaking of *Witchfinder* . . .

Henry Hood, coin-eyed living corpse, first appeared in the Hellboy series *Darkness Calls*. Just as the Hellboy world needed a '30s pulp hero and a Victorian occult detective, I felt it needed its own relentless, corrupt seventeenth-century persecutor of witches. Hood is modeled after a real-life Witch Finder General, Matthew Hopkins. Long-suffering Hellboy editor Scott Allie and I teamed with relative newcomer Patric Reynolds on "The Burial of Katharine Baker," to show that at least sometimes poor old Hood, like Grey, was working in the service of angels. This story originally appeared as a backup feature in issue #7 of *Hellboy: The Wild Hunt*.

There you go.

MIKE MIGNOLA

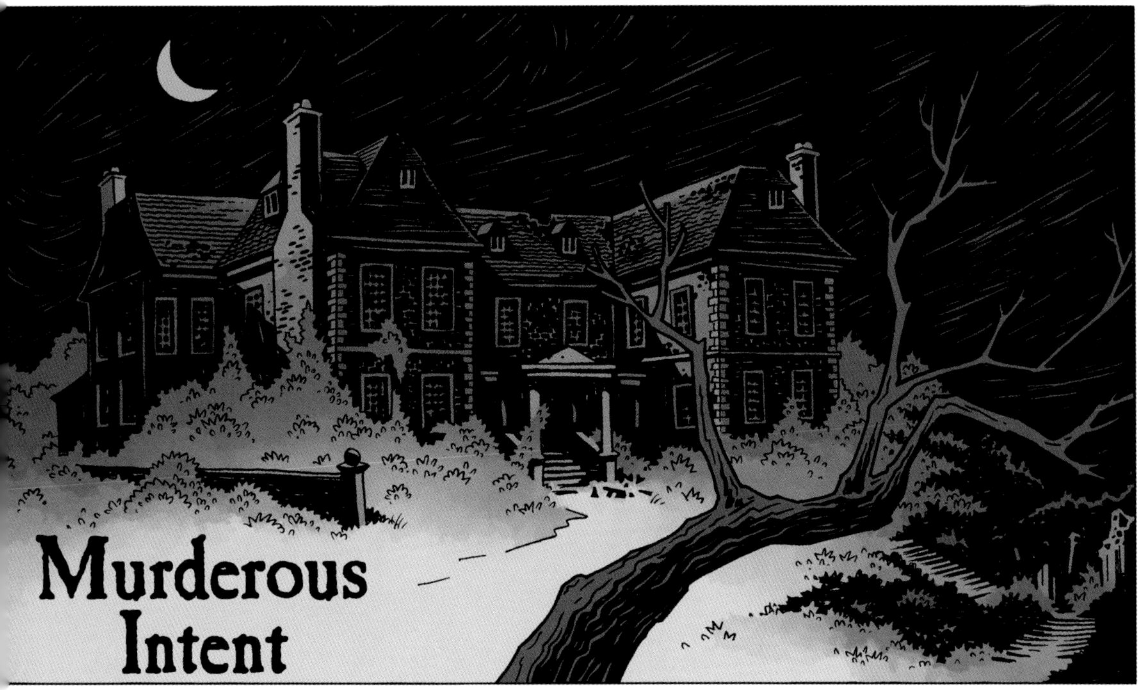
Murderous Intent

How an Attempt Was Made to Assassinate Her Majesty Queen Victoria of England on February 6, 1879, by Mary and Elizabeth Washbrook and Sara Webb, the Witches of Farnham.

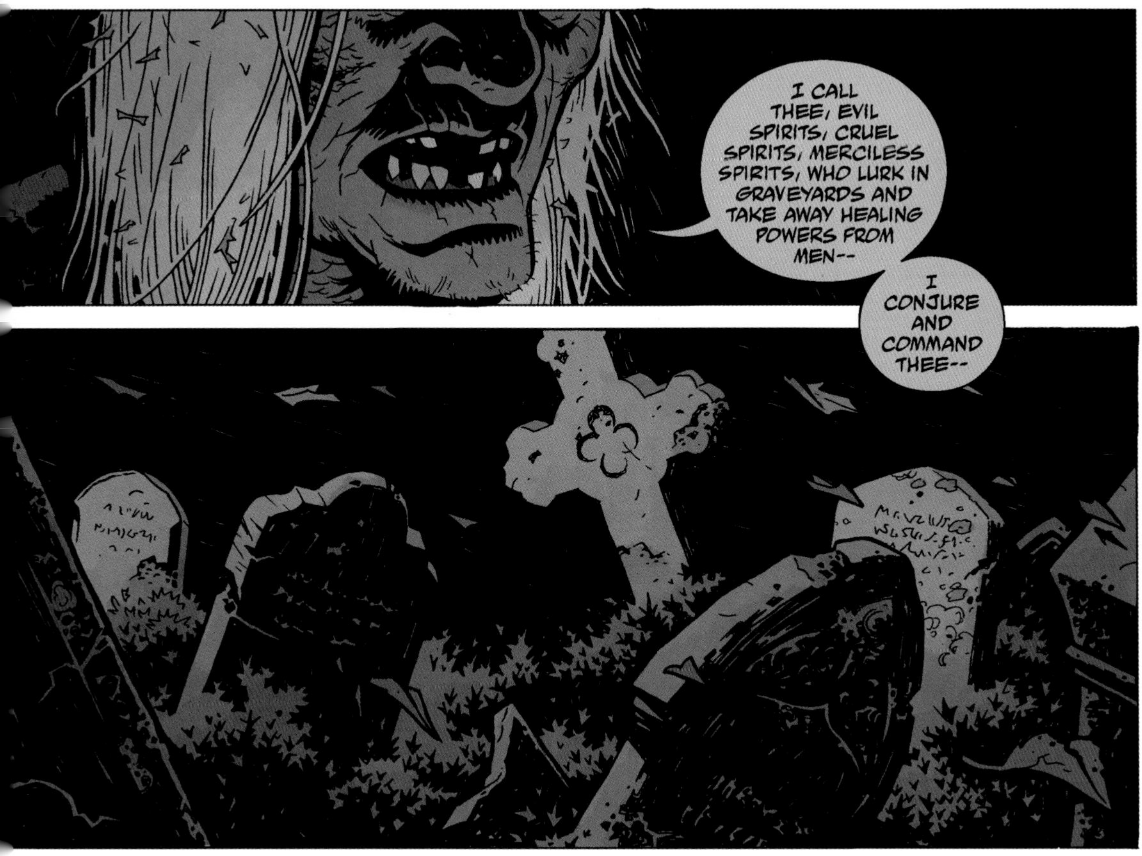
I CALL THEE, EVIL SPIRITS, CRUEL SPIRITS, MERCILESS SPIRITS, WHO LURK IN GRAVEYARDS AND TAKE AWAY HEALING POWERS FROM MEN--
I CONJURE AND COMMAND THEE--

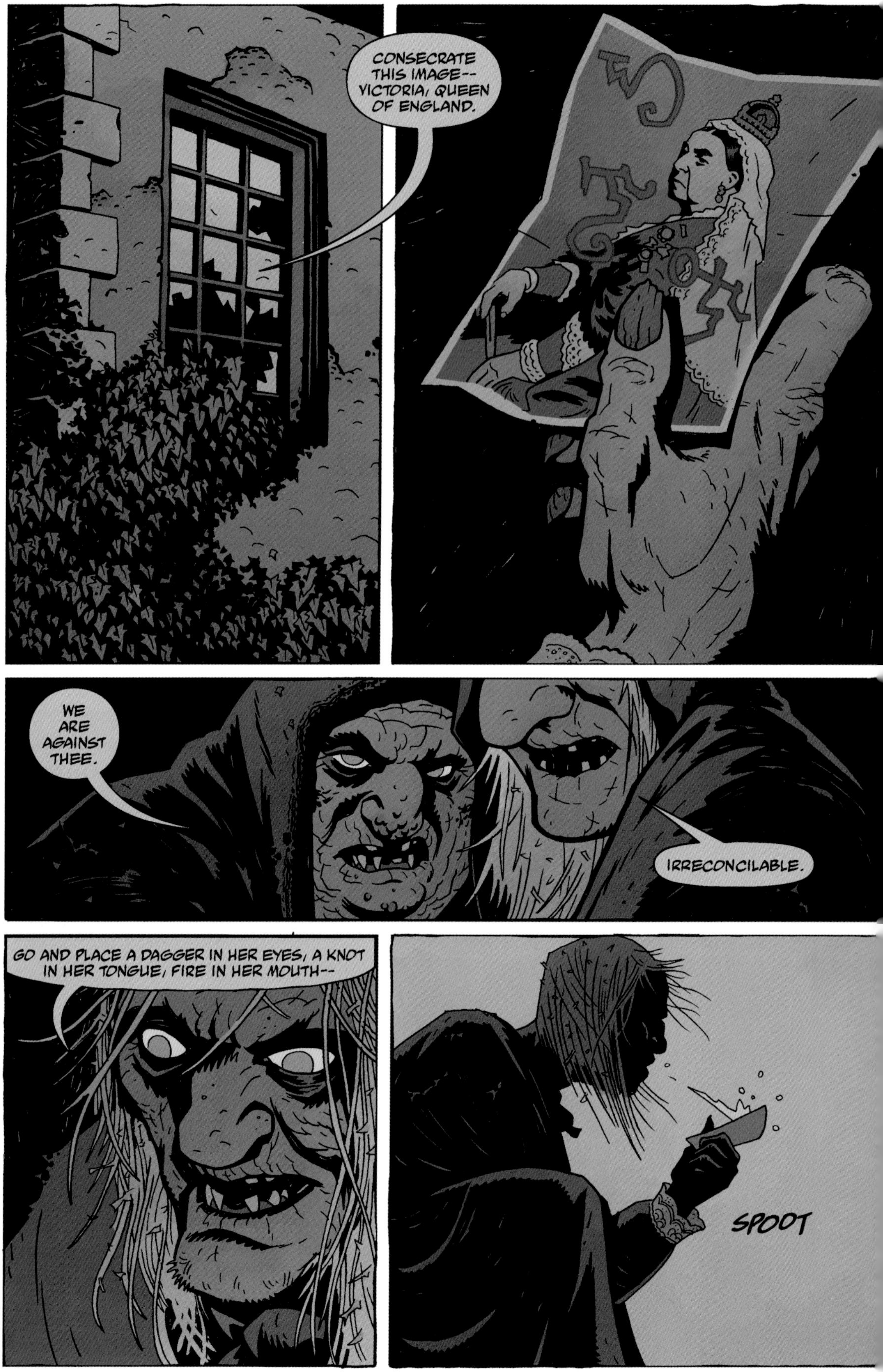
CONSECRATE THIS IMAGE-- VICTORIA, QUEEN OF ENGLAND.
WE ARE AGAINST THEE.
IRRECONCILABLE.
GO AND PLACE A DAGGER IN HER EYES, A KNOT IN HER TONGUE, FIRE IN HER MOUTH--
SPOOT

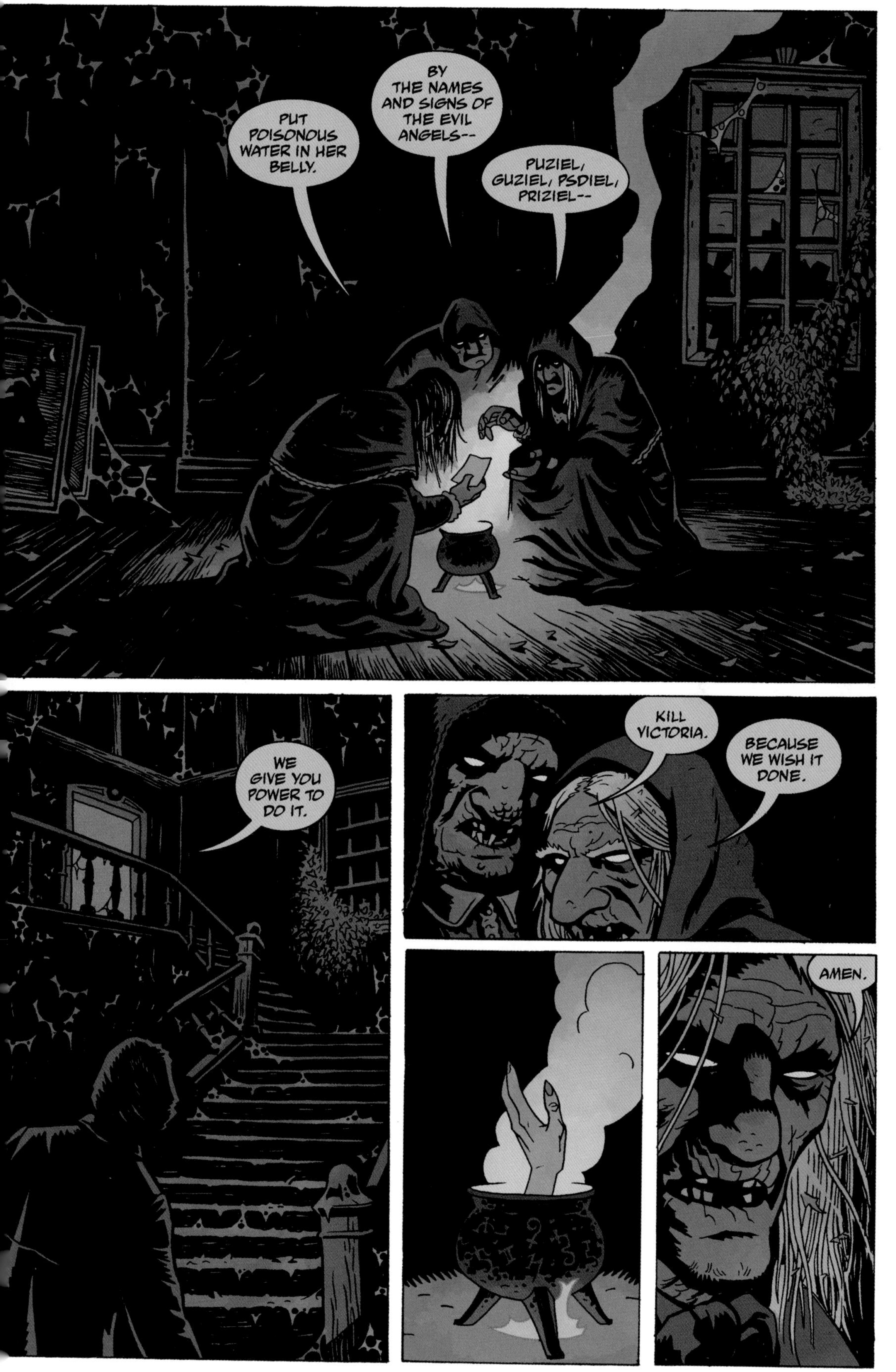
PUT POISONOUS WATER IN HER BELLY.
BY THE NAMES AND SIGNS OF THE EVIL ANGELS--
PUZIEL, GUZIEL, PSDIEL, PRIZIEL--
WE GIVE YOU POWER TO DO IT.
KILL VICTORIA.
BECAUSE WE WISH IT DONE.
AMEN.

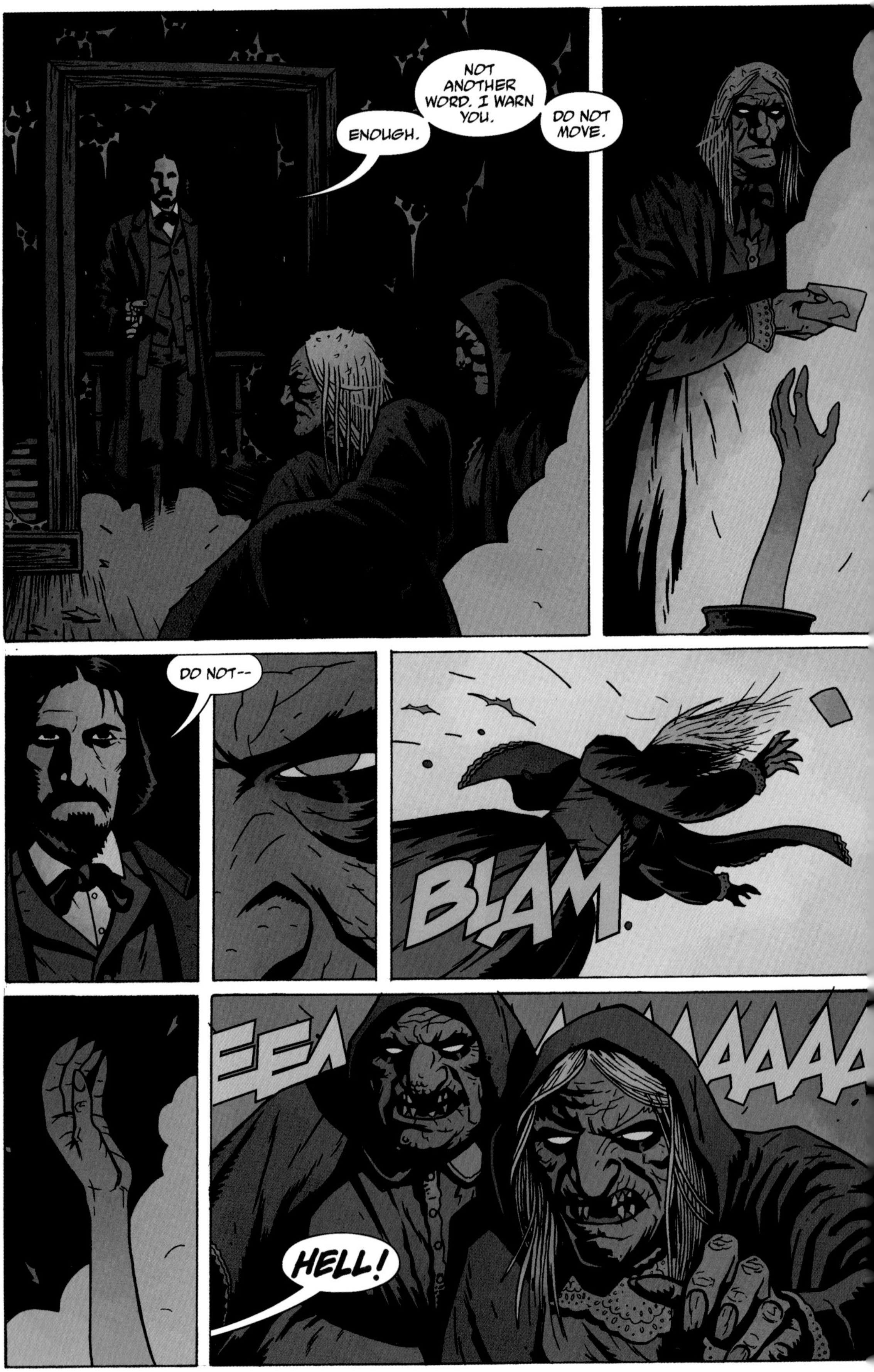
ENOUGH.
NOT ANOTHER WORD. I WARN YOU.
DO NOT MOVE.
DO NOT--
BLAM
EEA
AAAAA
HELL!

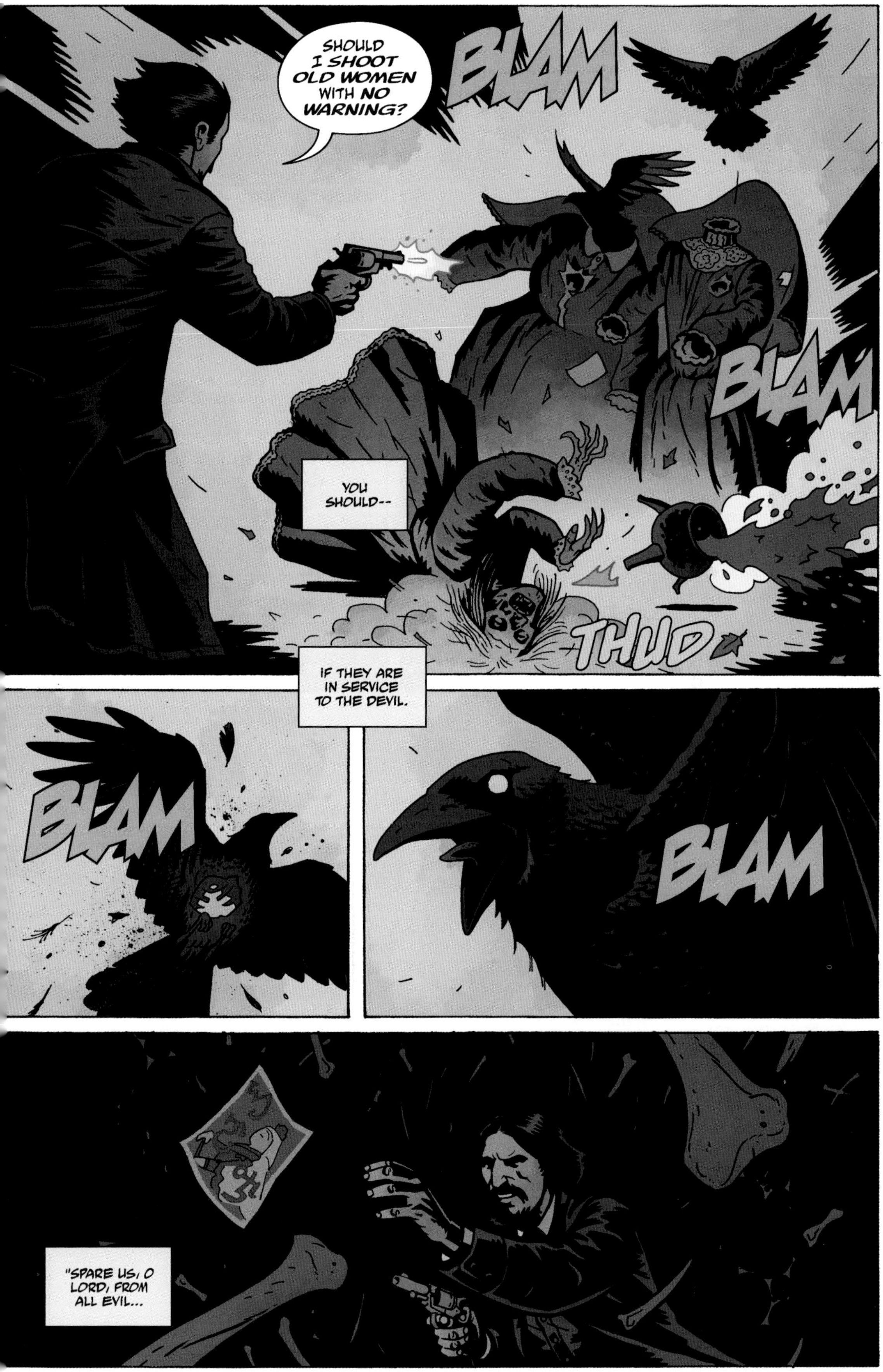
SHOULD I SHOOT OLD WOMEN WITH NO WARNING?
BLAM
BLAM
YOU SHOULD--
THUD
IF THEY ARE IN SERVICE TO THE DEVIL.
BLAM
BLAM
"SPARE US, O LORD, FROM ALL EVIL...

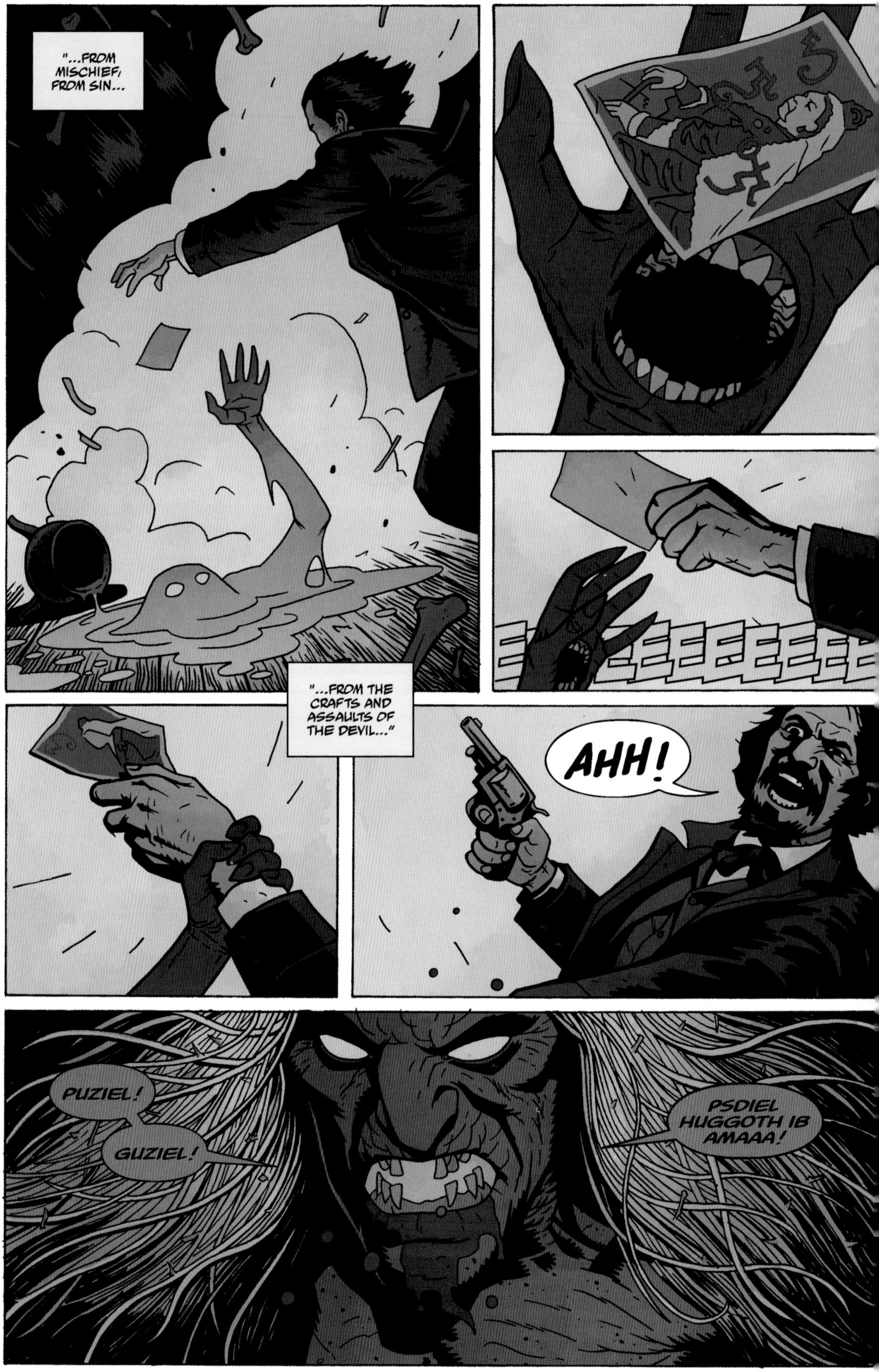
"...FROM MISCHIEF, FROM SIN...
EEEEEEEEEEEE
"...FROM THE CRAFTS AND ASSAULTS OF THE DEVIL..."
AHH!
PUZIEL!
GUZIEL!
PSDIEL HUGGOTH IB AMAAA!

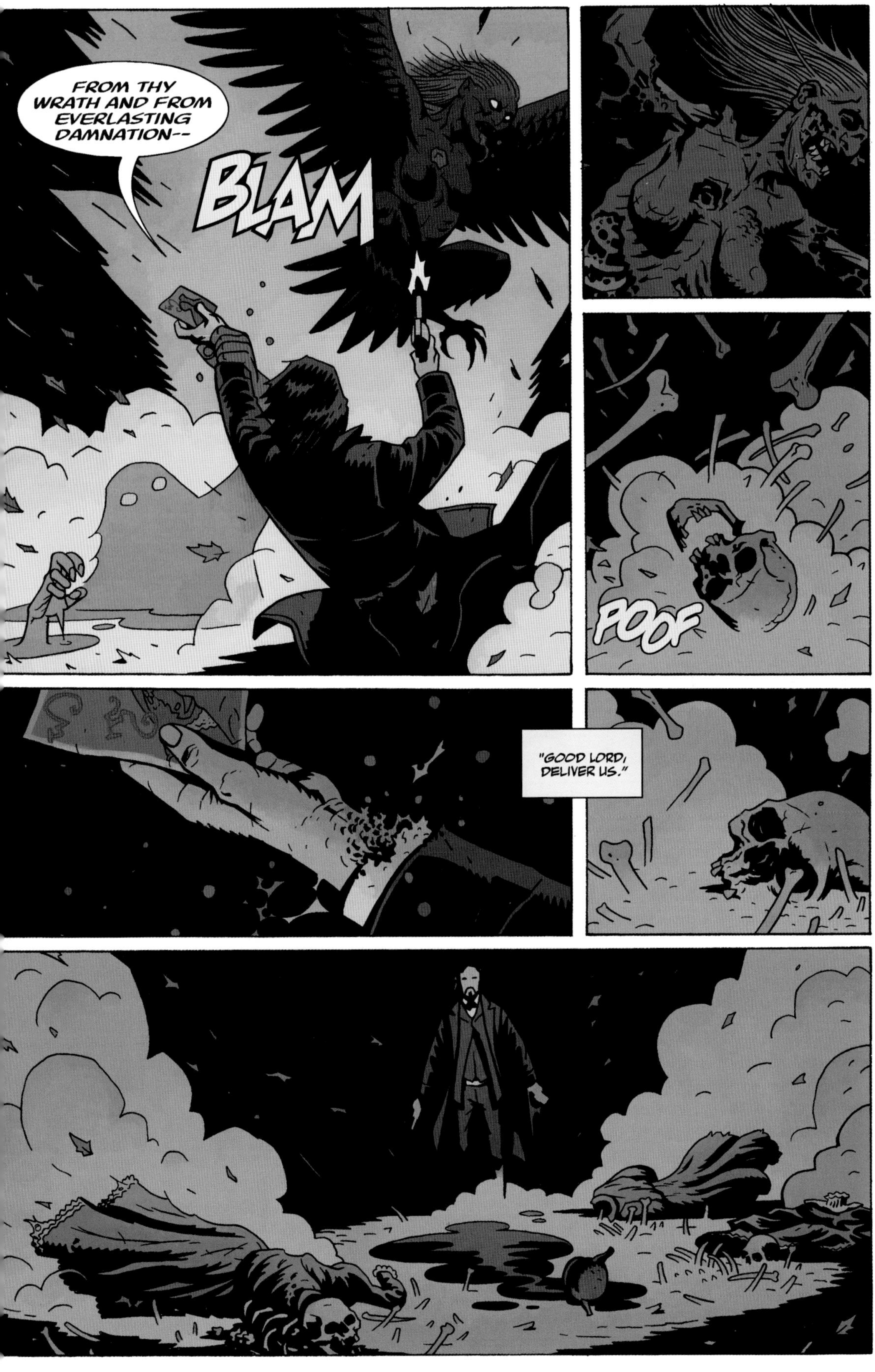
FROM THY WRATH AND FROM EVERLASTING DAMNATION--
BLAM
POOF
"GOOD LORD, DELIVER US."

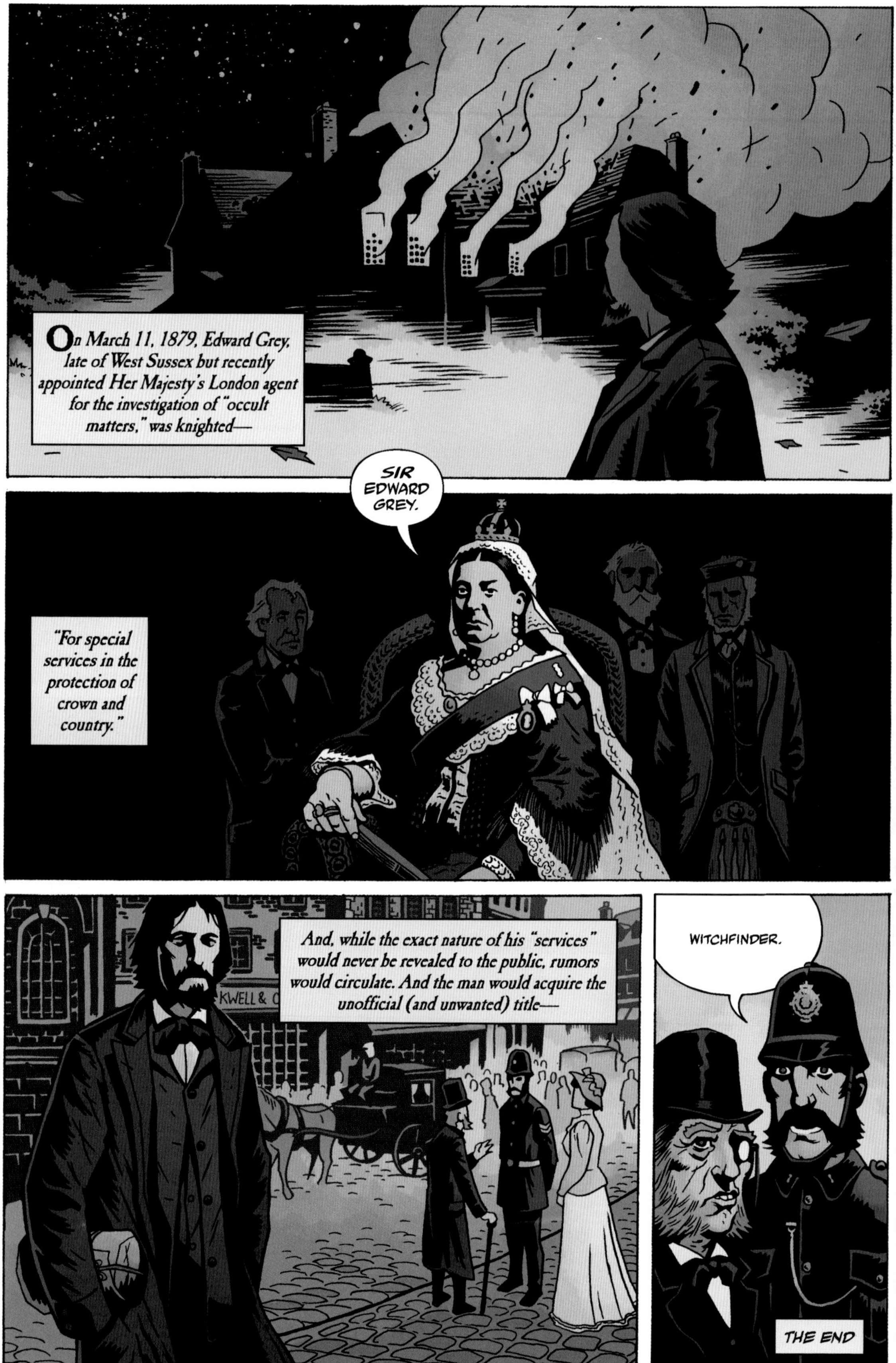
On March 11, 1879, Edward Grey, late of West Sussex but recently appointed Her Majesty's London agent for the investigation of "occult matters," was knighted—
SIR EDWARD GREY.
"For special services in the protection of crown and country."
And, while the exact nature of his "services" would never be revealed to the public, rumors would circulate. And the man would acquire the unofficial (and unwanted) title—
KWELL & C
WITCHFINDER.
THE END

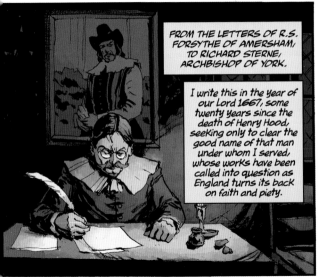

FROM THE LETTERS OF R.S. FORSYTHE OF AMERSHAM, TO RICHARD STERNE, ARCHBISHOP OF YORK.

I write this in the year of our Lord 1667, some twenty years since the death of Henry Hood, seeking only to clear the good name of that man under whom I served, whose works have been called into question as England turns its back on faith and piety.

In the spring of 1646 we traveled to Haverhill, where neighbors accused a young Katharine Baker of casting a plague on their crops, after her father's land bore a harvest while all others were worm eaten.

The boy she loved had died that winter, and her lack of grief had attracted suspicion. Her sin was found to be far worse, though, when she was seen visiting the boy in the cemetery beyond the town.

We tried the girl in the usual manner, confirming her guilt.

As we left the town, the girl's family blocked the road to Essex.

The Burial of Katharine Baker

WHAT DID YOU DO WITH HER, YOU BASTARD?

YOU FACE A SERVANT OF THE *CROWN*, SIR, CHARGED WITH FREEING ENGLAND FROM THE *CLUTCHES OF THE DEVIL.*

IF *YOU* OPPOSE ME, WHAT CONCLUSION MUST I DRAW?

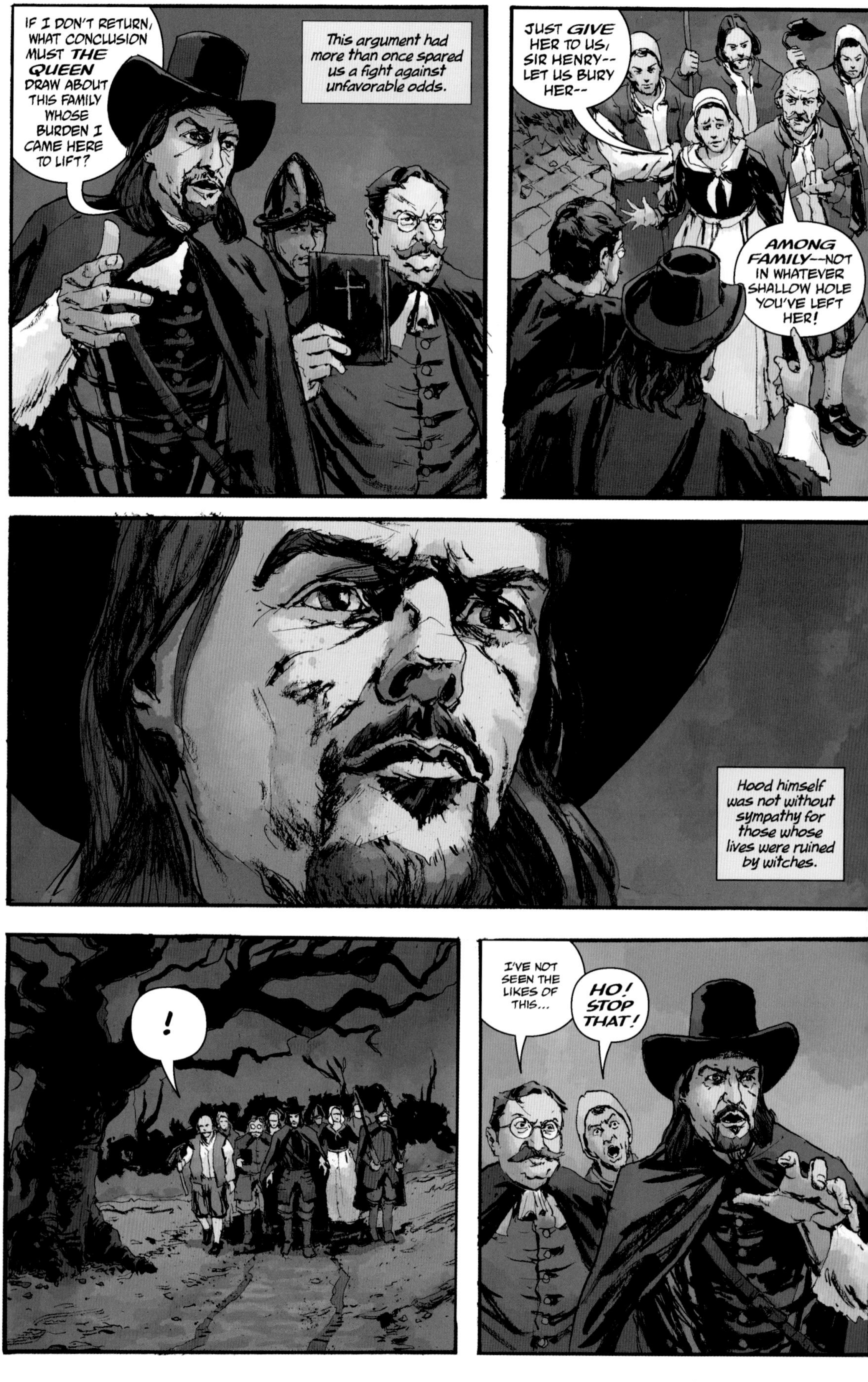
IF I DON'T RETURN, WHAT CONCLUSION MUST THE QUEEN DRAW ABOUT THIS FAMILY WHOSE BURDEN I CAME HERE TO LIFT?
This argument had more than once spared us a fight against unfavorable odds.
JUST GIVE HER TO US, SIR HENRY--LET US BURY HER--
AMONG FAMILY--NOT IN WHATEVER SHALLOW HOLE YOU'VE LEFT HER!
Hood himself was not without sympathy for those whose lives were ruined by witches.
!
I'VE NOT SEEN THE LIKES OF THIS...
HO! STOP THAT!

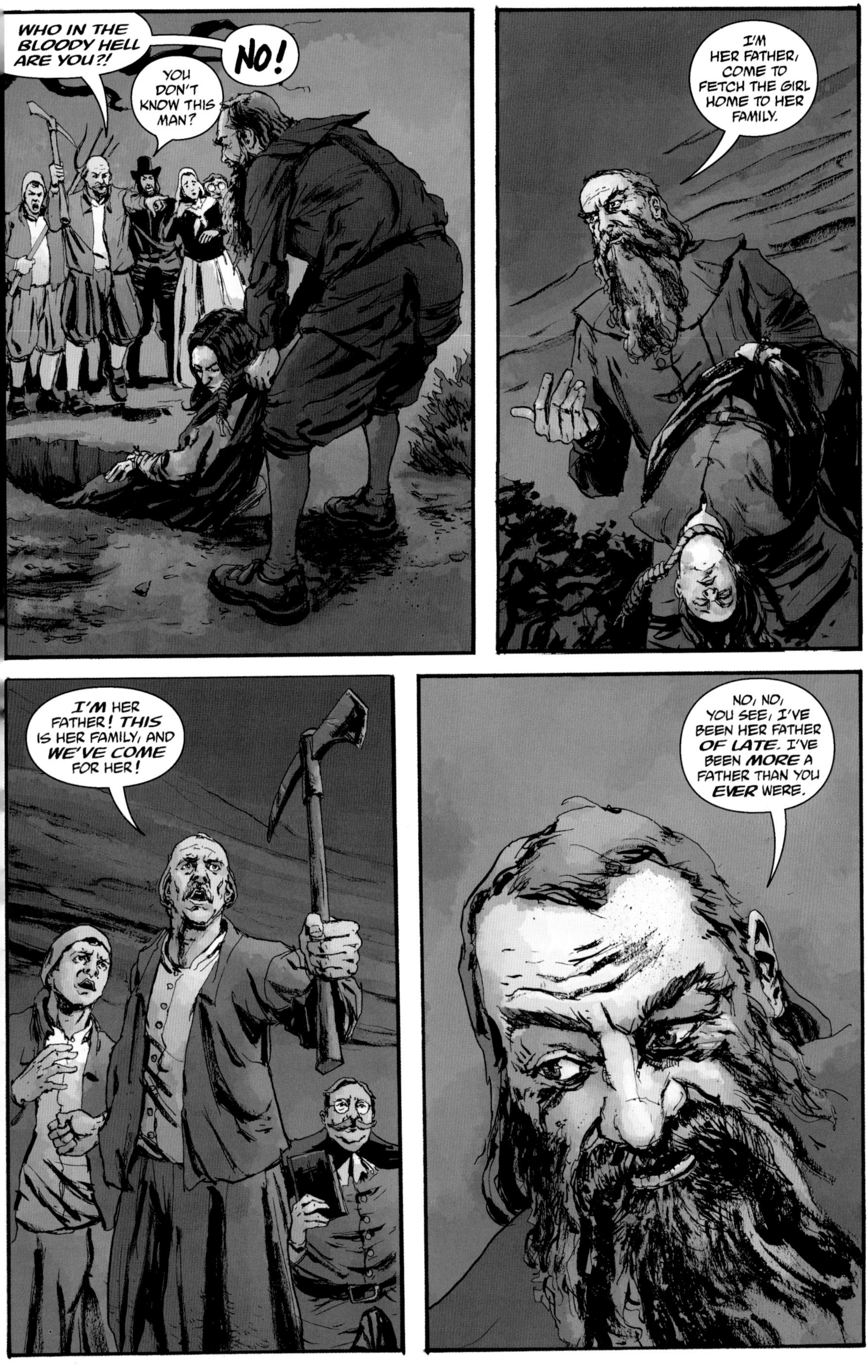
WHO IN THE BLOODY HELL ARE YOU?!
NO!
YOU DON'T KNOW THIS MAN?
I'M HER FATHER, COME TO FETCH THE GIRL HOME TO HER FAMILY.
I'M HER FATHER! THIS IS HER FAMILY, AND WE'VE COME FOR HER!
NO, NO, YOU SEE, I'VE BEEN HER FATHER OF LATE. I'VE BEEN MORE A FATHER THAN YOU EVER WERE.

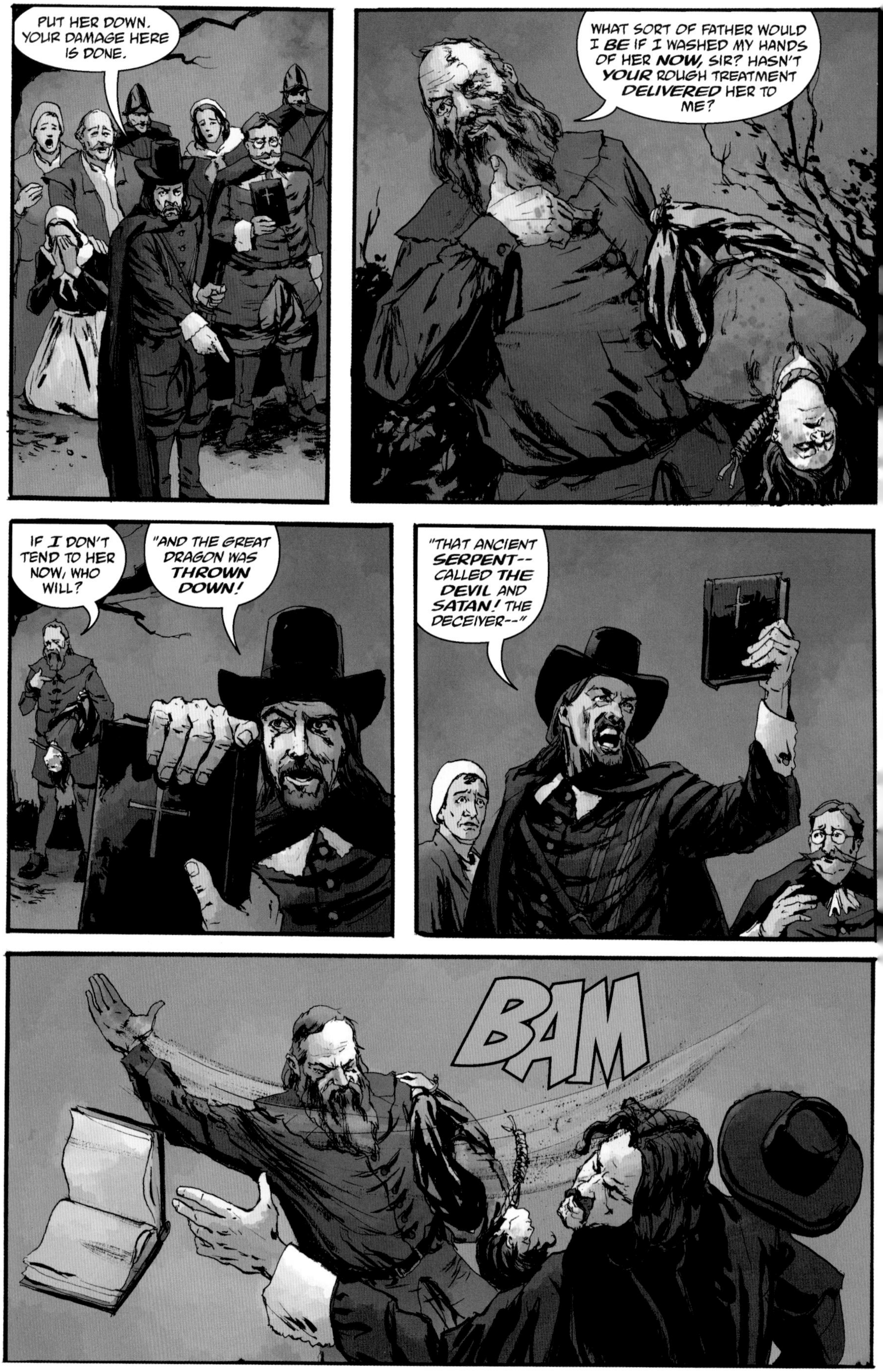

PUT HER DOWN. YOUR DAMAGE HERE IS DONE.
WHAT SORT OF FATHER WOULD I BE IF I WASHED MY HANDS OF HER NOW, SIR? HASN'T YOUR ROUGH TREATMENT DELIVERED HER TO ME?
IF I DON'T TEND TO HER NOW, WHO WILL?
"AND THE GREAT DRAGON WAS THROWN DOWN!
"THAT ANCIENT SERPENT-- CALLED THE DEVIL AND SATAN! THE DECEIVER--"
BAM

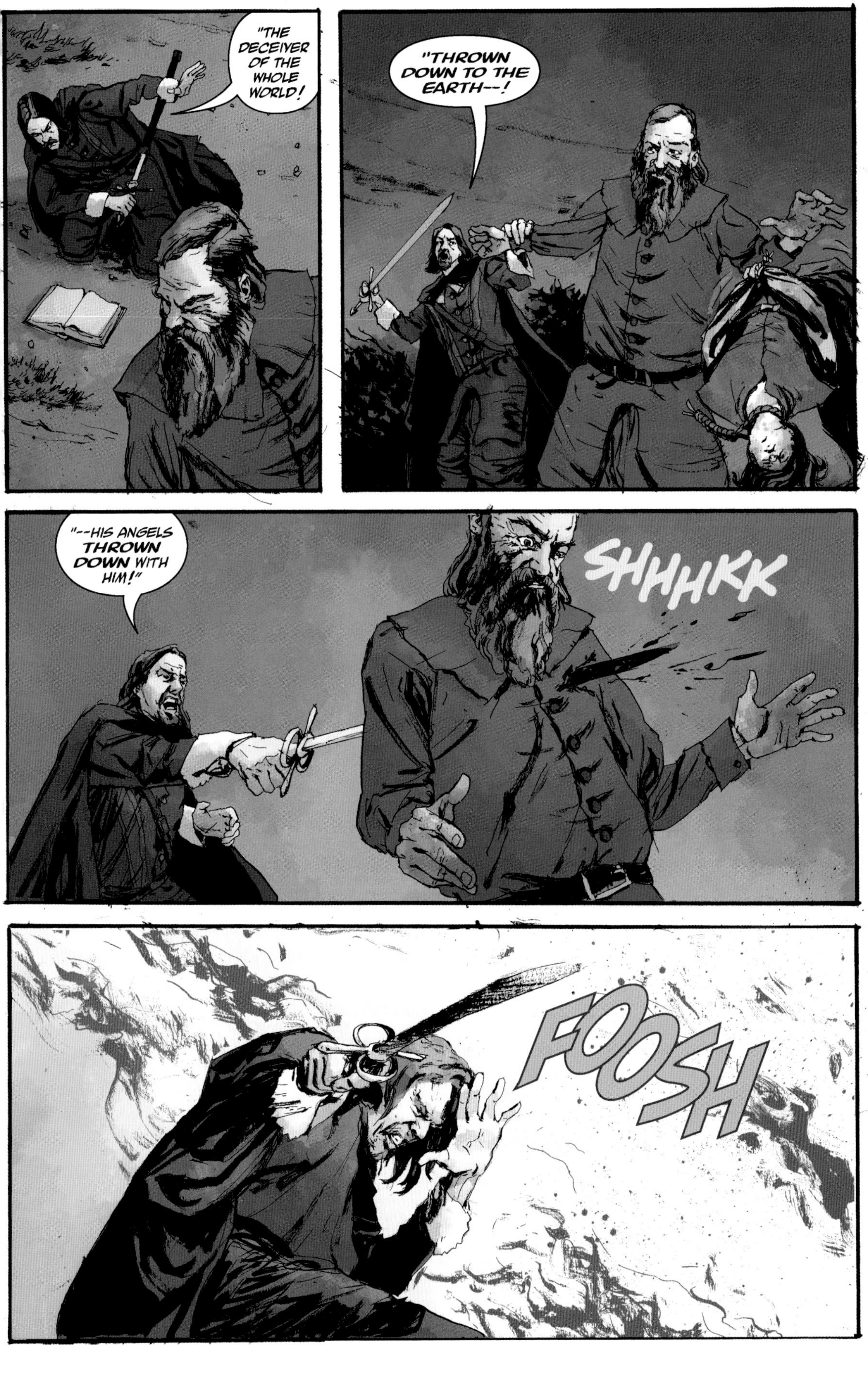
"THE DECEIVER OF THE WHOLE WORLD!
"THROWN DOWN TO THE EARTH--!
"--HIS ANGELS THROWN DOWN WITH HIM!"
SHHHKK
FOOSH

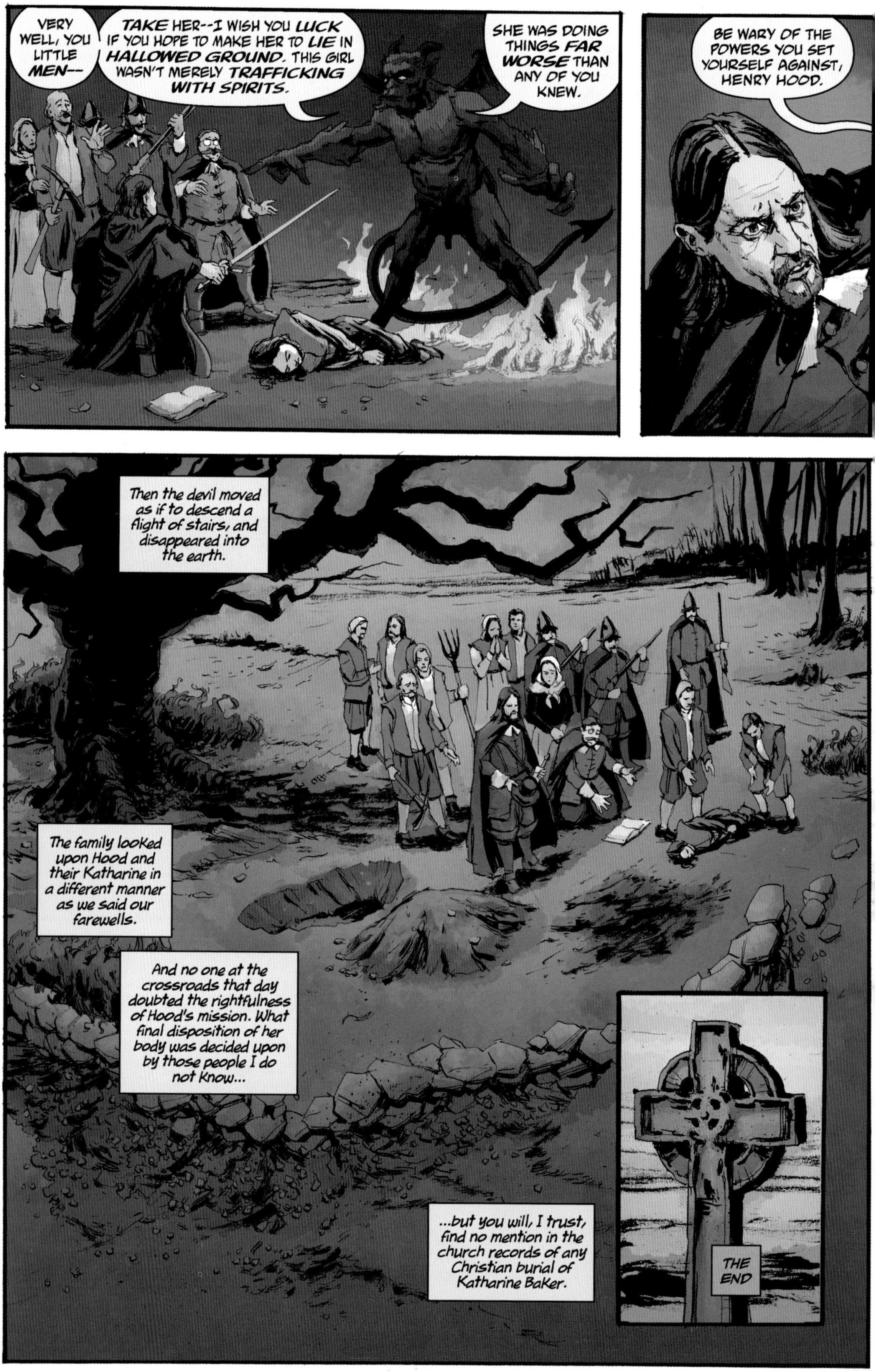
VERY WELL, YOU LITTLE MEN--
TAKE HER--I WISH YOU LUCK IF YOU HOPE TO MAKE HER TO LIE IN HALLOWED GROUND. THIS GIRL WASN'T MERELY TRAFFICKING WITH SPIRITS.
SHE WAS DOING THINGS FAR WORSE THAN ANY OF YOU KNEW.
BE WARY OF THE POWERS YOU SET YOURSELF AGAINST, HENRY HOOD.
Then the devil moved as if to descend a flight of stairs, and disappeared into the earth.
The family looked upon Hood and their Katharine in a different manner as we said our farewells.
And no one at the crossroads that day doubted the rightfulness of Hood's mission. What final disposition of her body was decided upon by those people I do not know...
...but you will, I trust, find no mention in the church records of any Christian burial of Katharine Baker.
THE END

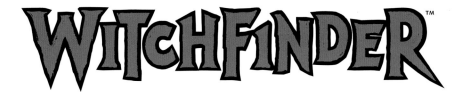

WITCHFINDER™

SKETCHBOOK

with notes from the artists

BEN STENBECK: I've wanted to draw a Victorian horror comic written by Mike Mignola ever since reading the first issue of *Jenny Finn* (by Mike and Troy Nixey). And now I have. Thanks for having me onboard, Mike!

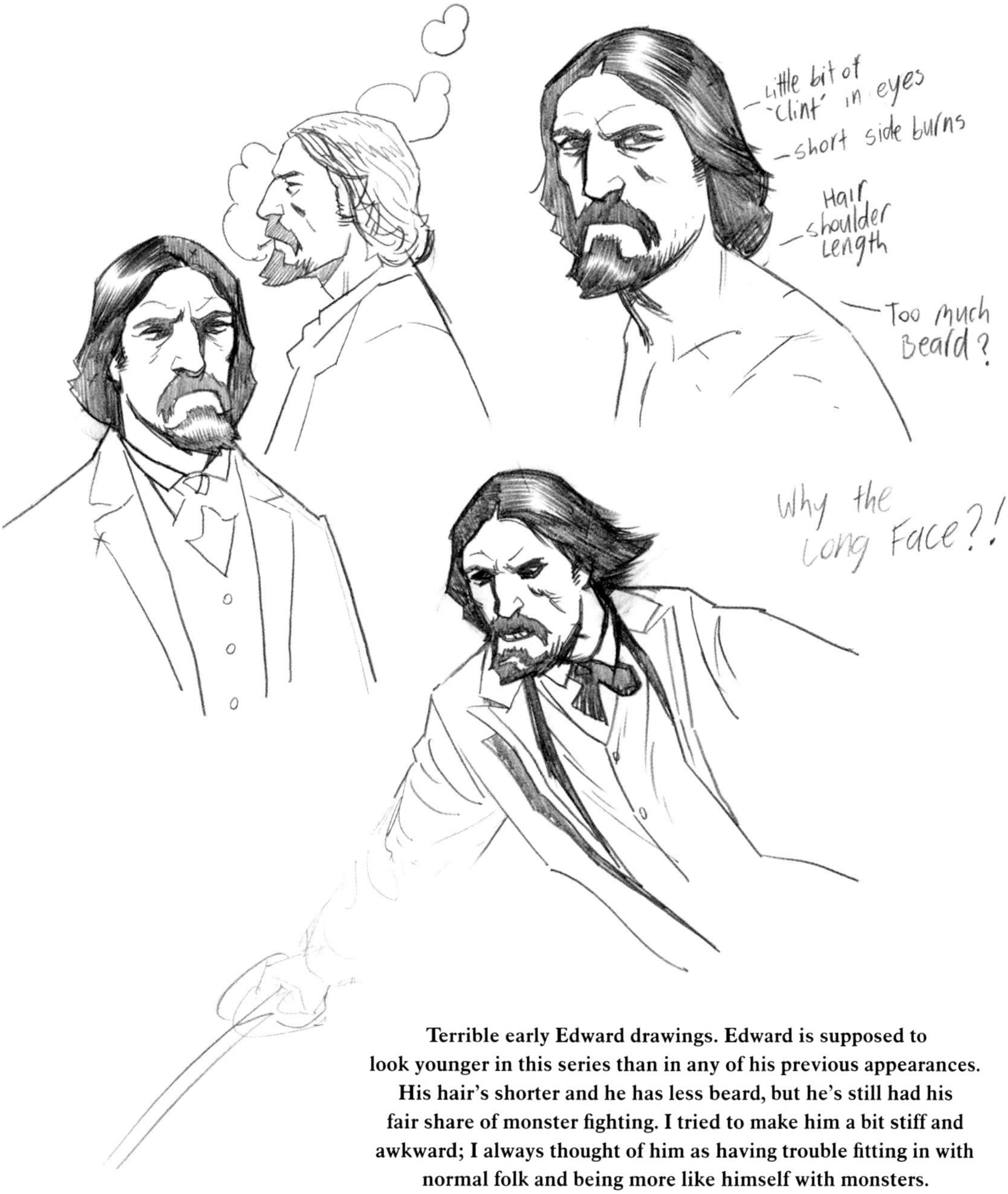

Little bit of 'Clint' in eyes
short side burns
Hair shoulder length
Too much Beard?
Why the long Face?!

Terrible early Edward drawings. Edward is supposed to look younger in this series than in any of his previous appearances. His hair's shorter and he has less beard, but he's still had his fair share of monster fighting. I tried to make him a bit stiff and awkward; I always thought of him as having trouble fitting in with normal folk and being more like himself with monsters.

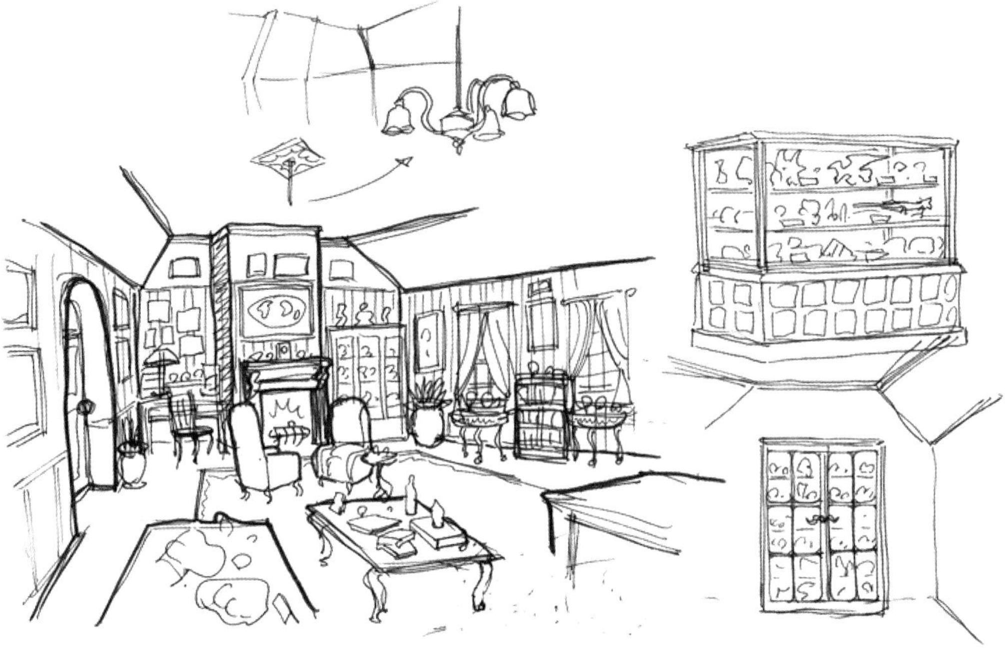

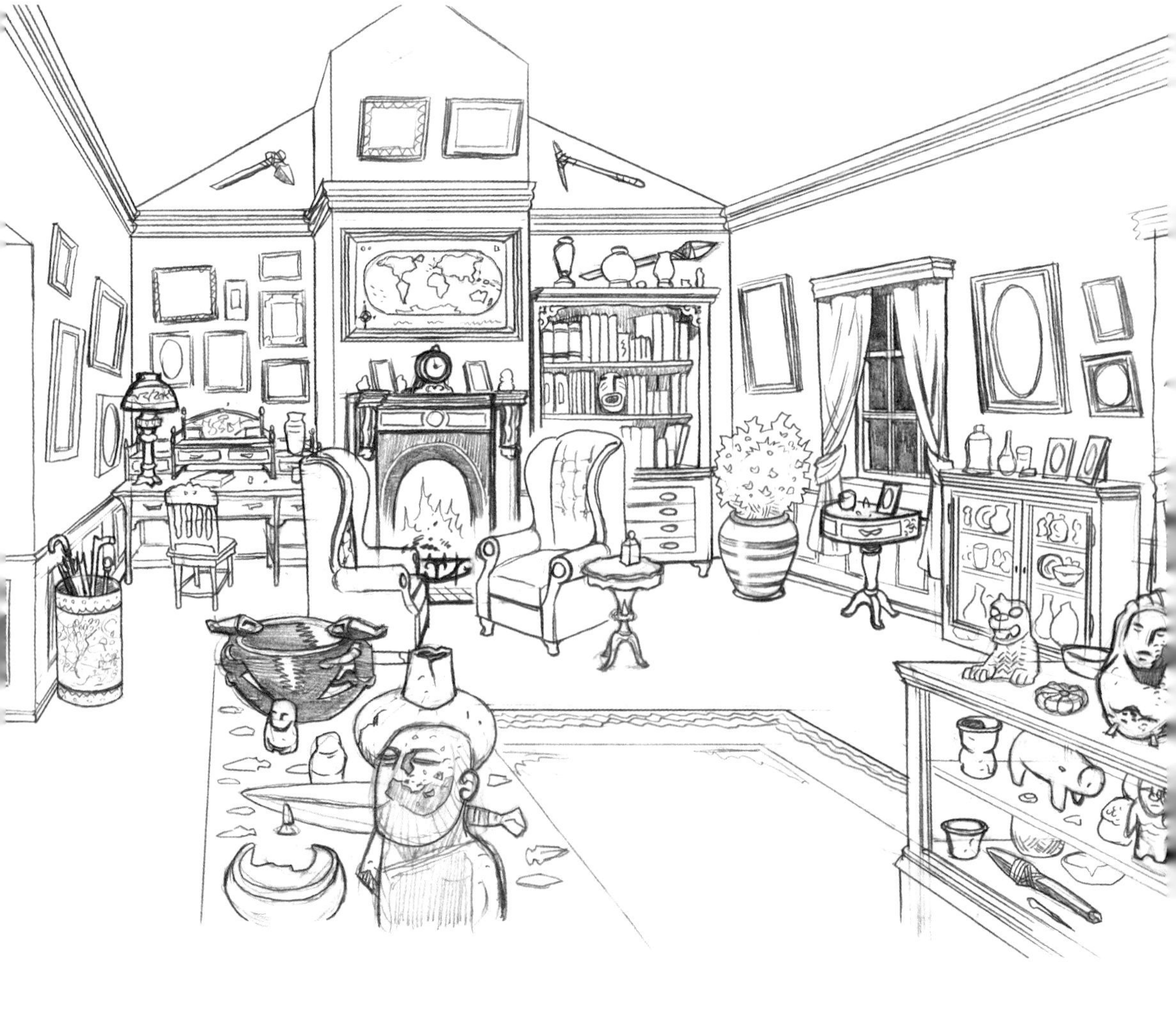

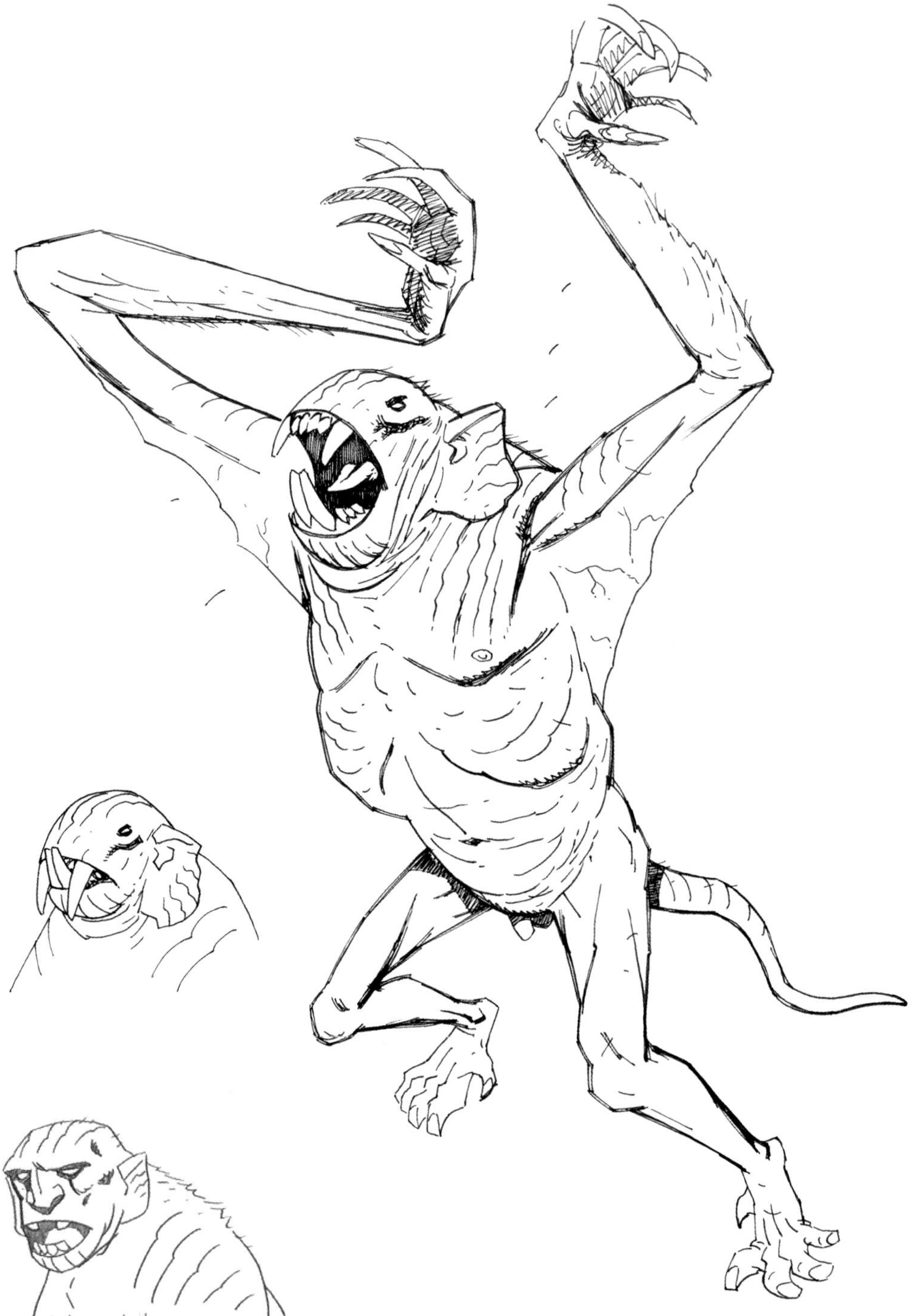

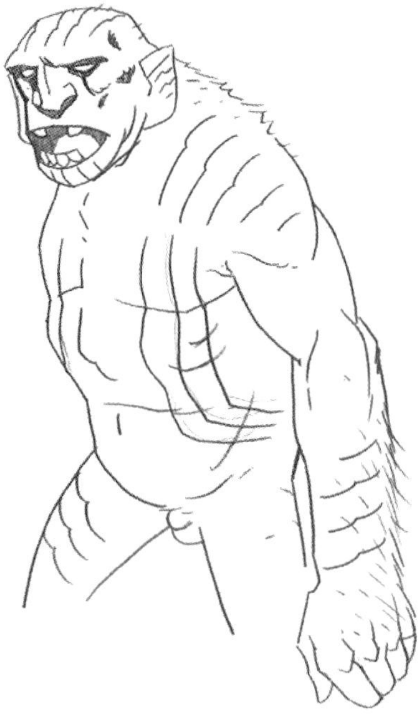

I have an "I'll get it right on the night" attitude when it comes to design, which hardly ever works out for the best. Anyway, originally I was thinking of the creature being a bit more pathetic and awkward. And the thing that stuck was those goofy mole-rat teeth. I don't know. It seemed like a good idea at the time.

CREATURE

① "Child" version

Almost flat nose-

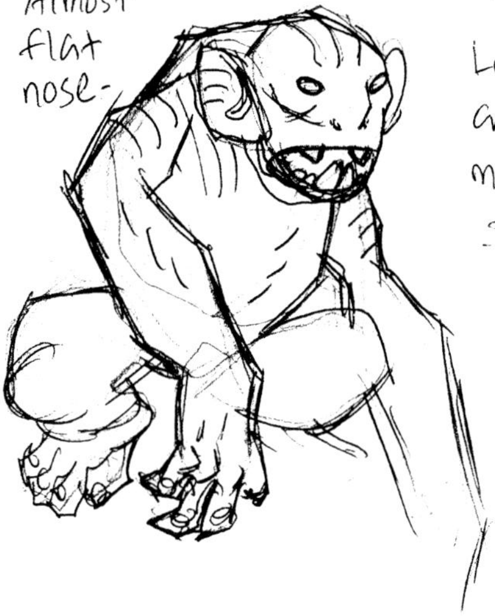

Let's keep his face and body in shadow as much as possible -- ~~play up~~ pop out eyes and mouth -- like he's lit from inside.

- Heavy powerful hands and forearms
- Downplay teeth -- maybe lower-middle fangs are more prominent than upper fangs.

Creature ②

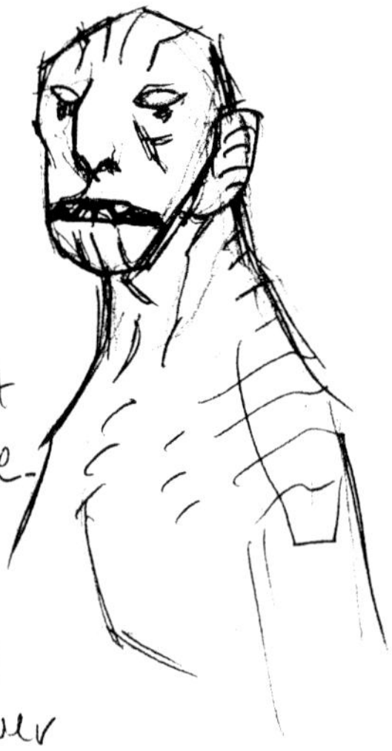

As he appears

- at the Hollow Earth Church --
- More human shaped -- Almost Abe Sapien-like.
- Fangs are down-played, but we still see upper and lower ones (small) in his partially opened mouth.
- Nose more pronounced
- Ears are still large, but closer in to head.
- As Noble as you can make him.

-Eyes more almond shaped.

- Not so much in shadow -- But we will never see full figure.

MIKE MIGNOLA: I first designed these underground slave guys for the first B.P.R.D. series, *Hollow Earth*. Here, since we are dealing with the *spirit* of one of these guys, I wanted him to assume different forms at different times. At first, since he hasn't killed too many people yet, he's like a scrappy little monkey. Later he appears almost human in order to seduce Reverend Blum. As he kills more, takes more blood, he becomes not just bigger, but more monstrously apelike.

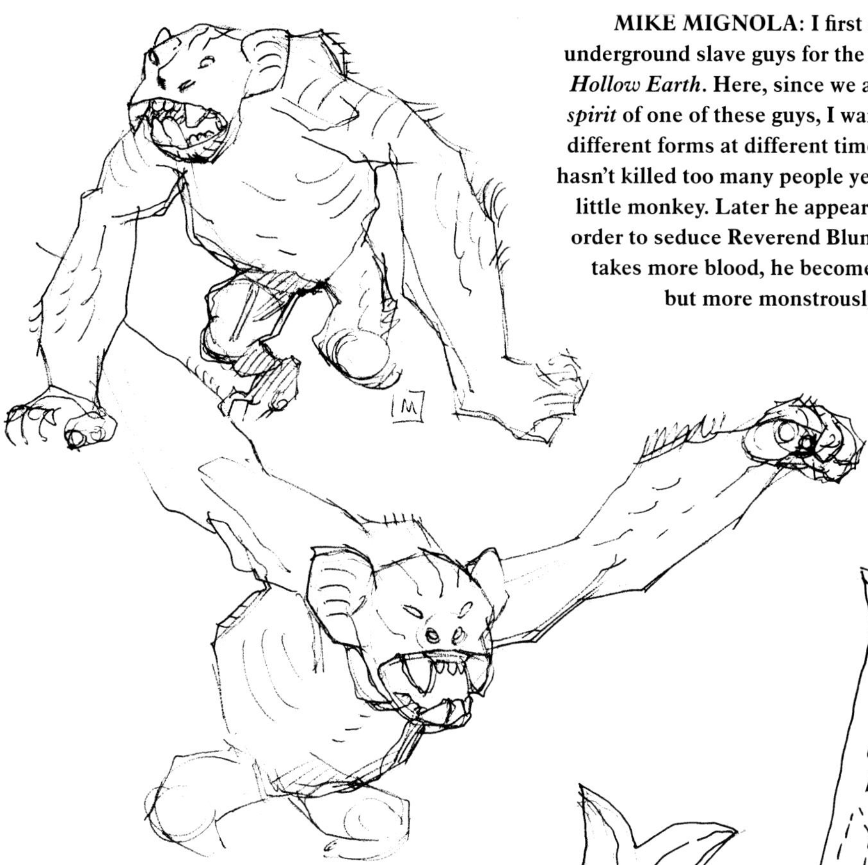

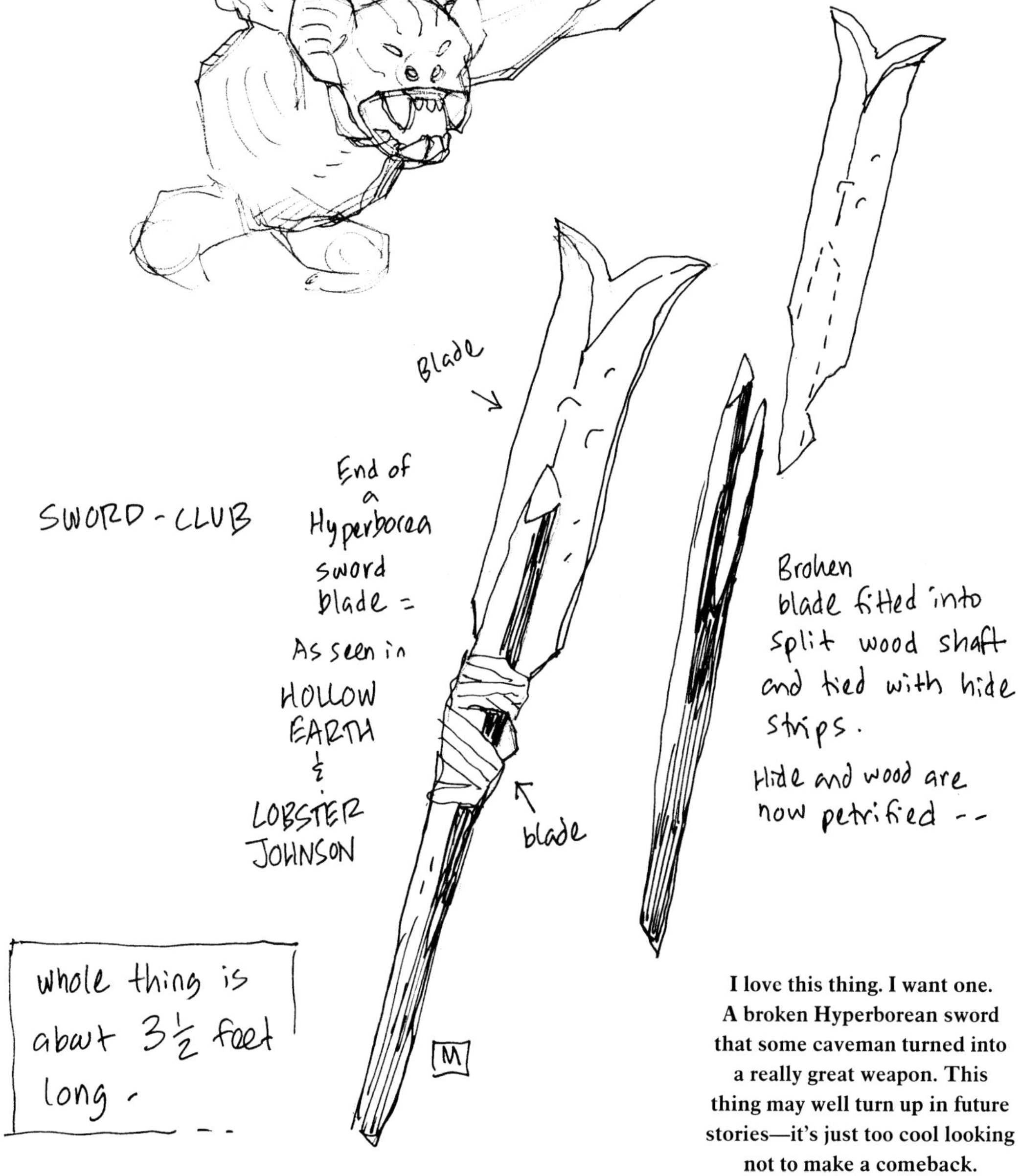
SWORD-CLUB
Blade
End of a Hyperborea sword blade =
As seen in HOLLOW EARTH & LOBSTER JOHNSON
blade
Broken blade fitted into split wood shaft and tied with hide strips.
Hide and wood are now petrified --
whole thing is about 3 1/2 feet long.

I love this thing. I want one. A broken Hyperborean sword that some caveman turned into a really great weapon. This thing may well turn up in future stories—it's just too cool looking not to make a comeback.

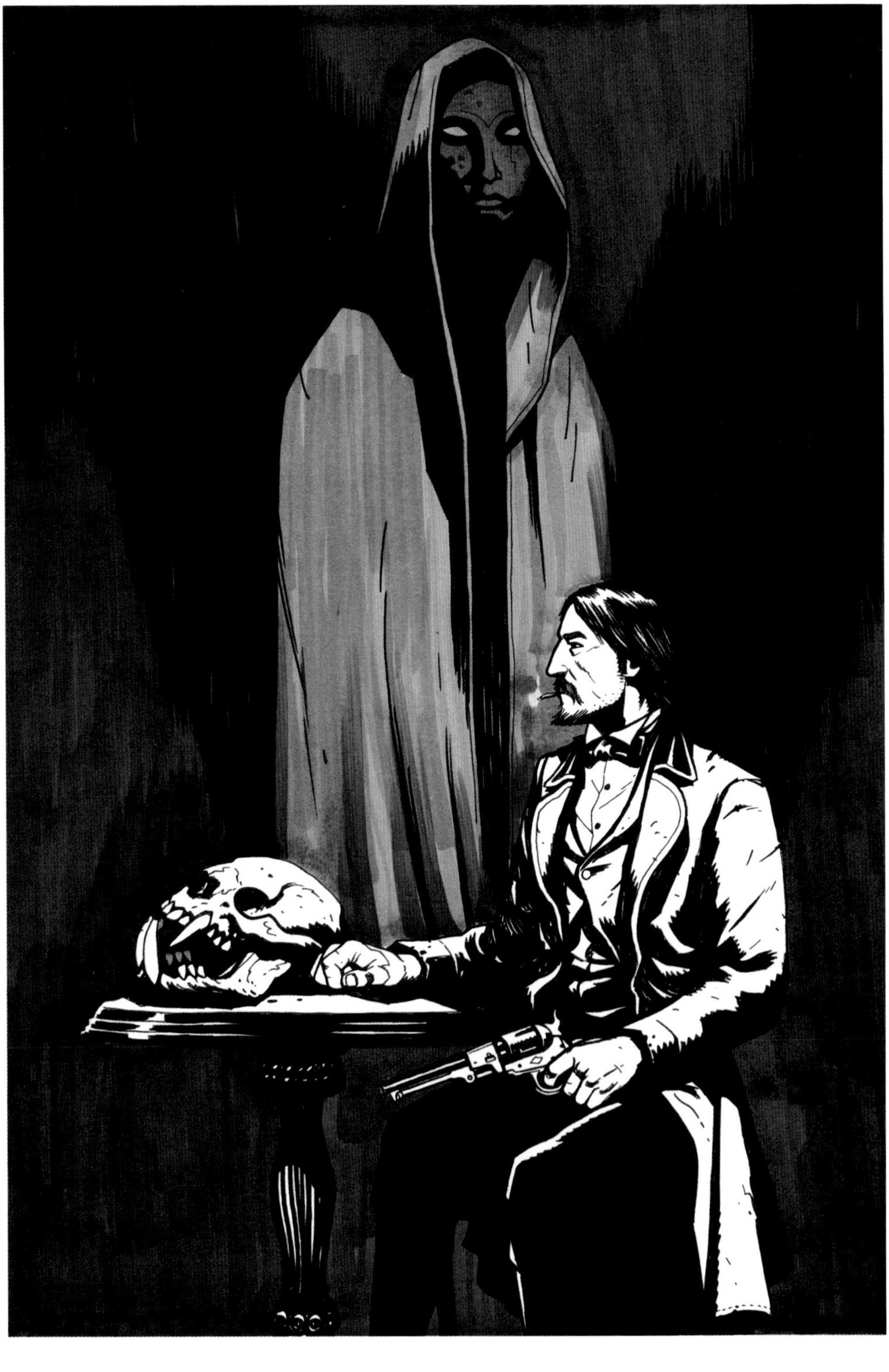

BS: I made someone wait a year for his commissions while I drew *Witchfinder*.
This was done as an apology.

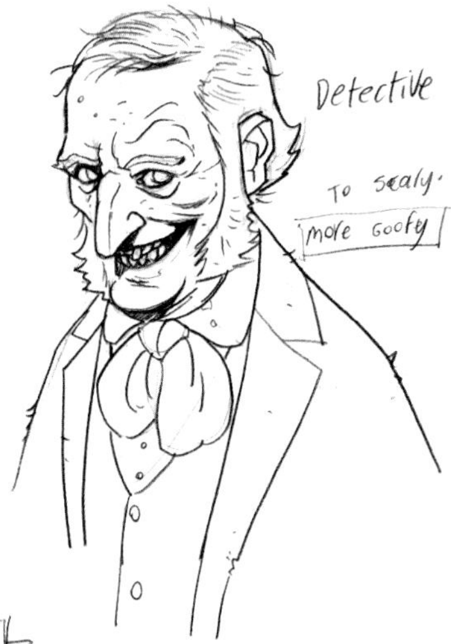
Detective
To scaly·
more goofy

The Captain (formerly "the Detective"), loosely based on Peter Cushing. The H.B.R. guy that gives Edward his card is based on Christopher Lee (as he appears in *The Devil Rides Out*).

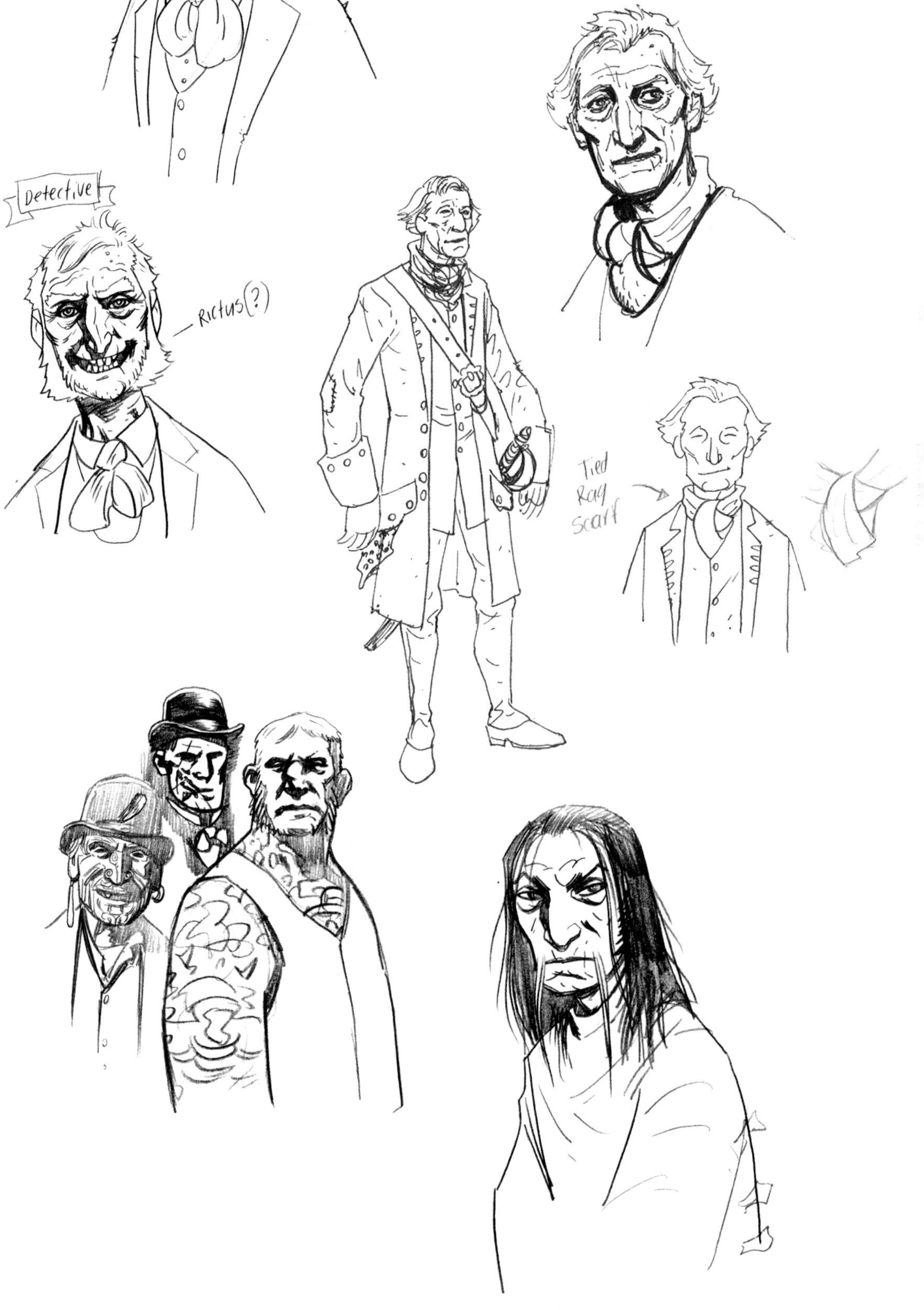
Detective
Rictus(?)
Tied
Rag
scarf

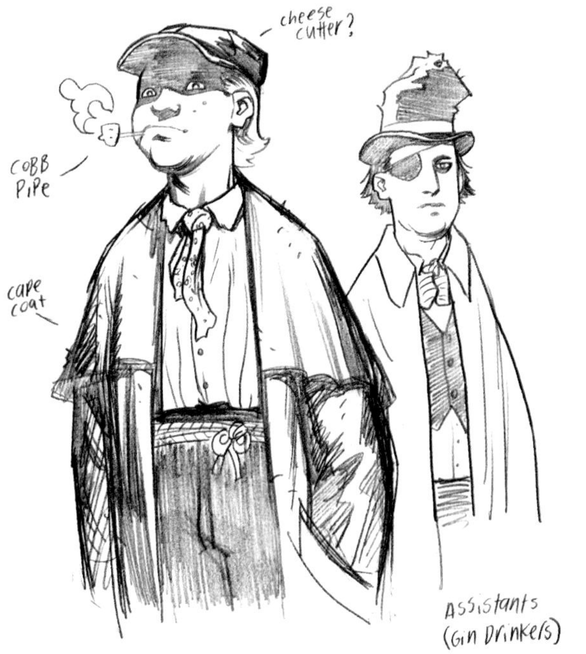
cheese cutter?
COBB Pipe
cape coat
Assistants (Gin Drinkers)

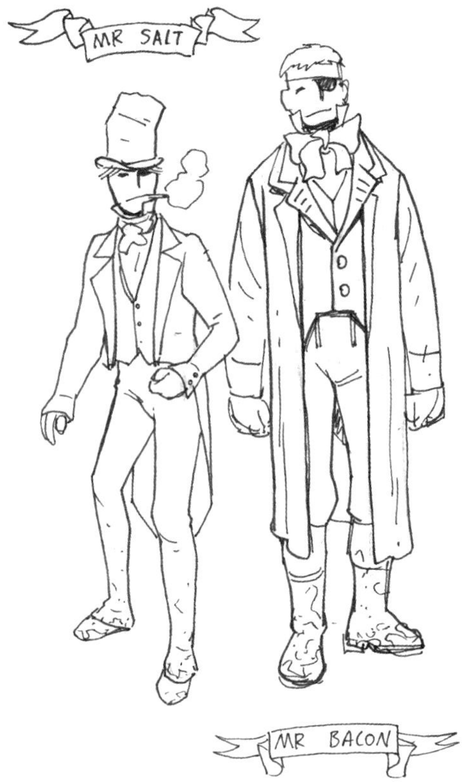
MR SALT
MR BACON

Quick sketches of Bacon and Salt. I really liked these guys. Wish we'd had room to do more with them.

For Mary, I didn't want to go with a typical elaborate Victorian dress; she's a simple country girl. The dress she wears is a mix of various references.

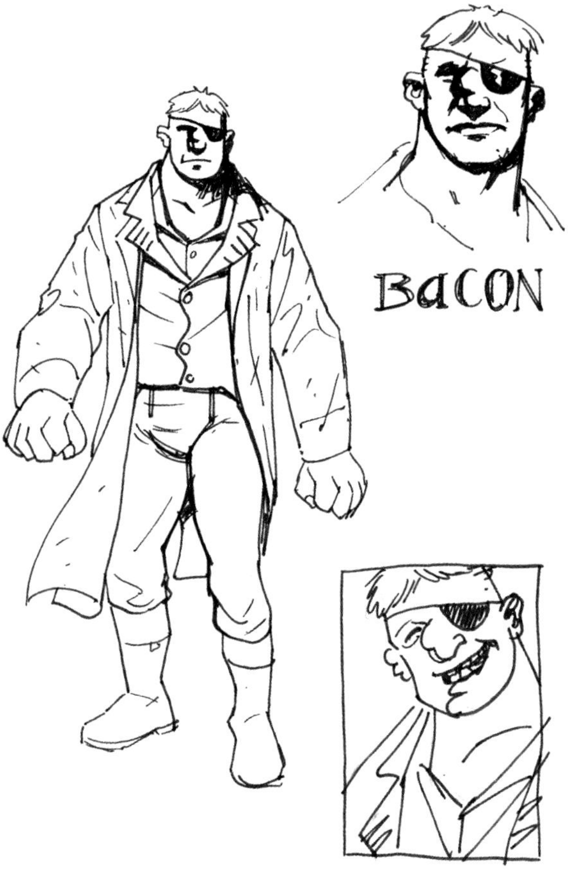
BACON

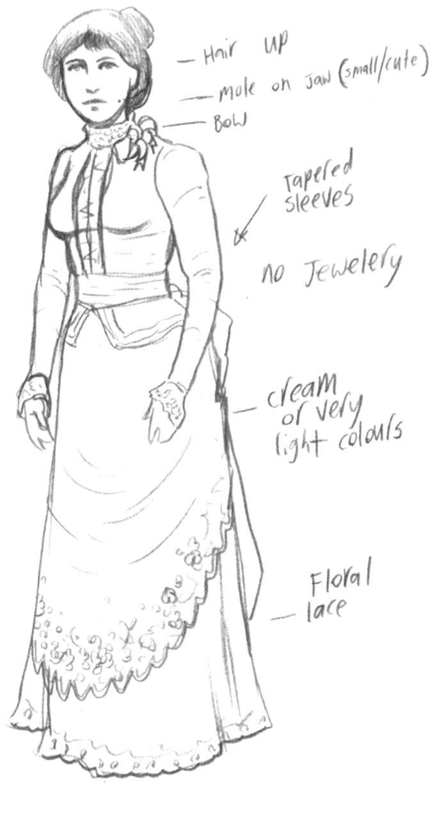
Hair up
mole on Jaw (small/cute)
Bow
Tapered sleeves
no Jewelery
cream or very light colours
Floral lace

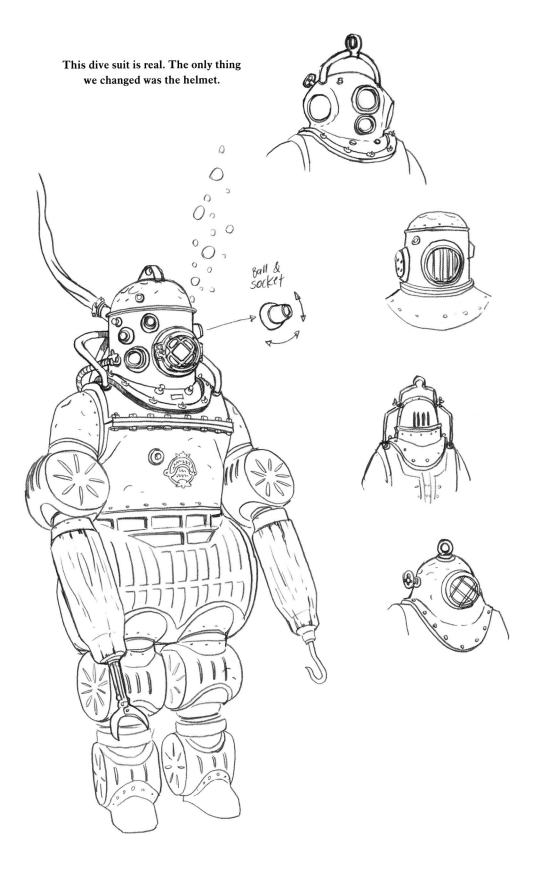

This dive suit is real. The only thing we changed was the helmet.

Ball & socket

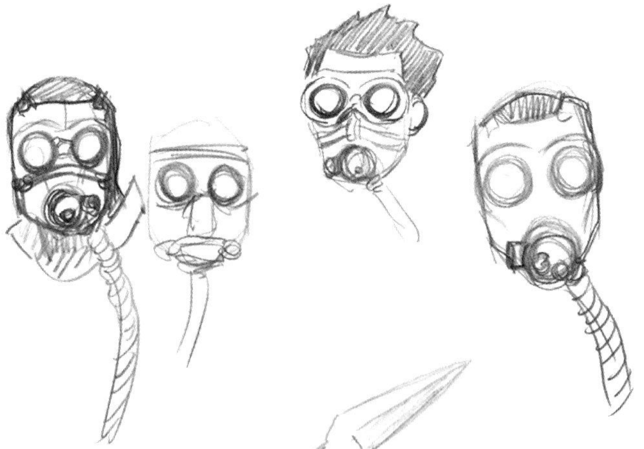

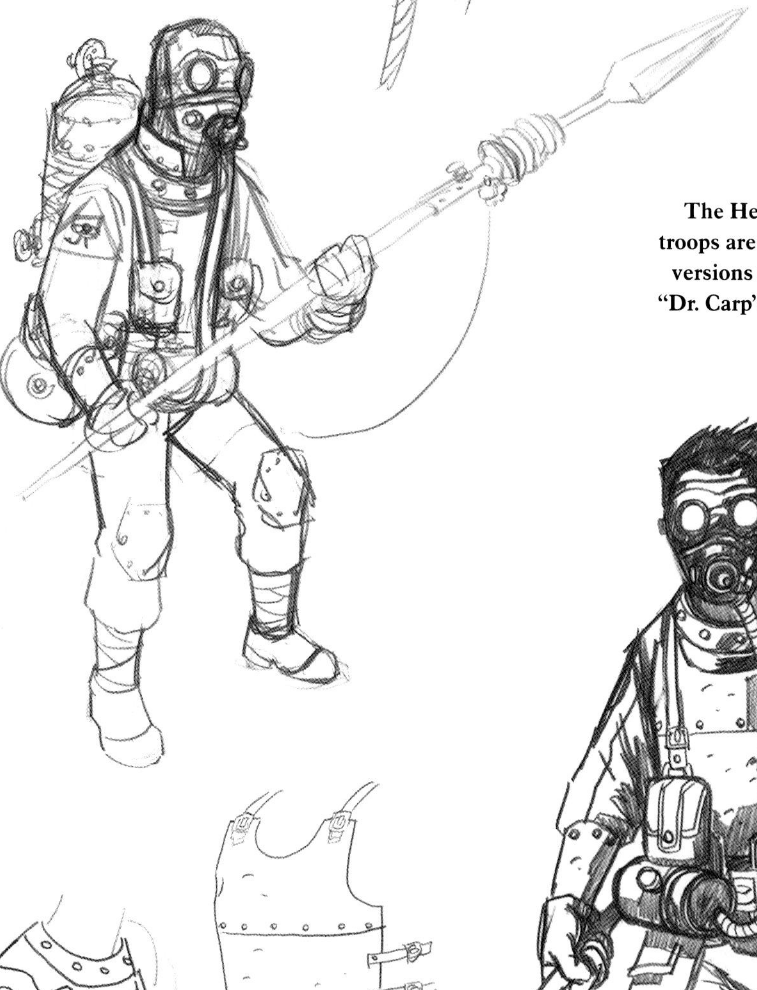

The Heliopic shock troops are more-armored versions of the guys in "Dr. Carp's Experiment."

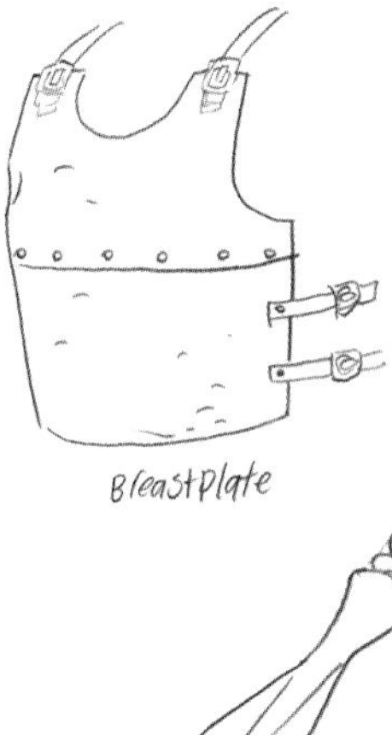
Breastplate

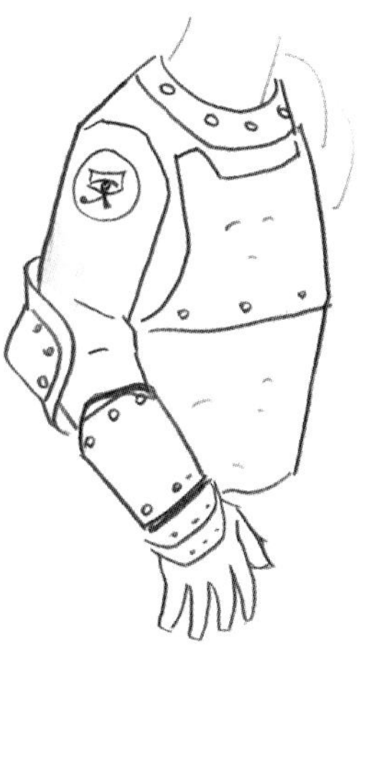

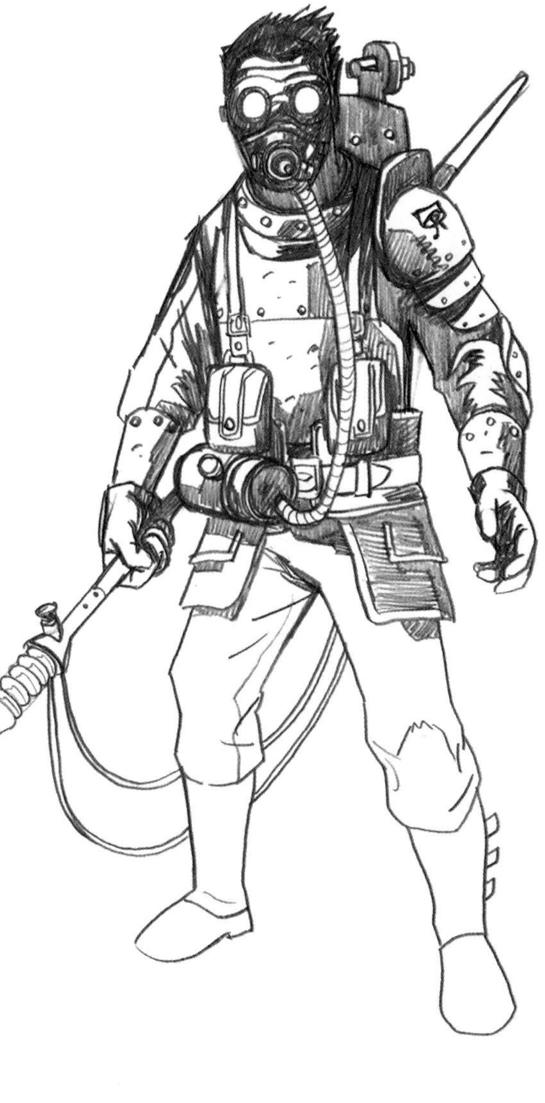

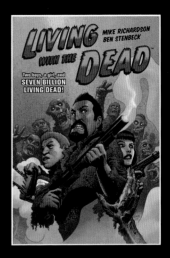
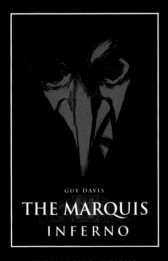

HELLBOY™

by MIKE MIGNOLA

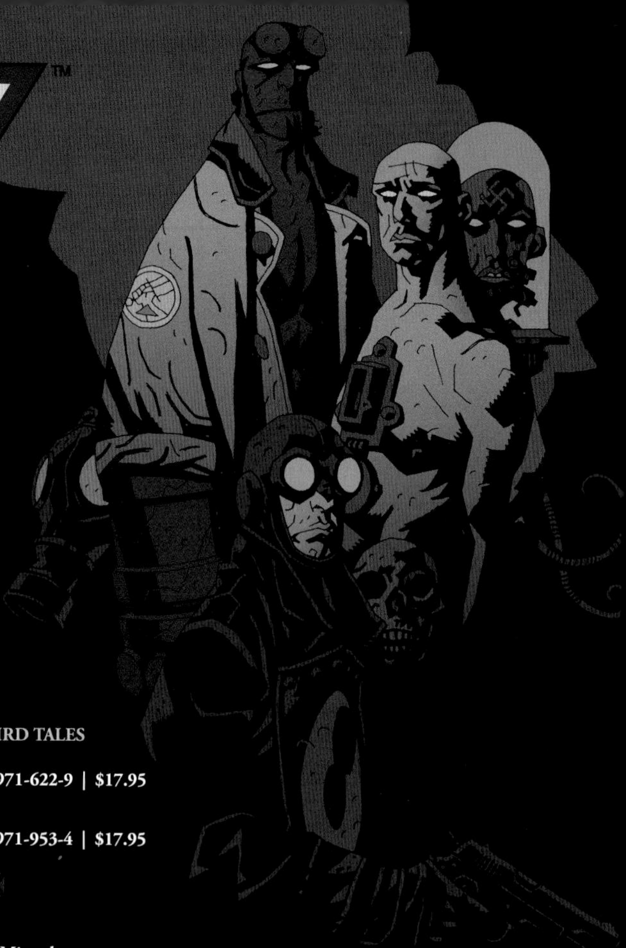

HELLBOY LIBRARY EDITION VOLUME 1:
SEED OF DESTRUCTION
AND WAKE THE DEVIL
ISBN 978-1-59307-910-9 | $49.95

HELLBOY LIBRARY EDITION VOLUME 2:
THE CHAINED COFFIN
AND THE RIGHT HAND OF DOOM
ISBN 978-1-59307-989-5 | $49.95

HELLBOY LIBRARY EDITION VOLUME 3:
CONQUEROR WORM AND STRANGE PLACES
ISBN 978-1-59582-352-6 | $49.95

SEED OF DESTRUCTION
with John Byrne
ISBN 978-1-59307-094-6 | $17.95

WAKE THE DEVIL
ISBN 978-1-59307-095-3 | $17.95

THE CHAINED COFFIN
AND OTHERS
ISBN 978-1-59307-091-5 | $17.95

THE RIGHT HAND OF DOOM
ISBN 978-1-59307-093-9 | $17.95

CONQUEROR WORM
ISBN 978-1-59307-092-2 | $17.95

STRANGE PLACES
ISBN 978-1-59307-475-3 | $17.95

THE TROLL WITCH AND OTHERS
By Mignola, Corben, and Russell
ISBN 978-1-59307-860-7 | $17.95

DARKNESS CALLS
ISBN 978-1-59307-896-6 | $19.95

THE ART OF HELLBOY
ISBN 978-1-59307-089-2 | $29.95

HELLBOY II: THE ART OF THE MOVIE
ISBN 978-1-59307-964-2 | $24.95

HELLBOY: THE COMPANION
ISBN 978-1-59307-655-9 | $14.95

HELLBOY WEIRD TALES
Volume 1
ISBN 978-1-56971-622-9 | $17.95

Volume 2
ISBN 978-1-56971-953-4 | $17.95

ODD JOBS
Short stories by Mignola,
Poppy Z. Brite, Chris Golden, and others
Illustrations by Mignola
ISBN 978-1-56971-440-9 | $14.95

ODDER JOBS
Short stories by Frank Darabont,
Guillermo del Toro, and others
Illustrations by Mignola
ISBN 978-1-59307-226-1 | $14.95

ODDEST JOBS
Short stories by China Miéville,
Ken Bruen, Mark Chadbourn, and others
Illustrations by Mignola
ISBN 978-1-59307-944-4 | $14.95

B.P.R.D.: HOLLOW EARTH
By Mignola, Chris Golden,
Ryan Sook, and others
ISBN 978-1-56971-862-9 | $17.95

B.P.R.D.: THE SOUL OF VENICE
By Mignola, Mike Oeming, Guy Davis,
Scott Kolins, Geoff Johns, and others
ISBN 978-1-59307-132-5 | $17.95

B.P.R.D.: PLAGUE OF FROGS
By Mignola and Guy Davis
ISBN 978-1-59307-288-9 | $17.95

B.P.R.D.: THE DEAD
By Mignola, John Arcudi, and Guy Davis
ISBN 978-1-59307-380-0 | $17.95

B.P.R.D.: THE BLACK FLAME
By Mignola, Arcudi, and Davis
ISBN 978-1-59307-550-7 | $17.95

B.P.R.D.: THE UNIVERSAL MACHINE
By Mignola, Arcudi, and Davis
ISBN 978-1-59307-710-5 | $17.95

B.P.R.D.: GARDEN OF SOULS
By Mignola, Arcudi, and Davis
ISBN 978-1-59307-882-9 | $17.95

B.P.R.D.: KILLING GROUND
By Mignola, Arcudi, and Davis
ISBN 978-1-59307-956-7 | $17.95

B.P.R.D.: 1946
By Mignola, Dysart, and Azaceta
ISBN 978-1-59582-191-1 | $17.95

B.P.R.D.: THE WARNING
By Mignola, Arcudi, and Davis
ISBN 978-1-59582-304-5 | $17.95

B.P.R.D.: THE BLACK GODDESS
By Mignola, Arcudi, and Davis
ISBN 978-1-59582-411-0 | $17.95

ABE SAPIEN: THE DROWNING
By Mignola, Jason Shawn Alexander,
and Dave Stewart
ISBN 978-1-59582-185-0 | $17.95

LOBSTER JOHNSON:
THE IRON PROMETHEUS
By Mignola, Jason Armstrong,
and Dave Stewart
ISBN 978-1-59307-975-8 | $17.95

To find a comics shop in your area,
call 1-888-266-4226
For more information or to order direct:
• On the web: darkhorse.com
• E-mail: mailorder@darkhorse.com
• Phone: 1-800-862-0052
Mon.–Fri. 9 AM to 5 PM Pacific Time

DARK HORSE COMICS®
darkhorse.com
drawing on your nightmares™